Competition policy in the UK and EEC

Competition policy in the UK and EEC

Edited by

KENNETH D. GEORGE
Professor of Economics, University College, Cardiff

CAROLINE JOLL
Research Fellow, Department of Economics
University College, Cardiff

CAMBRIDGE UNIVERSITY PRESS

CAMBRIDGE

LONDON · NEW YORK · MELBOURNE

Published by the Syndics of the Cambridge University Press
The Pitt Building, Trumpington Street, Cambridge CB2 1RP
Bentley House, 200 Euston Road, London NW1 2DB
32 East 57th Street, New York, NY10022, USA
296 Beaconsfield Parade, Middle Park, Melbourne 3206, Australia

Library of Congress Cataloguing in Publication Data

Main entry under title:
Competition policy in the UK and EEC

'Contains six papers presented at a Social Science Research
Council Conference on "competition policy in the EEC," held at
Somerville College, Oxford, from 23–25 September 1974.'

Includes index

1. European Economic Community countries – Commercial
policy – Congresses. 2. Trade regulation – European Economic
Community countries – Congresses. 3. Great Britain –
Commercial policy – Congresses. 4. Trade regulation – Great
Britain – Congresses. I. George, Kenneth Desmond. II. Joll,
Caroline. III. Social Science Research Council.
HF1532.92.C67   382'.094   75–9285
ISBN: 0-521-20943-9

First published 1975

Printed in Great Britain at the
University Printing House, Cambridge
(Euan Phillips, University Printer)

CONTENTS

LIST OF CONFERENCE PARTICIPANTS

Professor T. Barna
University of Sussex
Professor A. Beacham
University of Liverpool
Miss P. Lesley Cook
University of Sussex
Professor K. Cowling
University of Warwick
Mr J. Cubbin
University of Warwick
Mr J. Driscoll
British Steel Corporation
Mr A. Dunning
Department of Prices and Consumer Protection
Professor K. D. George
University College, Cardiff
Mr J. D. Gribbin
Office of Fair Trading
Lady Margaret Hall
Somerville College, Oxford
Mr J. Hardie
Keble College, Oxford
Mr P. Harris
Office of Fair Trading
Professor P. E. Hart
University of Reading
Professor J. B. Heath
London Graduate School of Business Studies

Dr A. H. Hermann
Financial Times
Dr M. Howe
Monopolies and Mergers Commission
Professor A. Jacquemin
Université Catholique de Louvain, Belgium
Mr D. Jacobs
Shell International Petroleum Co.
Ms Caroline Joll
University College, Cardiff
Professor Dr H. W. de Jong
Instituut voor Bedrijfskunde, Netherlands
Mr J. F. Lever
All Souls College, Oxford
Mr L. Lightman
Office of Fair Trading
Dr Kurt Markert
Bundeskartellamt, West Germany
Professor P. Mathijsen
EEC Directorate General for Competition
Mr W. P. J. Maunder
University of Loughborough
Professor E. G. Mestmäcker
Bielefeld University, West Germany
Mr M. J. Methven
Office of Fair Trading
Miss E. Morgan
University of Reading

List of conference participants

Professor D. P. O'Brien
University of Durham
Mr R. G. Opie
New College, Oxford
Mr N. Owen
*Department of Trade and
Industry*
Professor Louis Philips
*Université Catholique de
Louvain, Belgium*
Professor S. J. Prais
*National Institute of
Economic and Social
Research*
Dr Willie Schlieder
*EEC Directorate General
for Competition*

Mr Z. A. Silberston
Nuffield College, Oxford
Mr A. Sutherland
Trinity College, Cambridge
Professor H. Townsend
University of Lancaster
Dr M. A. Utton
University of Reading
Professor J. M. Vernon
Duke University, USA
Mr D. G. Walshe
Office of Fair Trading
Professor T. Wilson
University of Glasgow

PREFACE

This book contains six papers presented at a Social Science Research Council Conference on 'Competition Policy in the EEC', held at Somerville College, Oxford from 23–25 September 1974, together with the comments made by the discussants. These papers cover the main areas of concern for competition policy in the context of the UK's national economy and the EEC's international common market, i.e. restrictive practices, monopolies and mergers. However 'the establishment of a system ensuring that competition in the common market is not distorted', which is the task of policy in the EEC, involves an approach which is broader than the traditional anti-trust policy. Professor Mathijsen's paper (chapter 7) draws attention to the fact that the EEC Commission has to regulate the behaviour of the governments of the member states as well as the market conduct of private firms if inter-state competition is not to be seriously distorted.

The Conference was opened by Mr John Methven who, as Director General of Fair Trading, now has overall responsibility for the administration of competition policy in the UK. We are grateful to Mr Methven for permission to include his opening address in this volume. The editors have contributed an introductory and a concluding chapter. Chapter 1 gives an account of the development of the legal framework within which competition policy is administered in the UK and in the EEC. Chapter 8 discusses some of the economic issues arising from the preceding papers. It is based largely on the views which were expressed during the general discussion which followed each paper, but the chapter is not entirely free of the editors' own prejudices on these matters.

The editors are grateful to the participants for entrusting them with the task of editing this book and hope that they will not be too disappointed with the outcome.

K.D.G.
C.L.J.

February 1975

Keynote Address

M. J. METHVEN

I was very pleased and highly flattered and honoured to have been given the opportunity to open this conference on competition policy in the EEC. While I have only comparatively recently taken up the job as Director General of Fair Trading, I am not by any means a stranger to competition policy. I was for some 18 months a part-time member of the Monopolies Commission and looking round this evening I am particularly pleased to see a number of ex-colleagues, both from among the Commissioners and the staff of the Commission who are attending this conference. I also had a number of years industrial experience with Imperial Chemical Industries and I hope that the cynics here don't think that my service there has made me an expert in anti-competition policy also! There are, however, advantages for a gamekeeper in knowing something of the skills and art of poaching! It is perhaps unfortunate that up to now, interest in competition matters, outside the United States at least, has been fairly limited although I believe that interest both in this country and elsewhere in competition matters is growing. I believe that the series of conferences, the last two of which were held in Cambridge in 1969 and in Tokyo in 1973, have contributed substantially to the growth of interest in competition matters; and conferences such as this one will stimulate interest even further. But the limited, though growing, interest in competition matters has one positive and happy result because it means that it is easier to keep contact personally with all those who are working or studying in the same field. Given the international operations of large business firms these days – and the number of large businesses and the scale of their operations continue to grow – it is important for those of us interested in competition matters, whether from an academic or an enforcement viewpoint, to keep in touch and to exchange our ideas and experiences across national frontiers. Among the European visitors, Professor Jacquemin, Dr Markert, Professor de Jong and Professor Mathijsen will be presenting papers. And I would like to extend a particularly warm welcome to all our overseas visitors who give an international flavour to this conference. The conference will, of course, be devoting much of its time to considering the relationship between national and European community action in the competition field. It therefore gives me, and I am sure all of us here, particular pleasure to see that Dr Schlieder will be taking part in our discussions. I still regard myself, because of my early training and work with local government and ICI, as at least partly a lawyer (a lapsed lawyer in fact!). And, as a lawyer I have found it difficult enough to understand even sections of the English law, let alone the law of the country from which I hail – Scotland. Indeed, if the truth be told I still do not know what some parts of the Fair Trading Act mean, let alone the Consumer Credit Act. I have never, therefore, ceased to be amazed at the facility that Dr Schlieder shows not only in understanding different legal systems, but in his ability to expound the law with clarity while switching effortlessly between two or three languages.

I am also glad to see present here a large number of economists. This is not only because it will ensure a lively discussion, since I understand it to be a basic law of economics that the number of economic opinions expressed always exceeds, by at least one, the number of economists present, but also because it is further evidence of the growing academic respectability, if I may so put it, of micro-economics. I am not an economist and so perhaps can venture sweeping opinions where trained economists would have to be much more cautious. But it seems to me that whatever the virtues of the broad macro-economic approach, or the intellectual delights of mathematical analysis and model building, the detailed analysis by economists of how specific firms or industries actually operate and detailed study of the workings of particular structures of the economy, have a much more important part to play in our understanding of economic behaviour than has sometimes been realised in the past.

I don't want in these opening remarks of mine to anticipate the discussions which will take place over the next 2½ days of the conference. But it is nearly the first anniversary of my appointment as Director General of Fair Trading and it seemed to me an opportune time to share with you some of the ideas to which my first year of Office have given rise. It used to be said that the best work of scientists and mathematicians was done in the first few highly productive years in their middle and late 20s soon after they had completed their university courses. I cannot lay claim to such youth. But it could be that the first year or two of my new job, when I am comparatively untrammelled by experience or the inevitable caution which it is said that public service produces, is the occasion of the most useful impressions and ideas about competition. My Office comprises, as you know, three divisions – monopolies and mergers, restrictive practices and consumer affairs. A fourth one is being added to take over wide responsibilities under the new Consumer Credit Act – a measure which has entirely reformed and largely rationalised the law relating to consumer credit in the UK and which could well be followed in other European countries.

When I started up the Office of Fair Trading last November I took over an already existing machine for dealing with monopolies, mergers and restrictive practices: and it was only my responsibility for consumer affairs which was entirely new and had to be built up from scratch. It is, therefore, inevitable that much of my time and attention has had to be given to the consumer affairs side of the Office and this was naturally the part of my work on which public attention tended to focus. This, after all, is the area which the general public can see most immediately influencing its day to day affairs.

There is one major point about the work of my Office which I should like to make. In US terms it combines the functions of the Anti-Trust Division of the Justice Department and the Federal Trade Commission. It is a regulatory agency. Further, I am working in an area where the same policies are, broadly speaking, supported by the main UK political parties. The Office was set up by a Conservative Government and has been given a major addition of work by the Labour Government. This should and does mean, therefore, that it is possible in the competition and consumer affairs fields to work out and implement policies on a long-term basis – something which I feel is very necessary when you consider how far, for example, monopoly and merger control, and restrictive practices legislation can and do affect industrial and commercial structure and profitability. Further, we have also found in the Office of Fair Trading over the last year that there are great benefits in having those responsible for the three different branches of legislation dealing with restrictive practices, monopolies and mergers all working closely together in one organisation.

Let me now turn in more detail to restrictive practices, monopolies and mergers. I think that the UK restrictive trade practices legislation has been remarkably effective in dealing with cartels and cartel agreements in manufacturing industry in this country and it is an important development that cartels in the service sector are shortly to be brought under the same regime. Not only have the bulk of cartel agreements been struck down or dropped, but in my view, just as importantly, the Restrictive Trade Practices Act seems to have changed the whole climate of thinking about cartel agreements. UK cartels are no longer respectable as they were in the thirties, forties or even the fifties. I think one can only gauge the scale of the change if one thinks back to the climate in industry in the thirties and in the post-war years. Two thoughts, however, occur to me in this field. The first is that it may well be that our success in abolishing restrictive agreements has been an important factor in encouraging merger activity and industrial concentration in the UK. Thus by 1970 one hundred firms controlled approximately 50 per cent of the net manufacturing output in the UK and if the concentration trend continues at the same pace, it could lead to 80–90 per cent of the net manufacturing output in the UK being controlled by 100 firms by the turn of the century. The second is that anyone concerned with competition policy is bound to wonder how far overt agreements have been replaced by more informal types of concerted behaviour which may not strictly fall within the statutory definition of a restrictive agreement (and thus become registrable under the Acts) or, if they do, are less easy to identify. The Monopolies Commission's report on parallel pricing explained how the structure of an industry and in particular high concentration, could itself lead to parallel behaviour or price leadership. High concentration may well be a necessary condition for parallel action and it could be that in some industries it is a sufficient condition. But this is an area in which the dividing line between what is lawful and unlawful may sometimes be crossed by those who sail close to the wind. Some interesting – and difficult – problems may arise. How far is the tendency to uniform behaviour reinforced by some sort of communication between the parties? Should we have wider and more readily available powers of inspection and enquiry? Would public opinion, and more particularly opinion in industry, be ready to accept this? And there is a wider question; assuming that parallel pricing arises, as it well may, without anything that remotely could be described as collusion, what should be done about it? How can you compel firms not to follow a leader?

On monopolies it seems to me that in spite of all the investigatory work that the Commission has done over the years, there is still not enough evidence to justify our assuming that monopolies, and I am using the word in the technical sense of the Fair Trading Act of a 25 per cent market share, are of themselves *against* the public interest. If this is right, and I think it is, it seems that we must continue with the case-by-case examination of individual monopoly situations. The setting up of my Office has meant that we are now able to devote more resources to an examination of structure, behaviour and economic performance of different industries. The economic information which we are collecting, recording and analysing, will be continuously added to and updated and will help us to a more systematic approach to selecting suitable references to the Monopolies and Mergers Commission than has been possible before. The case-by-case examination of the Monopolies Commission is, of course, a slow process, although the power to ask the Commission to report on a particular aspect of a monopoly will enable shorter reports to be produced in some cases. But if we are to have a Commission whose members have a wide range of experience and interests, it means that most of them will be part-time. Industry is not always anxious to co-operate in providing information quickly and thoroughness of investigation is important. This all takes time. A monopoly enquiry also imposes burdens on the firm and not least on senior management. This has sometimes led to suggestions that some enquiries could be conducted quickly and confidentially inside my own Office. This would be a mistake in my view. The fact that the Commission have to publish their reasoning and evidence helps to ensure a fair and thorough investigation, of which I can speak from my own experience on the Commission, and it ensures that the Commission's assessments and conclusions are open to public scrutiny and discussion.

Mergers seem to me to be the area with perhaps the greatest number of question marks. Ought we to be more worried than we appear to be about the trend in this country to greater overall concentration in the private sector as well as the trend towards increasing concentration in individual sectors of industry? And should this mean that we should be taking a tougher attitude on proposals to merge? If so should this be by referring more mergers to the Monopolies Commission (even if that means that the delay leads to some beneficial mergers not going ahead?) Or do we need to be even more radical and require the parties to all important mergers to demonstrate that the merger produces net public benefits before it can be allowed to go through? The problem seems to me to be most acute when dealing with conglomerate mergers. Horizontal or vertical mergers have, after all, clear effects on competition which are not too difficult to determine. Assessing these mergers involves deciding where the balance of advantage lies between the adverse effects on competition and the benefits, such as scale economies, or promotion of employment which the mergers might bring. The issues tend to be fairly clear. The effects of conglomerate mergers on competition are more difficult to see and the issues they raise are more difficult to identify. The strict application of merger control in the USA on vertical and horizontal mergers may well have led to a major conglomerate merger wave. Recently, however, the popularity of conglomerate mergers seems to be in decline as both business opinion and academic research have questioned whether they have, in fact, led to greater operating efficiency and profitability. Large conglomerate mergers bring problems of power in the market place and the exercise of managerial control. If the United States' experience suggests, as it seems to, that these problems are not outweighed by greater efficiency, we might need to adopt a more critical approach to conglomerate mergers in this country.

Then there is the particular problem of reconciling thoroughness and fairness of investigation with the need for the greatest possible speed in dealing with merger situations if beneficial, or at least harmless mergers are not to be unnecessarily impeded. We pride ourselves in the Office of Fair Trading on being able to give advice on a merger within two or three weeks of the information becoming available to us and I think our performance and that of our predecessors in the Department of Trade and Industry have been welcomed by industry and the City. The responsibility for deciding whether a merger should be referred to the Commission rests with the Secretary of State. If a reference is made the Monopolies Commission must report within six months and usually does so more quickly than that. But are there any ways in which the system could be speeded up? After all, things can change very quickly – look what has happened to the UK stock market in the last six months.

Finally, we know that there is increasing concern in the European Community about concentration, and the Commission's proposals for a new system of merger control are being studied by a group of officials set up by the Council of Ministers. Certainly there are some who would argue that the scale on which modern industry operates means that there will be some cases, at any rate, where national systems of merger control would not be adequate to deal with mergers affecting trade on an international or a European scale. And, of course, the European Commission have argued that a European competition policy must involve a European merger control more far-reaching than that provided by Article 86 of the Treaty of Rome. These are issues which will come up in our subsequent discussions. But whatever view one takes, if there is to be a European system of merger control there will be important problems in reconciling it with national systems of control and the efficient working of financial institutions capital markets; and the same kind of problems that one also comes up against in a national system of control, speed and fairness.

Had I been addressing another kind of audience I might have thought that I have just reached the point where I should start an impassioned peroration about the virtues and benefits of competition, but this would just be preaching to the converted. So since I have been posing questions rather than seeking to answer them, I wonder if I might end my remarks by asking whether we are right in the UK to adopt an agnostic view generally about monopoly and mergers and to operate on a system of assessing the pros and cons in each case, or whether we should adopt the same approach as we and the EEC have to cartels, namely to regard all of them, subject to some specific exceptions, as bad in themselves. Does the one lead to too much uncertainty or the other to too much rigidity? And perhaps most difficult of all, when you have set up all your investigatory bodies and regulatory agencies, can you do more than identify and try to stop or control specific abuses of market power, and have we all in the end got to admit that we have not yet found a way of preventing people following a leader or of making people compete? The value of a seminar of the kind we have just started is that it enables national and international civil servants, businessmen and economists to discuss and pool their ideas about our common problems. I know that this conference which Professor George and Mr Silberston have worked so hard to organise, will be a great success.

1
The legal framework

K. D. GEORGE AND C. L. JOLL

In this introduction we trace the development of competition policy in the UK and the EEC. This provides the background to the specific issues discussed in the six papers contained in this book, and a guide to the complex succession of laws and statutory bodies involved in the administration of competition policy. It also gives an explicitly comparative view of policy towards monopolies, mergers and restrictive practices as separately evolved by the UK and the EEC. Thus we look at the relative scope of UK and EEC laws, the procedures and sanctions provided for enforcing the law and the extent to which these have been used successfully. This serves to point out any difference in the attitudes towards the competitive process adopted by the UK and the EEC authorities respectively.

Some difference is to be expected in view of the different objectives pursued by competition policy in a single national economy and in an international common market. Thus while the objectives of UK policy in this area are rarely spelt out explicitly and may seem to be dictated at least in part by the prevailing concerns of macro-economic policy it may be taken that policy is aimed at improving some aspects of national economic performance. Indeed it has been said that the only specific guidance on 'the public interest' provided by the 1948 Monopolies and Restrictive Practices (Inquiry and Control) Act (the first piece of UK legislation in this area) was its emphasis on a nationalistic approach. EEC competition policy, on the other hand, is given an important role in achieving the fundamental aims of the Common Market as laid down in Article 2 of the Treaty of Rome: 'a harmonious development of economic activities, a continuous and balanced expansion, an increase in stability, an accelerated raising of the standard of living and closer relations between the states belonging to it'. In other words the aims of EEC competition policy are primarily international in character – the economic integration of Europe.

This fundamental difference manifests itself in a number of ways: one of the obvious ones being the difference in scope between UK legislation and that of the EEC. Thus UK policy is concerned with restrictive agreements and monopolistic abuses which have consequences for the UK economy: restrictions in the export market are not prohibited. EEC policy, conversely, is concerned only with anti-competitive behaviour which 'may affect trade between member states' and not with purely domestic restrictions. Given this difference in attitude a conflict in interest between the EEC and national authorities is quite likely to arise on competition policy matters.

Thus a restrictive agreement or merger which would have the effect of strengthening the balance of payments of the country in which the firms are situated, and so would be considered by the national authorities to be in the public interest, could be prohibited by EEC law as inhibiting inter-state trade. This possibility of conflict between the EEC and its constituent states is strengthened when one realises that, in the attempt to ensure fair competition throughout the Common Market, the EEC's competition policy is not confined to measures affecting private firms but also includes control over Governmental aids to industry and those aspects of fiscal policy which affect industry. Thus the term 'competition policy' must be broadly interpreted in the context of the EEC and in fact only one part of the Commission's annual reports on competition policy is about 'competition policy towards enterprises' with which this book is mainly concerned. Chapter 7 on the EEC's competition policy towards member states looks at these broader aspects, which in the UK have been regarded as part of industrial or regional policy, although they obviously affect competition. Since there are many ways in which the interests of a single member state may conflict with those of the Common Market, and since the actions of private firms or national Governments can do much to block integration, the power to take competition policy decisions is firmly centralised in the EEC Commission, and representatives of the member states have only a consultative role.

The member countries of the EEC have national competition policy laws and enforcement apparatus developed to varying degrees – most highly in the UK and Germany. Thus restrictive agreements, monopolistic practices and mergers which affect inter-state trade as well as one or more national economies may be subject to EEC law as well as at least one set of national laws. Harmonisation and the avoidance of unnecessary and time-wasting duplication has some way to go: meanwhile, should conflicting decisions be reached as to the legality of some form of anti-competitive behaviour, EEC law has priority.

EEC policy has from the start taken the US approach of separating the problems arising from agreements between firms from those arising from a single firm of large size, and such a dichotomy has also been evident in UK law since 1956. Policy is in general more hostile towards the former group of problems since restrictive practices seem to involve restricting competition without the prospect of any compensating economies of scale. Most activity in EEC competition policy has in fact been directed against restrictive practices under Article 85 of the Treaty of Rome: the EEC's policy towards single firm monopolies is contained in Article 86 of the Treaty of Rome which has been relatively little used. However, a two-pronged attack on restrictive practices and monopolistic abuses has been found inadequate to maintain a competitive industrial structure in the UK and the EEC, which has led in both cases to the introduction of measures to control merger activity. Since restrictive practices have accounted for the bulk of EEC competition policy decisions to date, it is these we examine first.

Policy in the UK and the EEC towards restrictive practices

As stated in the previous section, competition policy is in general more hostile towards restrictive practices than towards the large-firm problems posed by monopolies and mergers and the following sections will show that this is certainly true of both the UK and the EEC. However, although restrictive practices are in general condemned for restricting competition without creating any gains in efficiency from increased scale of output, in neither system are restrictive practices subject to blanket prohibition and illegality. Thus, as will be seen, both UK and EEC policies contain provision for exemption from prohibition for agreements which fulfil certain conditions, and also in certain circumstances agreements of particular kinds or with particular objectives may be actively encouraged by the authorities. In the UK various government bodies, notably the National Economic Development Office, have promoted agreements in certain industries to increase efficiency and rationalisation; and the EEC Commission has always made it clear that not all forms of agreement are prohibited. Its annual reports on competition policy contain a section 'Encouragement of permitted forms of co-operation' – these are mainly agreements concerning specialisation or joint research by smaller firms, which may enable the firms concerned to compete more effectively.

UK legislation

UK legislation on restrictive practices is contained in a number of Acts of Parliament: the Monopolies and Restrictive Practices (Inquiry and Control) Act 1948, the Restrictive Trade Practices Act 1956, the Resale Prices Act 1964, the Restrictive Trade Practices Act 1968 and the Fair Trading Act 1973. To some extent this can be seen as a gradual extension of the scope of restrictive practices policy, although as indicated above this policy has not been unswervingly in favour of competition.

UK policy towards restrictive practices made a tentative start with the passing of the 1948 Act. This marked the end of a period in which the favourable attitude to restrictive agreements distinguished above predominated in the conditions of the inter-war years. The introduction of this legislation was called for by the famous 1944 White Paper 'Employment policy' which considered that restrictive practices and monopolistic behaviour might frustrate the Government's new determination to secure a high level of employment and economic growth. Whatever the merits of this argument, the success in subsequent years in maintaining high levels of demand and employment in turn provided a favourable economic climate for an attack on the more blatant forms of restrictive agreements.

Various official committees reporting in the inter-war period recommended that there should be investigation into the extent of monopolistic situations and restrictive practices in the UK economy in order to discover whether they had undesirable effects, and the 1948 Act was primarily designed to elicit this information. To this end, it created an administrative tribunal to be called the Monopolies and Restrictive Practices Commission – at this stage of UK policy the necessity for having different machinery for single and multi-firm forms of anti-competitive behaviour was not recognised. Although investigations into various forms of restrictive practice occupied most of the Monopolies and Restrictive Practices Commission's time during the first eight years of its existence, the part played by the Commission in the development of restrictive practice policy was largely preliminary and exploratory. In 1956 restrictive practices were removed from the jurisdiction of the Commission which, however, continued to have responsibility for monopoly situations and will be discussed in more detail later.

Suffice it to say here that the 1948 Act empowered the Board of Trade to refer to the Monopolies Commission any good supplied, processed or exported by two or more persons who 'conduct their respective affairs so as to prevent or restrict competition in connection with the production or supply of goods of the description in question' provided that the firms concerned account for at least one-third of the UK supply of the good. Between 1948 and 1956 the Board of Trade made some 13 restrictive practice references to the Monopolies Commission, designed to cover a wide variety of restrictions, and these revealed the prevalence of restrictive practices in the UK economy. The most influential of the Commission's reports was that on *Collective Discrimination* published in 1955 (Cmnd 9504) in which the Commission looked at exclusive dealing, collective boycotts, aggregated rebates and other discriminatory trade practices, and concluded that all these types of agreement were likely to adversely affect the public interest. The report considered that sufficient evidence about the extent and effects of restrictive practices had now been collected and recommended new tougher legislation, but while the majority favoured general prohibition with specific provisions for exemption a minority report recommended the registration of agreements and the examination of individual cases.

The minority report was adopted by the Board of Trade as the basis of the Restrictive Trade Practices Act, passed in 1956, which marks the beginning of UK restrictive practices policy proper. Thus the 1956 Act separates monopolies and restrictive practices in terms of both policy attitude, which was more adverse to restrictive practices, and procedure: monopolies were left in charge of the reconstituted Monopolies Commission while a judicial system was established to deal with restrictive practices. The Act established compulsory registration of agreements, defined as 'the acceptance by two or more persons of restrictions relating to such things as prices to be charged, terms or conditions on which goods are to be supplied, processes of manufacture to be applied and persons and areas to be supplied' between two or more persons operating in the UK. Such agreements are initially assumed to be against the public interest. The register, which was to be open to the public, was kept by the Registrar of Restrictive Trading Agreements who was also to prosecute individual agreements before the Restrictive Practices Court. The Fair Trading Act passed in 1973 transferred the responsibilities of the Registrar of Restrictive Trading Agreements to the newly created Director General of Fair Trading and extended the coverage of restrictive practice legislation slightly (see below) but made no other substantial changes.

Under the 1956 Act restrictive agreements are presumed contrary to the public interest and this may seem to represent a descent from the fence and a commitment to competition in comparison with the neutral attitude of the 1948 Act. However, the presumption in the latter Act is not universal and may be reversed under certain conditions. These are (*a*) that the agreement must have beneficial effects falling into one of seven categories laid down in the Act and (*b*) these benefits must outweigh the detrimental effects of the agreement in reducing competition. The circumstances in which an agreement may be found to have beneficial effects, known as the 'gateways', are

(*a*) where the restriction is necessary to protect the public against injury in connection with the consumption, installation or use of the goods in question;

(*b*) where removal would deny the public other benefits or advantages arising from the restriction or arrangements or operations resulting from it;

(*c*) where the restriction is necessary to counteract measures taken by a non-party to prevent or restrict competition in relation to the goods in question;

(*d*) where the restriction is necessary to negotiate fair terms for the supply of goods to, or the acquisition of goods from, a non-party who controls a preponderant part of the trade in such goods;

(*e*) where the removal of the restriction would have a serious and persistent adverse effect on unemployment in an area in which a substantial part of the trade in question is situated;

(*f*) where the removal of the restriction would cause a reduction in exports;

(*g*) where the restriction is required for the maintenance of any other restriction found by the Court not to be contrary to the public interest.

The onus of proof is on the firms concerned to show that their agreement is not against the public interest, unlike merger and mono-poly legislation, but the inclusion of these gateways severely qualifies the commitment of UK policy to competition as the best way of achieving desired objectives. This conclusion is strengthened by the subsequent Restrictive Trade Practices Act of 1968 which introduced additional grounds on which a restrictive agreement might be allowed. The Act introduced an eighth 'gateway':

(*h*) where the restriction does not directly or indirectly restrict or discourage competition to any material degree in any relevant trade or industry and is not likely to do so.

The Board of Trade was also given the power to exempt from registration an agreement calculated to promote a project or scheme of national interest designed to create or promote efficiency or to create or improve production capacity as long as the agreement is no more restrictive than necessary to achieve the purpose and is on balance in the national interest. Finally, a 'competent authority' (this includes a number of Government departments) can exempt from registration agreements designed to prevent or restrict price increases or secure price reductions.

Before introducing for comparison the grounds on which a restrictive agreement may be exempt from the general prohibition of EEC law a few points may be made about the UK attitude. First, there are a large number of ways in which an agreement which restricts competition may nevertheless not be found to operate against the public interest. These include contribution to other areas of government policy, e.g. full employment, price stability, balance of payments equilibrium. The wisdom of including such considerations in competition policy de-cisions, rather than making the latter on more limited grounds of competition and efficiency and using other and more effective policies to deal with macro-economic problems, may well be questioned.

Second, UK legislation is quite ready to concede that a restrictive agreement may promote efficiency more than competition would – such an attitude would be totally alien in the US where many types of restrictive practice are '*per se* illegal'. Gateway '*b*' of the 1956 Act (which is the widest, having let through seven of the ten agreements upheld by the Court) has been criticised in this respect since it appears to invite balancing the advantages from a restriction against those from competition with no presumption in favour of either. However, gateway '*b*' was somewhat superseded by the 1968 Act which enables the Board of Trade to license restrictive agreements which contribute to efficiency and are, on balance, in the public interest – indeed these do not have to be registered. This means that one of the main advantages of the UK restrictive practice system – its openness to public opinion and scrutiny – is weakened since a government department can decide that an agreement is 'on balance' in the public interest, or will keep prices down, without having to prove this in front of the Court and enable the public to see exactly what restrictions are being permitted. This clause reflects increased Governmental reliance on planning rather than free competition to promote industrial efficiency in the late 1960s.

Third, the procedure of the Restrictive Practices Court has been criticised for being open-ended: a large number of agreements are terminated voluntarily without trial. In this case no order is made not to form another agreement to like effect although this is exactly what may occur in many cases.

Fourth, for various reasons – including pressure from the business community which was suspicious of the Monopolies and Restrictive Practices Commission and thought it too slow – the UK has adopted a judicial rather than an administrative framework for dealing with restrictive practices. The formation of a special branch of the High Court raises the important questions of the justiciability of the primarily economic issues raised in restrictive practices cases (none of the members of the Court is an economist, although economic evidence is presented), and in particular about whether the 1956 Act leaves the Court too much discretion in deciding whether an agreement should be upheld or struck down. If this were the case, so that the Court has in fact to make policy rather than judicial decisions, then many of the advantages claimed for a legal procedure, such as consistency and legal security, will in fact be substantially eroded.

EEC legislation

The principles of EEC restrictive practices policy are contained in Article 85 of the Treaty of Rome, and were translated into an effective policy by various implementing regulations, notably no. 17 which came into force in 1962. Article 85 states that 'agreements between undertakings, decisions by associations of undertakings and concerted practices which may affect trade between Member States and which have as their object the prevention, restriction or distortion of competition within the

Common Market shall be prohibited as incompatible with the Common Market'. The Treaty goes on to give examples of such agreements, e.g. price-fixing, and to state that prohibited agreements will be automatically void and then to specify the conditions for exemption from prohibition. An agreement, decision or concerted practice may be allowed if it contributes to improving the production or distribution of goods, or to promoting technical or economic progress, while allowing consumers a fair share of the resulting benefits, as long as the restriction is necessary for attainment of the objective and the firms concerned are not thereby enabled to eliminate competition in respect of a substantial part of the products in question.

How does the attitude towards restrictive practices and competition shown here compare with that discussed earlier in connection with UK legislation? The difference is one of degree rather than of kind. In both the UK and the EEC, restrictive practices are in general prohibited with provision for exemption, rather than being illegal *per se* (as in the US), or being judged solely in terms of effects (as with monopolies and mergers in the UK). However, the last-mentioned condition for exemption in the EEC implies that an agreement will not be allowed, however beneficial its effects, if it eliminates competition for a substantial part of the product. Thus benefits from restriction can be weighed against reduction in competition to only a limited extent, beyond which the detriment to competition is presumed to outweigh any other considerations. The UK legislation contains no such 'cut-off' provision in favour of competition, although the difference made in practice will depend on the Commission's interpretation of the conditions for exemption.

Also the range of benefits which can be claimed to ensue from an agreement in Article 85 is narrower than that encompassed by the gateways and other grounds for exemption of UK legislation. Under EEC law only improvement of production, distribution and technical progress are grounds for allowing an agreement and it may reasonably be supposed that such efficiency grounds are the correct ones on which to take competition policy decisions.

In general then the EEC legislation may be said to take a tougher attitude than the UK legislation: restrictive practices are prohibited, with a narrower range of benefits which can be offset against restriction of competition, and reduction of competition will be tolerated only up to a certain point. This tougher line is to be expected, given the different objectives governing competition policy for a nation state and for an international community – indeed most of the original member countries of the EEC had less legislation against anti-competitive behaviour than the UK at the time of the formation of the Community.

It should be emphasised that the prohibition of Article 85 expressed a principle of the EEC: the effectiveness with which this principle is applied depends very much on the procedure established for administering the law on restrictive practices, which procedure was laid down in a number of implementing regulations, notably Regulation 17 which came into force in March 1962. This means that between 1957 and 1962 competition policy was not administered on a community level and decisions were made by national authorities, who applied the principle of Article 85 with varying degrees of stringency.

Regulation 17 states that agreements and concerted practices as defined in Article 85 are prohibited. The EEC Commission, which is the enforcement agency in EEC competition policy (one of the Commissioners has responsibility for competition policy and there is a Directorate General for Competition under him), has wider powers to seize evidence than those afforded the Registrar of Restrictive Trading Agreements. If it uncovers an infringement of Article 85 the agreement is automatically null and void and fines of up to one million units of account or 10 per cent of turnover can be levied on each of the participating firms. The Commission can initiate investigations where a complaint has been made by an interested party or where the performance of an industry gives cause to suspect the existence of an anti-competitive agreement. Firms which wish to continue operating an agreement without threat of discovery and fine have two options open to them: they can apply for 'negative clearance', i.e. a declaration by the Commission that their agreement is not prohibited by Article 85 – usually because it does not affect competition between member states. Alternatively they can notify the Commission of their agreement and ask for exemption under 85(3). Regulation 17 did not make notification compulsory and although by the end of 1972 the Commission had been notified of some 37000 agreements estimates of the proportion of agreements covered by Article 85 which have not been notified vary from 50 per cent to 95 per cent.

The Commission's hearings are held in secret. Firms and member governments are legally obliged to render up all relevant evidence, and all interested parties have the right to be heard. The Commission also has to consult the Consultative Committee on Cartels and Monopolies which consists of one official from each EEC member state and was set up to give the states a voice in decisions taken at the Community level. The Commission can terminate an agreement by issuing informal recommendations to the firms concerned or by reaching a formal decision which legally enforces abandonment of the agreement. Conditions can be attached to the granting of exemptions or negative clearance, and exemption decisions may be revoked if the conditions are abused. Firms or member states can appeal against a decision of the Commission to the European Court of Justice on legal grounds or on matters of fact only against an exemption decision.

In the EEC then where, as we have seen, the law allows less room for discretion in decisions about whether an agreement should be upheld, such decisions are made in an administrative framework with the EEC Commission playing a role analogous to that of the Monopolies and Restrictive Practices Commission under the 1948 Act: it is judge, jury and prosecutor at the same time. Whether the administrative procedure of the EEC has produced less consistent decisions than those of the UK is not easy to say: both systems have been accused of fluctuating in attitude to certain sorts of restrictive practices.

How do these powers and sanctions compare with those provided by the UK legislation? It will be remembered that the 1956 Restrictive Trade Practices Act unlike EEC Regulation 17 makes registration of agreements compulsory and an unregistered agreement which comes to light may be treated as though all its restrictions are against the public interest. Where the Registrar has reasonable cause to believe that such an agreement exists he can ask whether this is so, but may not receive the truth – unlike in the EEC, he cannot seize documents. Thus firms operating an agreement unlikely to be exempted by the Court may well decide not to register since the worst consequence of non-registration – discovery and trial – is the same as that of registration. The 1968 Act attempted to improve this situation. It did not increase the Registrar's powers of discovery but made the duty to register statutory, and provided that an unregistered agreement which came to light was automatically void and could not be enforced.

The Restrictive Practices Court's hearings are open to the public so that there is less secrecy about its decisions than with the EEC Commission, although as noted above this particular difference has been reduced as a result of the 1968 Act. Firms have the right to present evidence. If an agreement is judged contrary to the public interest the Court can issue an order forbidding the parties to operate the agreement in its original form or another to like effect. The Court cannot impose fines as can the EEC Commission (in neither case are participants to an agreement liable to imprisonment as they are in the US). Appeal against a decision of the Court can be made on grounds of fact only and, as in the EEC, exemptions granted can be reviewed if the circumstances in the industry change.

Finally, we should consider the relative scope of the UK and of the EEC legislation in terms of types of agreement and of commodities covered by the prohibition, which affects the comprehensiveness of the law and how easily it can be evaded. EEC law is wider than that of the UK in both respects. Thus Article 85 prohibits agreements between undertakings, decisions of associations of enterprises and concerted practices. This may be broadly interpreted as covering all forms of anti-competitive co-operative behaviour by firms and the Commission has shown itself ready to make such a broad interpretation. The range of agreements made registrable by the 1956 Restrictive Trade Practices Act was somewhat unclear but a sufficient number of firms took refuge from the provisions of that Act in 'information' or 'open price' agreements which they considered non-registrable for such agreements to be explicitly brought into the scope of the legislation by the 1968 Act. The 1973 Fair Trading Act gave the Court power to look into restrictions arising from designs and patents (which have always come under EEC law), restrictive export agreements and collective agreements to recommend prices. Part II of the 1956 Restrictive Trade Practices Act dealt with resale price maintenance: collective agreements were made registrable and enforcement of such agreements prohibited, but individual resale price maintanance was made legally enforceable. In the EEC collective but not individual resale price maintenance comes under the prohibition of Article 85. However, individual agreements are only allowed if they are not exclusive and the dealer is allowed to buy from any supplier: this fulfils the EEC's purpose of breaking down national systems of resale price maintenance by allowing imports between the EEC countries. In 1964 the Resale Prices Act was passed in the UK, which made individual resale price maintenance illegal. Firms wishing to apply for exemption had to register their agreement with the Registrar of Restrictive Trading Agreements and prove that the resale price maintenance offers specified benefits to the public which outweigh the benefits to be expected from abandonment of the agreement. For this one type of restrictive practice then, UK policy is tougher than EEC policy though the EEC may be thought to have taken action against the aspects of resale price maintenance likely to affect trade between member states.

EEC law prohibits agreements in respect of goods and services, including in principle those supplied by public enterprises or in regulated markets. Labour is not covered in either system, although since the Fair Trading Act 1973 restrictive labour practices can be referred to the Monopolies and Mergers Commission for investigation only. The 1956 Act covered goods only although the 1973 Act extends this to cover commercial (but not professional) services.

Policy in the UK and the EEC towards monopolies

We turn now to examine the policies of the UK and the EEC towards those restrictions on competition which are due to the presence in the economy of large firms rather than to agreements between a number of firms. UK policy in this respect is contained in the Monopolies and Restrictive Practices (Inquiry and Control) Act 1948, the Monopolies and Mergers Act 1965 and the Fair Trading Act 1973. Monopolistic situations are examined in an administrative framework, unlike restrictive practices, by the Monopolies Commission which has had responsibility in this area since 1948, although the title of the Commission has changed to show its loss of jurisdiction over restrictive practices in 1956, and the addition of that over mergers in 1965. We shall refer to it as the Monopolies Commission throughout. EEC policy towards large firms is expressed by Article 86 of the Treaty of Rome but, in sharp contrast to the policy of Article 85 on restrictive practices, this policy remained an empty threat for many years, was first applied in 1971 and has been rarely used subsequently.

In general the attitude of competition policy in the UK and the EEC towards large single firms in the economy is more favourable than towards restrictive agreements between firms. Although the existence of large firms in a market may mean a high level of concentration and limited competition, there may be offsetting gains in the shape of greater efficiency in production, marketing or research and development to be reaped from increasing size, which are not available from agreements. The EEC, in particular, has welcomed the integration of the members' economies into a common market as affording an opportunity for European firms to grow to a size competitive with US firms without greatly increasing concentration. (In fact concentration in the EEC has increased considerably and concern at this has prompted the proposals for control over mergers which will be discussed later.) Thus UK policy towards monopolies is 'neutral' – no presumption is made as to their desirability and each case is answered separately. Likewise, EEC policy prohibits only the undesirable consequences which may ensue from a monopolistic situation: 'the abuse of dominant position'.

UK policy

The 1948 Act defines a monopoly situation as existing where one-third of the UK supply of any good is supplied, processed or exported by a single firm, or by two or more inter-connected firms corporate, or by two or more persons who 'conduct their respective affairs so as to prevent or restrict competition in connection with the production or supply of goods of the description in question'. Several points need to be made about this criterion (the 'monopoly' market share was reduced to 25 per cent in the Fair Trading Act). Obviously it does not define 'monopoly' in the conventional sense, since it includes oligopolistic situations, termed 'complex monopoly' in the 1973 Act. Nor is one-third presumed to be the market share at which a firm assumes a dominant position and may abuse its power. The intention rather is to define 'the conditions to which the Act applies' since these must be fulfilled before a market can be investigated. The use of a quantitative market-share criterion avoids some of the problems involved in establishing the existence of a dominant position as called for by EEC law but the problem of defining the appropriate market which will determine whether or not a firm's position fulfils the conditions to which the Act applies, remains a major problem.

Under the 1948 Act it was the Board of Trade which took the initiative in referring a good which fulfils the above conditions to the Monopolies and Restrictive Practices Commission for investigation, and this continued to be the case until 1973 (although the Department of Trade and Industry and subsequently the Department of Prices and Consumer Protection became the responsible departments). For convenience the various Government departments which have held responsibility for monopoly legislation are hereafter referred to as 'the Department'. Since 1973 the independent Director General of Fair Trading has also been able to make monopoly references. Members of the public can make requests or suggestions to the Department about markets to be referred to the Commission, but the Department is not obliged to take any notice of such suggestions, although they are made public. The Department can ask the Commission merely to determine whether the conditions to which the Act applies are fulfilled by the market for a particular good and if so, what practices the conditions lead to, or the Commission may also be asked to report on whether the conditions and things done by the parties concerned as a result of, or for the purpose of, preserving these conditions operate or may be expected to operate against the public interest. Section 14 of the Act contains guidance as to the sort of factors relevant to the 'public interest' implications of monopolistic practices:

> all matters which appear in the particular circumstances to be relevant shall be taken into account and amongst other things regard shall be had to the need...to achieve
>
> (*a*) the production, treatment and distribution by the most efficient and economical means of goods of such types and qualities, in such volume and at such prices as will best meet the requirements of home and overseas markets;
>
> (*b*) the organisation of industry and trade in such a way that their efficiency is progressively increased and new enterprise is encouraged;
>
> (*c*) the fullest use and best distribution of men materials and industrial capacity in the UK; and
>
> (*d*) the development of technical improvements and the expansion of existing markets and the opening up of new markets.

These considerations are obviously very general, and leave the Monopolies Commission a great deal of discretion in deciding whether a firm's behaviour is or is not against the public interest: such latitude has been attacked on the grounds that it may lead to inconsistency. The Commission had to wait until 1973 for a clearer definition of the public interest. Clause 84 of the Fair Trading Act states

> the Commission shall have regard to the desirability
>
> (*a*) of maintaining and promoting effective competition between persons supplying goods and services in the UK
>
> (*b*) of promoting the interests of consumers, purchasers and other users of goods and services in the UK in respect of the prices charged for them and in respect of their quality and the variety of goods and services supplied
>
> (*c*) of promoting, through competition, the reduction of costs and the development and use of new techniques and new products and of facilitating the entry of new competitors into existing markets
>
> (*d*) of maintaining and promoting the balanced distribution of industry and employment in the UK
>
> (*e*) of maintaining and promoting competitive activity in markets outside the UK on the part of producers of goods, and of suppliers of goods and services, in the UK.

Thus the 1973 Act, unlike earlier UK legislation, explicitly cites 'effective competition' as being in the public interest and also states that UK firms should behave competitively outside UK while the 1948 Act may be said to have taken a purely nationalistic attitude. However, the 1973 Act did not change the basic requirement that the Commission decides whether a firm's behaviour is against the public interest, the firm is not required to show that it operates to the benefit of the public interest and the onus is on the Commission to show otherwise, unlike the restrictive practice procedure.

UK monopoly procedure thus requires the Monopolies Commission to investigate the market for any good referred to it by the responsible Government department, identify any practices resulting from the monopoly situation and decide in each case whether such practices are against the public interest. How does this compare with the EEC's attitude towards monopolies as shown by Article 86?

EEC policy

Article 86 states that 'any abuse by one or more undertakings of a dominant position within the Common Market or in a substantial part of it shall be prohibited as incompatible with the Common Market in so far as it may affect trade between Member States' and goes on to give examples of abuse, such as the imposition of unfair prices, which parallel the types of restrictive agreements prohibited by Article 85. In some respects this policy stance is similar to that of the UK legislation – it is the abuse of a dominant position or non-competitive market conduct – which is condemned rather than the existence of such a position, i.e. the market structure which makes such conduct possible. Thus in both cases the possibility of a dominant firm which does not abuse its position is envisaged, and this differs from the USA where 'monopolisation' – the wilful acquisition or consolidation of a mono- polistic situation – is illegal *per se*. However, the possibility of identify- ing such a 'good' monopolist or dominant firm is more problematic in the EEC than in the UK. In the UK a monopolistic firm is fairly straightforwardly identified by reference to its market share and the firm's behaviour is then examined to see whether it operates against the public interest. However, the EEC Commission has taken the view that a dominant position may not be established simply with reference to market share, or in fact to other structural features since some evidence is needed that the firm is able, by virtue of its dominance, to exert an independent influence on the other firms in the market. If evidence of anti-competitive behaviour is required there seems to be no way to establish the existence of a dominant position without at the same time establishing its abuse. Article 86 was first used in 1971, when Article 85 had already been in use for many years and Professor Jacquemin suggests in chapter 5 that the problems involved in interpret- ing the Article are one reason for this delay.

UK and EEC policy – scope, procedure and powers

If we examine the scope of UK and EEC anti-monopoly legislation, it is obvious that both may be extended to the control of oligopoly situations, provided that the firms concerned account for a quarter of the market (UK) or have each or between them a dominant position and are likely to affect trade between member states (EEC). The concept 'abuse of a dominant position' has been considered by the Commission to cover merger proposals by a dominant firm which would have the effect of increasing its dominance; however Article 86 has not been found an adequate measure for merger control and only one merger case has been tried under this Article.

Export monopolies, when the firm's behaviour has no effect on the domestic market, were brought under the UK legislation in 1973, while the EEC is concerned only with practices which affect international trade. Until 1956 the Department could make 'general' references to the Monopolies Commission, for investigation of a practice rather than a market. Since 1965 this possibility has been reinstated for practices or agreements not covered by the separate restrictive practices legislation. The 1973 Act also provided that the Monopolies Commission can be asked to concentrate on one particular aspect of a reference in order to expedite its findings. The original UK legislation covered monopolies in the supply of goods only and excluded monopolies authorised by enactment. EEC legislation from the start covered services as well as goods and public enterprises except in so far as the latter are providing services of 'general economic interest' (see chapter 7). The range of markets which can be referred to the Monopolies Commission has been gradually extended: services were added in the 1965 Monopolies and Mergers Act, and the Fair Trading Act allows the Commission to look at the nationalised industries and at restrictive labour practices, although there is no provision for action on the latter.

The procedure followed by the Commission in an action under Article 86 is similar to that under Article 85 and was originally laid down in the same implementing regulation – no. 17 passed in 1962 – although less detail is given in the case of Article 86, probably because 86 does not provide for exemption with the consequent need for a complex notification procedure. Thus the Commission initiates an investigation *ex officio* or on request, holds hearings in private at which the firms concerned have the right to be heard, has the same extensive powers to elicit evidence, and consults the member states' representatives on the Consultative Committee on Cartels and Monopolies before reaching a decision. The Monopolies Commission in the UK operates with a similar administrative procedure when a reference has been received: hearings are held in two stages – 'factual' to uncover the facts and 'public interest' to assess the implications of these facts for the public interest. Interested parties can submit evidence at both stages and the Commission can require persons to attend and to give evidence. The Commission then reaches its conclusions, which need not be unanimous, and recommends action as suggested by its 'public interest' findings. The Commission has the supply of certain goods or services referred to it. It then has to determine, using a somewhat arbitrary definition of the market (in terms of both product and geography) whether the 'conditions to which the Act applies' are met. However, in examining the implications of the situation a more extensive structural analysis will be needed and the 'reference' market may turn out not to be the economically relevant market (see chapter 4 for some problems of market definition in merger cases). In addition, some examination of market behaviour or conduct will be needed to establish the existence of a 'complex monopoly' situation. The Commission's work is completed by submitting a report to the Government department responsible: the Minister has to lay the report before Parliament but doesn't have to accept the Commission's recommendations.

The powers of the EEC Commission to take action against proven abuses of dominant position are similar to those given to the Department in the 1948 Act to deal with practices found by the Monopolies Commission to operate against the public interest. Thus in both cases the authority can seek voluntary undertakings from the firms concerned to desist from practices considered undesirable and the Department in particular relies heavily on such informal dealings. Alternatively, more formal measures are available in both cases: the EEC Commission can take a decision which legally enforces abandonment of abusive practices (in the Continental Can case of 1971 since the abuse in question was a merger proposal this amounted to forbidding the merger) and in the UK Parliament can issue a statutory order compelling firms to desist from any practices considered to be against the public interest. Such statutory orders are rarely used, but the UK legislation also provides for a 'follow-up' reference to be made to find out whether firms are sticking by voluntary undertakings made to the Government, and two such references have in fact been made. In the EEC, firms or member governments can appeal against the Commission's decision, but no such appeal against the Department's decision, based on the Monopolies Commission's recommendation, is possible in the UK.

The remedies discussed so far would tend to support the view that the concern of UK and of EEC competition policy authorities in the area of monopolies is to regulate market conduct and stop bad behaviour, rather than to control underlying market structure. This is certainly true of the EEC, and may be thought to show a continuing favourable attitude towards large firms, but the 1965 Monopolies and Mergers Act in the UK gave the Department the power to influence industrial structure, by preventing the acquisition or providing for compulsory sale of undertakings or assets. This Act also extended the Department's regulatory powers: it could declare unlawful an agreement not covered by the restrictive practices legislation, ban certain practices (e.g. discrimination), require the publication of prices and regulate prices where those charged had been found to be against the public interest. Thus the remedies available against a large firm exerting its market power are potentially more radical in the UK than in the EEC, but the Department is most reluctant to exert its statutory power to break up monopolies, and has never in fact done so, even when such a course of action was recommended by the Monopolies Commission.

Policy in the UK and the EEC towards mergers

Finally, we examine the policies of the UK and the EEC towards mergers. This is the newest area of competition policy and the EEC still has no law relating specifically to mergers although the Commission has put forward proposals for a system of merger control which are now under consideration by the Council of Ministers. Thus any comparison between UK and EEC policies must be made on the basis of proposals which may be modified before becoming law. The control of merger activity is in a sense a logical counterpart to anti-monopoly policy, aimed at prevention rather than cure, since by controlling mergers the build up of monopoly positions can be prevented and the need to control the behaviour of large firms relieved. However, the control of mergers is a more radical policy than the types of monopoly policy pursued in the UK and the EEC, which have been confined to the regulation of abusive market conduct, since merger control means the prevention of concentration rather than of the adverse effects of concentration, and thus intervention in market structure.

Both in the UK and in the EEC, control over mergers was instituted some years after measures to deal with monopolistic abuses. This suggests that the attitude of policy towards mergers was somewhat ambivalent compared to that on, say, restrictive practices, and this has indeed been the case. The reason for this ambivalence is partly the same as that for the relatively more lenient attitude towards monopolies than towards restrictive practices – mergers between firms in the same or related industries may, it is argued, increase efficiency by increasing the scale of output, eliminating duplication of activities and so on. Moreover, mergers between small or medium-sized firms may actually increase competition within an industry. Furthermore, the threat of take-over can provide a spur to efficiency since it should be the more efficient who take over the less efficient firms, thereby improving industry's performance. Thus one strand of merger policy in both the UK and the EEC has been concerned to encourage beneficial mergers: in the EEC this includes particularly mergers between firms in different member countries as these contribute to integration, and also mergers are seen to offer a quick way for firms to grow to a size comparable with US competitors. In the UK the pro-merger strand of policy was briefly institutionalised in the Industrial Reorganisation Corporation which existed from 1966 to 1970, and has continued less formally since.

The co-existence of the Industrial Reorganisation Corporation and the Monopolies Commission emphasises the pragmatic UK approach to mergers which is neutral in the same sense as its monopoly policy – mergers as such are not presumed to be either good or bad, but each case is examined on its own merits – indeed the principles of UK merger policy are in many ways adopted from monopoly policy. The importance attached to control of mergers has however increased considerably in recent years, which have seen a surge of merger activity and increased concentration in many industries and has led to the intended introduction of merger control in the EEC, where monopoly policy is itself in its infancy. As previously mentioned the EEC anti-monopoly provision, Article 86, which prohibits the abuse of a dominant position has been interpreted to include the prohibition of acquisitions by dominant firms. However, Article 86 has only been used on one occasion against a proposed merger and its use in this area is inherently limited since the article applies only to firms which have already a dominant position, and so cannot be used to preserve the competitive structure of an industry. There is an additional asymmetry between merger and monopoly policies in the EEC since, whereas a firm can be prevented from merging so that industry structure is affected, if it grows to dominant size entirely by internal expansion only its conduct, and not its size, will be subject to control. In practice, although the 1965 Act allows for a structural policy approach, the same asymmetry has applied to the UK.

UK merger policy

Provision for the control of mergers in the UK was first made in the Monopolies and Mergers Act 1965, but had been advocated by a wide variety of groups for some years. This Act basically made mergers above a certain size liable to investigation in the same way as monopolies – the Board of Trade could refer a merger to the Monopolies Commission and ask the Commission to report on whether the merger would, or would be expected to, operate against the public interest. The Fair Trading Act 1973 which gave the Director General of Fair Trading the power to make monopoly references allows him only to *advise* the Department of Prices and Consumer Protection (now the responsible Department) on what mergers to refer to the Monopolies Commission. This asymmetry has been ascribed to the greater political sensitivity of mergers. Also, since 1973, as for monopoly references, the Department can ask the Monopolies Commission to concentrate on one aspect of a merger reference.

The size criteria specified for reference were either that assets taken over should exceed £5 million or that the merger would create or strengthen a monopoly situation (then one-third of the market, reduced in 1973 to one-quarter). Special conditions apply to newspaper mergers. The question asked of the Monopolies Commission is the same 'negative' one as in the case of monopolies – firms which wish to merge do not have to show that their merger will operate positively in the public interest. In the case of a merger which hasn't taken place the Monopolies Commission's examination of its effects must necessarily be speculative and this makes the Commission's task more difficult. The guidance given on how to interpret the 'public interest' by the 1965 Act was very vague, the Commission being instructed to 'take into account all matters which appear in the particular circumstances to be relevant', but the 1973 Act contains more explicit and pro-competitive considerations. These considerations are the same as those laid down for monopoly references (see p. 22).

EEC merger policy

The EEC's draft proposal for a Regulation on the control of concentrations between undertakings, which is the subject of chapter 3, appears to take a firmer line against mergers than the UK policy. Article 1(1) states that 'any transaction which has the direct or indirect effect of bringing about a concentration between undertakings...whereby they acquire or enhance the power to hinder effective competition in the Common Market or in a substantial part thereof, is incompatible with the Common Market in so far as the concentration may affect trade between Member States'. In other words, mergers which destroy effective competition will be prohibited. Several qualifications have to be made to this statement. First, as with the rest of EEC competition policy, this proposal covers only those mergers which affect inter-state trade. Second, like the UK legislation, it applies only to mergers above a certain size: the criteria laid down here are that the aggregate turnover of the firms is at least 200 million units of account or that the firms between them account for 25 per cent of turnover of the goods or services concerned in any member state. Third, there is provision for exemption: Article 1(3) of the draft proposal states that 'Article 1(1) may be declared inapplicable to concentrations which are indispensable to the attainment of an objective which is given priority treatment in the common interest of the Community'.

Thus the proposed merger policy of the EEC, like its policy on restrictive practices and unlike its monopoly policy, allows for exemptions from the general prohibition of anti-competitive mergers, but the grounds for exemption are wider and vaguer in this case. The inclusion of such a potentially wide open exemption clause reflects the ambivalence of EEC policy towards mergers in the past, which could hardly be expected to turn suddenly into an outright prohibition. Thus it is universally accepted that it must be possible to exempt some mergers from prohibition, on e.g. regional and social grounds, even if they do have adverse effects on competition. This is not the same attitude as in the UK where anti-competitive mergers may be justified by performance tests and appeal does not have to be made to the overriding aims of areas of policy other than competition. However, until the draft regulation becomes law and the first cases are heard it is not possible to say how easily 'public interest' exemptions will be granted and the force of the proposal eroded.

The draft regulation forbids mergers which 'create or enhance the power to hinder effective competition' and one can foresee controversy surrounding the interpretation of this criterion. As with the 'abuse of dominant position' prohibited by Article 86 this does not seem to be a purely structural concept although the regulation says 'the power to

hinder effective competition shall be appraised by reference in particular to the extent to which suppliers and consumers have a possibility
of choice, to the economic and financial power of the undertakings
concerned, to the structure of the markets affected, and to supply and
demand trends for the relevant goods and services.' In other words, by
reference to a broad set of structural features. Dr Markert (chapter 3)
expresses concern that to find out whether a merger will hinder
effective competition, data on conduct over a period of time is needed
and thus it may be impossible to reach a decision based on this
criterion within the legal time-limits. This appraisal will not be made
easier by the need for prediction in merger examinations.

The EEC regulation has evidently been drafted to cover all types of
merger like the UK legislation, since the size criteria in both cases are
cast in terms both of market share and of size *per se* (of assets in the
UK and turnover in the EEC). Neither system goes as far to prevent
mergers as the US anti-trust laws, which lay down 'guidelines' specify-
ing structural changes, i.e. certain increases in market share which are
presumed illegal.

UK and EEC procedure

The fact that in the majority of merger cases the competition policy
authorities are deciding on the desirability of an event which has not
yet taken place necessitates certain differences in procedure from
investigations into the already existing facts about restrictive agreements or monopolistic practices. In the case of mergers there is greater
pressure on the authorities to decide quickly, so that the merger can
either proceed or be abandoned before the circumstances which led to
the proposal are completely changed. Thus in both the UK and the EEC
a maximum time period is set, within which the decision on whether
to allow the merger must be made, and the merger can be held up until
the decision is reached. The EEC draft regulation proposes compulsory
pre-notification for mergers involving a combined turnover of one
billion units of account, unless the acquired firm has an annual turnover
of less than 30 million units of account. This does not include all
mergers covered by the proposal and other mergers may be notified
voluntarily. The EEC Commission has three months after notification
to decide whether to commence proceedings against the merger which
cannot take place during this time unless the Commission decides not
to proceed. If proceedings are decided on, the automatic 'stand still'
ends but the Commission can order suspension of the merger until
proceedings are concluded and a decision has been reached, which must
be within nine months of commencement. Merger proposals voluntarily
notified to the Commission can also be suspended. Thus mergers may
be delayed for a year. Mergers which are not compulsorily notifiable

are also subject to examination *ex post* by the Commission so it seems likely that firms contemplating a merger which would be covered by the regulation will prefer to notify the Commission and receive 'advance clarification' rather than go ahead with the merger and run the risk of subsequently being ordered to dissolve.

The same considerations mean that in the UK the Government department concerned will be informed of merger proposals covered by the 1965 and 1973 Acts although the UK has no formal pre-notification system. Such mergers are subjected to an initial scrutiny by a 'mergers panel' within the Department of Prices and Consumer Protection but with the Director General of Fair Trading as Chairman. This normally takes two to three weeks. The panel advises the Secretary of State, but he alone decides whether to refer a merger proposal to the Monopolies Commission. Mergers which have taken place within the last six months can also be referred. The Commission has to report within six months and a 'stand still' order can be made preventing the merger from completion during this time. In practice this has not been necessary as firms are most unlikely to enter finally into a merger which is still under investigation – in fact the acquiring company normally withdraws its bid when a reference is made to the Monopolies Commission and on several occasions the proposal has been abandoned although the Monopolies Commission is still obliged to complete its report. Thus the maximum delay likely to be imposed on a proposed merger is considerably shorter in the UK than in the EEC, although it must be recognised that the latter is dealing with a larger and more heterogeneous system. Nevertheless even the delays involved in the UK system have understandably been unpopular with the firms concerned.

The actual investigations of the EEC's Directorate General for Competition and the Monopoly Commission in the UK are much the same in merger as in monopoly cases in terms of hearings, power to call evidence, consultations etc. with the two differences already mentioned, namely that there is a time-limit on the proceedings and that the evidence relevant to assessing the effects of a proposed merger consists largely of forecasts.

The legal powers to control – i.e. prevent or dissolve – mergers are similar in the UK and the EEC. Thus in the event of the EEC Commission's finding that a proposed merger comes under Article 1(1) of the draft regulation it could issue a decision declaring the concentration incompatible with the Common Market and if the merger had already taken place it can be legally broken up. Exemptions under Article 1(3) may be granted only on certain conditions. As with decisions under Articles 85 and 86 appeal may be made to the Court of Justice. The 1965 Monopolies and Mergers Act gave the Department substantially greater powers than it previously possessed, including the power to prevent the acquisition of firms or assets, and to compel dissolution. In contrast to the situation in monopoly cases the responsible department has accepted the Monopolies Commission's recommendation in all merger cases so far examined. Of course there is less scope for negotiation since the merger has simply to be authorised or forbidden. An adverse finding is usually accepted by the firms concerned without recourse to legal steps to prevent the merger. Conditions may also be attached to the authorisation of mergers, and there is no provision for appeal. However, the EEC proposal also includes the possibility of fines, for giving incomplete or misleading evidence, for failing to notify where this is compulsory, or if a merger is completed during the standstill period or after it has been prohibited.

Obviously it is difficult to say in advance how successful the EEC's proposals will be in preventing increased concentration, since this depends very much on how 'the power to hinder effective competition' is interpreted and how easily exemptions are granted for mergers which are 'indispensable to the attainment of an objective which is given priority treatment in the common interest of the Community'. Dr Markert discusses the proposals in some detail in chapter 3, and makes various suggestions for rendering the control over mergers more effective. In particular he suggests that the regulation may 'catch' so many mergers that sheer volume will threaten the efficiency of the system, and that with the available resources and hierarchical structure of the EEC's Directorate General for Competition only superficial decisions will be reached in the time available. This may result in many mergers with anti-competitive effects being allowed to proceed simply because there isn't time to examine them all. This process has been observed in the case of restrictive practices where the Directorate General's workload is also very heavy. But the costs involved in delaying examination of a merger are greater than in delaying restrictive practices cases since in the meantime the merger will proceed and it is more difficult to break up a firm than to dissolve an agreement.

Finally, Article 86 will continue to apply to mergers by firms in dominant positions not covered by the new regulation, and it appears that, although the Continental Can case remains the only formal merger decision reached under Article 86, the Directorate General for Competition, which monitors the process of concentration in the Common Market, has intervened informally to prevent other mergers taking place.

APPENDIX

Most of the papers in this book contain references to and quotations from relevant pieces of legislation. There follows for the reader's convenience a complete list of the major UK and EEC competition policy Laws.

United Kingdom Statutes
>1948. Monopolies and Restrictive Practices (Inquiry and Control) Act
>1956. Restrictive Trade Practices Act
>1964. Resale Prices Act
>1965. Monopolies and Mergers Act
>1968. Restrictive Trade Practices Act
>1973. Fair Trading Act

EEC

(*a*) Laws contained in the Treaty of Rome, 1957
>Article 7. Discrimination on the basis of nationality
>Article 37. State Monopolies
>Article 85. Restrictive agreements, decisions and concerted practices
>Article 86. Abuses of dominant positions
>Article 90. Public undertakings
>Articles 92–94. Aids granted by Member States

(*b*) Implementing Regulations

EEC Regulation no. 17/62 – procedure for administering Article 85
>(proposed) EEC Regulation on the control of concentrations between undertakings (being considered by the Council of Ministers, January 1975)

2
EEC competition policy towards restrictive practices

H. W. DE JONG

The essence of European economic integration obviously lies in the conversion of the pre-war closed economies of Western Europe into a system of free-exchange economies bound together by rules. The market process has been given the chance to work within a joint Common Market formed initially by six and later by nine national states. The acid test of the success of this concept is the degree to which interpenetration of trade and industry has occurred. The record bears out the striking progress which has been made – between 1957 and 1972 the share of trade between the initial six member countries in their total trade rose from 30 per cent to 52 per cent, which is twice as much as in the early 1950s. (On the basis of 1958 = 100, intra-Community trade rose to 721 in 1971, measured in units of account.) Calculations made by the Dutch Central Planning Bureau indicate that the elasticity of intra-EEC trade, with respect to the gross domestic expenditure of the national economies during the fifties and sixties was between 2.5 and 3.0, or nearly double the level of elasticity for world trade.[1]

Understandably, the degree to which trade flows increased between the various countries of the EEC has varied. In a previous study it was found that interpenetration of trade between countries in the period 1958–70 varied according to the previous 'openness' of the countries concerned; i.e. trade between Benelux countries and West Germany rose to a lesser degree than that between Benelux and Italy or between West Germany, Italy and France.[1]

Also, the number of cases in which a firm in one member country has established a subsidiary in another one has risen fast: the index on the basis of 1966 = 100 stood at 187 in 1971, indicating that member countries' firms have increasingly felt the necessity to establish themselves in partner countries.[2]

Thus the economies of the former six member states, and now those of the enlarged Community, are becoming an increasingly unified market due to the efforts of business firms. As a result, competition has intensified because firms encroach upon each other's traditional markets, in an effort to seize new opportunities. To a large extent this has taken the form of price competition based on the need to break into member countries' markets and to 'internationalise' price cuts.[3] The challenge confronting EEC firms was to benefit from the welding together of national economies and expand: to enlarge market shares, to capture the strategic points of production and distribution, to supply fast growing new products, to apply new production processes in order to cut costs and to streamline organisation; in short, the classic virtues of the competitive process made themselves apparent. Growing firms were aided in their efforts by the cyclical events of the first ten years: because of the divergent rhythms of economic fluctuations in the national economies, a period of recession or stagnation in the home market could be used to push sales in other member countries' markets. Apart from the macro-economic effects of this phenomenon, such as contribution to price stability, these divergent cycles tended to facilitate the interpenetration of trade, while in reverse, growing interpenetration dampened to some extent the cyclical fluctuations. European firms which made the 'forward leap' were therefore rewarded, instead of penalised as was often the case in the UK; they could not only gain stronger market positions, but also hold their costs down in recessions to the extent that they were able to remain fully employed by means of exports.

Moreover, competition was stimulated by two other events. First, the entry of a great number of firms from other countries, of which American firms had initially the lion's share; this share fell when other (mainly British) firms started operations in the Common Market later in the sixties and in the early seventies.[4] Second, the unsettling effects on firms of the uncertainty resulting from confrontation with unknown competitors in other member countries, with different goals and strategies, and pursuing different policies. Also, the increasing diversification of the larger firms made an impact, and this diversification seems to be increasing which adds to the instability of market relationships.

It is against this background that EEC competition policy has to be appraised. Governments may create a new institutional environment and express the desire that competition should be the pivot upon which the system hinges, but business must play the game. The fact that firms have seized the opportunities offered, driven by increased uncertainty, is of central importance. Competition policy in the EEC has therefore had a silent, powerful ally right from the beginning and it is as well to keep this in mind if in future years the degree of uncertainty were to decline because of the growth of firms into established positions.

The primary goal of competition policy in the EEC has been to ensure that the establishment of the Common Market will not be frustrated and distorted by firms bent on erecting or maintaining barriers to entry into their markets, regulating output and prices, splitting up markets, tying customers, etc., in short changing the uncertainty of competition for the security of regulated behaviour. Such privately regulated behaviour would tilt the balance between seller and buyer, old seller and new seller, producer distributor and customer, to the benefit of the former in each case, and may impede realisation of the aims of the Treaty. Competition policy can therefore be considered to be the necessary complement of a unified Common Market, devised to keep the market functioning and to safeguard the aims of the Treaty: freedom of movement for goods, services, persons and capital through-out the Community without barriers, and the harmonious develop-ment of economic activities (Articles 2 and 3). Freedom, the market and competition policy belong to each other as do the members of a Victorian family.

The pivotal role of the Commission

Competition policy therefore occupies a central place in the system; it has to ensure that economic agents continue to have a choice open to them. But high-sounding principles do not normally convince the economist. He is interested in the way these principles are applied and if necessary enforced.

It is eminently logical that the powers to take decisions relating to competition policy have been taken out of the hands of national states and been centralised at community level. Since Regulation 17 was issued on 21 March 1962, the Commission of the EEC is for all practical purposes exclusively empowered to issue firms or associations with recommendations and decisions designed to end infringement of Articles 85 and 86 and to exempt agreements or concerted practices.[5]

Though the Commission is expected to act 'in close and constant liaison with the competent Authorities of the Member States' and its decisions remain subject to review by the Court of Justice, the organ-isational centre of gravity in the EEC's competition policy is the Commission. Its role may be subdivided into two parts, legislative and executive. The legislative role is exercised by means of initiatives, laid before the Council of Ministers, which then empower the Commission to issue block exemptions. Two such initiatives have been made: in 1965 bilateral agreements relating to exclusive dealing and licensing were put into the hands of the Commission to be exempted from the prohibition of agreements under Article 85(1) and in 1971 a similar power to exempt was conferred upon the Commission with respect to agreements for standardisation, research and development and specialisation (of which only the last-named has so far been the subject of a block exemption regulation issued by the Commission).

The executive function of the Commission is geared to the examination of individual cases. Several stages are necessary: (1) the discovery of restrictive practices, and the supervision of prohibitions, conditions and obligations laid down with respect to former decisions; (2) the individual probing of a case and its possible solutions, as well as the making of the proposed decisions; (3) the harmonisation of proposed individual decisions with general competition policy aspects and with the legal structure of the Treaty; (4) the taking of a decision by the highest officials, the Members of the Commission and the Director General for Competition Affairs.

This general procedure ensures that competition rulings are harmonised with the economic, monetary, industrial and other policies of the Community and that some flexibility remains to allow for individual circumstances. The powers of the Commission are far reaching. It may seek any information considered necessary (including accounts, documents, verbal explanations, etc.) from the enterprise concerned or the association's offices or it may acquire this information from the national government or competent authorities. It may act upon information provided by individuals, companies or bodies, with a justified interest in a specific case. It may also conduct general enquiries into industries or sectors of the economy if there arises a presumption that competition is restricted; the firms in these sectors are then obliged to furnish the required information. Fines may be imposed on those unwilling or omitting to submit evidence or who give incomplete evidence, as the largest Belgian sugar refinery, which was fined 4000 units of account, found out to its cost. Member states are likewise obliged, according to Article 14(6) of Regulation 17 to assist investigations, to the extent of making available police officers to open closed doors.

However, the Treaty has not been so harsh as to leave firms or their defenders unarmed. Before a decision is taken by the Commission it has to consult some wise men, grouped into a Consultative Committee on Restrictive Practices and Monopolies, and it is obliged to hear the interested parties. The latter come first and in two rounds: interested parties may give both written and oral comments on the Commission's notice of objections, which indicates the important facts relating to an infringement. Hearings take place behind closed doors. After the accused men come the wise men and they make a written statement on the case which remains unpublished. The only way for that poor creature, the curious university researcher, to get some precise, factual information on what is going on, is to get himself appointed as an assistant of the accused party, in the role of a qualified person.[6] If, finally, the Commission takes a decision (that is a measure which has legal consequences for the interests of the parties concerned and imposes obligations) an appeal may be lodged with the Court of Justice within two months. Such an appeal may be wholly or partially successful.

Article 173 of the Treaty specifies the grounds for annulment of the decision: lack of competence, infringement of an essential procedural requirement (for example the absence of adequate reasons), infringement of the Treaty or of a rule of law, and misuse of powers (*détournement de pouvoir*). In cases of exemption under Article 85(3) grounds for annulment are restricted to questions of fact and the adequacy of stated reasons, because the Commission often has to make complex economic appraisals in such cases. If an appeal is wholly or partially successful, the Court of Justice may cancel or reduce the fines imposed. It may also increase them if it thinks less highly of the offenders than does the Commission.

Most cases have ended without a formal decision. This touches upon the important distinction between formal and informal cartel policy, well known in Continental European countries. Informal cartel policy refers to the ways in which the cartel authority deals with cartels which are not made public. If a cartel agreement is considered unimportant, or does not fall under the competition rules, or will have to be adapted if it is to qualify for exemption, the Commission will communicate this fact to the firms or associations concerned. Such a procedure enormously increases the flexibility of the system. Formal decisions which require lengthy preparations are avoided. Whereas 57 formal decisions were given in the period 1964–72, the Commission's file, which stood at some 37000 cases in 1963/64, was reduced to 2873 cases at the end of 1972. Thus about 34000 cases were cleared without formal decisions, partly because of the termination of agreements, partly because of block exemptions especially in the years 1967–9 after the issue of Regulation 67/67, and partly because of the informal cartel policy.

The changing nature of competition

What do restrictive practices restrict? The obvious answer will be that they restrict competition between firms. This is in a general sense considered to be rivalry between firms buying and selling goods, services and resources under conditions of uncertainty. There are however several varieties of competition, and restrictive practices are devised accordingly.

The problem is that competition is a many faced phenomenon which depends on the changing structure and growth of the economy. Industrial organisation economists have come to realise that structure and growth to a large extent determine the competitive market conduct and performance of sellers and buyers, while in reverse structure (and to a much lesser extent growth) can be changed by conduct and sometimes by performance. An adequate competition policy should therefore be aimed at the structural features of the economy and EEC policy has consistently been so aimed from the beginning.

Initially the main policy goal was to open national frontiers to foreign competitors and to prevent the consolidation of existing market structures in each of the member states. Now another function of competition policy is becoming increasingly important: the preservation of effective competition throughout the Community in order to ensure the efficient co-ordination of individual market decisions. The former task was a reflection of the need to create the Common Market and to establish it as a going concern. The latter task of competition policy takes into account the fundamental structural change which has taken place in recent years: the wave of mergers, leading to increasing concentration in many sectors, growth in absolute and relative size of the dominant European firms and increasing diversification. Firms will no longer feel the need to protect their own national markets, but will increasingly try to adapt their restrictive policies towards the new market structures which have emerged. Competition policy in the future will therefore have to be guided by such structural changes. It will have to look at types of restrictive practices designed for these structures such as international price cartels crossing national boundaries, concerted practices between dominant firms, international boycotts, restrictions of a conglomerate nature comprising reciprocal dealing, cross-subsidisation and price discrimination, and vertical squeezing operations in their various forms.

The review which follows of the 'old' and 'new' competition policies is necessarily confined to the main events. It does not seek to be exhaustive. It is moreover an economist's summary, foregoing many points which the lawyers – who until now have reigned supreme in the discussion of EEC competition policy – would consider of major importance.[7] A few essential terms will be defined as we go on; minor attention will be paid to the institutional and regulatory framework of the policy decisions and none to their application in particular areas such as agriculture or transport, or to the problems raised by state aids to industry, public enterprises or national commercial monopolies. A short glance at the essential points of Articles 85(1) and 85(3) will precede the review.

The prohibitions and exemptions of Article 85

Article 85(1) forbids all agreements between firms, decisions by firms or associations of firms and concerted practices which restrict competition in trade between member countries.

Agreements may be enforceable agreements, gentlemen's agreements, consisting of unsigned documents, or conditions of sale. Such agreements are generally considered in their legal and economic context in order to determine whether they are restrictive. Even a tiny requirements contract, tying an inn-keeper to a brewery (Brasserie de Haecht) was considered by the Court of Justice to fall under the prohibition of Article 85(1) because the national market (in this case Belgium) could well be pre-empted for foreign breweries if the system became generalised. The concept of concerted practice is more difficult and we will come back to it later on.

'Restriction of competition' may refer to the competition between contracting parties as well as to that involving outsiders (internal and external competition effects). It may be practised at a single stage of production or distribution (horizontal) or between different stages (vertical). It may also refer to various types of competition, such as price competition, product differentiation, new products or processes, etc. A further requirement is that trade between member states should be affected, either directly or indirectly, actually or potentially (Grundig/Consten Case, 1966). Thus ingenious devices limiting imports or exports, such as compensation schemes, collective rebates discouraging imports and terms of sale which eliminate the benefits derived from importing from a cheaper source of supply can be forbidden, as well as export bans or market divisions along national boundary lines. An agreement between firms in a single member state may well affect inter-state trade. This may happen when a requirements contract is concluded, when export bans are imposed on national customers or when an aggregate rebate cartel materially excludes imports. The inter-state trade clause thus has a wider application than is commonly thought and the Commission and Court of Justice have repeatedly surprised narrow-minded lawyers. The restriction must also have a 'noticeable effect' on the market. In a notice on agreements of minor importance issued in 1970 the Commission stipulated that if the participating firms have a market share of less than five per cent of the product concerned or an aggregate turnover of less than 15 million units of account (20 million units of account for companies involved in distribution) the infringement is considered to be insignificant. The idea was to promote co-operation between small firms not capable of restricting competition.

Companies have to decide for themselves whether their agreements or decisions infringe the competition rules. They may be helped, however, in cases of doubt by a pronouncement from the Commission, issued on their request, as to whether Article 85(1) is applicable to their case. The agreement, decision or practice is then tested and if found unobjectionable is given a 'negative clearance', pursuant to Article 2 of Regulation 17. The whole procedure described earlier including hearings, consultations and publication of the request, goes through before an agreement is cleared.

The powers of the Commission become clearly visible in Article 85(3) which deals with suspensions (individual cases) and exemptions (in group cases) from the prohibition of Article 85(1). Only the Commission is entitled to apply such dispensations, and it is restricted by the conditions of Article 85(3) which stipulate that dispensation may be given if agreements, decisions or concerted practices contribute to the improvement of the production or distribution of goods or to technical or economic progress and allow the consumer or customer a fair share of the resulting benefit. Moreover, it is also laid down that the restrictions must be indispensable to the attainment of these objectives (i.e. superfluous restrictions are considered inadmissible) and that competition must not be eliminated from the product market in question. Since Regulation 17 introduced a notification system, only agreements that have been duly notified are eligible for exemption; non-notified agreements which constitute serious restrictions under the prohibition of Article 85(1) (the so-called 'heavy cartels') will therefore not be reviewed for dispensation. This was the case with the quinine and sugar cartels in 1969 and 1973.

The Treaty thus acknowledges that some agreements may have such beneficial effects of an objective economic nature[8] that they can be approved. But the Commission is left with an appreciable amount of discretionary power. It determines whether agreements between firms lead to 'improvements' and 'progress', it may require the amendment of agreements before granting suspensions or exemptions, it can lay down conditions and obligations if dispensation is allowed (for example the provision of information) and can withdraw a dispensation previously given. It can do so for various reasons such as a change of circumstances, firm behaviour which does not comply with a condition made by the Commission, abuse of dispensation and so on.

Economists can easily think of improvements which are achieved by agreements between firms, such as specialisation, longer output series and the consequent reduction in costs, concentration of sales activities, broadening of the product range, faster and continuous supply, joint research and development work, exchange of information, etc. The balancing of such advantages against the restriction of competition is a more difficult job, however, and it is interesting to see how the Committee has approached this task. Both approvals and rejections of applications for dispensation are instructive. Table 1 shows the Commission's refusals, up to the end of 1973. According to the classification, in 10 out of 13 cases no appreciable objective advantages could be discerned, while in six cases it was found that the restrictions imposed were not indispensable to the attainment of the stated objectives.

T..e Table should not be read as meaning that in the majority of cases the Commission has refused dispensation because no advantages could be claimed, but that these advantages (if any) were not sufficient to outweigh the disadvantages from the restriction of competition between

Table 1. *Refusals of exemptions under Article 85(3) to end 1973:
conditions for exemption not met in each case*

	A	B	C	D
1. Grundig/Consten	—	x	x	—
2. Julien/Van Katwijk	x	—	—	—
3. German tile manufacturers	x	—	—	—
4. VCH	x	—	—	—
5. NCH	x	x	x	—
6. Central Heating	x	—	—	—
7. Pittsburgh Corning	x	—	x	—
8. Cement agreement Nederland	—	—	x	—
9. Cimbel	x	—	x	—
10. Cut polyester fibres	x	—	x	—
11. SCPA–Kali und Salz	—	—	—	x
12. Kali und Salz/Kali – Chemie	x	—	—	x
13. Hot water boilers and geysers	x	—	—	—

A = Improvement of production or distribution or the promotion of technical
or economic progress; B = fair share of the resulting benefit for customers;
C = no imposition of restrictions which are not indispensable; D = no elimination of substantial amount of competition.

the firms concluding the agreement, or could have been achieved by
means of competition rather than restriction. In the Julien/Van Katwijk
case (1970) it was held that improvements in production or distribution
or technical and economic progress cannot be promoted if competition
is eliminated; in Central Heating (1972) similar claims advanced on
behalf of an exclusive collective purchasing agreement were disposed
of by the argument that the advantages were hardly discernible, while
international trade was artificially curtailed; in the four cement cases
(VCH, 1971; Cement Agreement Nederland, 1972; NCH, 1971; Cimbel,
1972) improvements were considered as possibly present (ranging from
'extremely doubtful' in CAN to 'some improvements' in NCH), but
could not outweigh the effects of the restraint on competition, which
were clearly visible, and so on. Co-ordination of investments in order
to avoid excess capacity was not allowed in the Cimbel case or in the
polyester fibre case (agreement cancelled without formal decision) –
the cartel was not considered to be more able than competition to solve
the existing problems. Likewise, price and quota agreements and
reciprocal exclusive dealing arrangements have hardly qualified for
exemption so far.

On the positive side, the exemptions approved demonstrate the same
principle. A specialisation agreement between French cigarette paper
manufacturers having a market share of 80 per cent in France and

70 per cent in Benelux, was exempted because the Commission found real competition from West German and Italian producers and potential competition from third-countries' producers. Moreover, the agreed specialisation was not irreversible so that competition between the contracting partners could be revived. Countervailing power was also found to exist in the form of the French and Italian tobacco monopolies and other large cigarette producers. In the Henkel/Colgate decision (1971), the argument was that the agreement could be exempted because the companies did not have a dominant position in the products concerned, even though they had important market shares in several countries. In view of the tight oligopolistic market structure, the Commission was of the opinion that developments had to be watched, and both companies were therefore obliged to inform it of all licence agreements concluded by the joint venture as well as interlocking directorates and participations between the two groups. The latter decision was a borderline case and not everybody was happy with the decision to allow exemption. The joint venture, charged with research for both the mother companies, was considered to be able to promote economic and technical improvements, but it was not indicated how and why it would actually do so, nor how the exemption fits in with the requirements of Article 85(3). The absence of market domination as an argument for exempting companies of the size of Henkel and Colgate is moreover rather curious if at the same time the tight oligopolistic market situation is referred to in order to justify continuing supervision.

The Man/Saviem case (1972) and the ACEC/Berliet case (1968) also related essentially to agreements for joint research and development, though the former contained other clauses. Though the Commission was satisfied that the first condition of Article 85(3) would be satisfied, it was in doubt as to the fair share of consumers in the benefits. In ACEC/Berliet the companies had only planned to pool resources so that no benefit to consumers was yet discernible; in Man/Saviem the Commission maintained that consumer choice was reduced. In both cases the Commission relied on the forces of competition to look after the fulfilment of the exemption requirements. Sufficient has been said to draw the overall conclusion that both prohibitions under Article 85(1) and exemptions under Article 85(3) have to comply with the golden rule that effective, rivalrous competition under conditions of uncertainty within the Common Market is guaranteed by the final clause of Article 85(3). The clauses in this Article referring to improvements, progress, consumer benefits and indispensability of restrictions have therefore no independent existence, but will be considered against the background of the presence or absence of a competitive market structure. This rule holds both for block exemptions and for individual suspensions and it continues to hold for dispensation given in the past, which may be withdrawn or amended as we have seen. The whole of Article 85 therefore constitutes a powerful weapon in the hands of the Commission. The erstwhile hotly debated distinction between per-se and abuse principles in cartel policy no longer applies, because agreements and practices restraining or distorting competition in respect of a substantial part of the product in question are prohibited *per se* and cannot be exempted. Exemptions may be granted, however, for those agreements and practices which do not conflict with this general rule; they are afterwards supervised for possible abuses.[9] Our next step therefore is to review the different types of agreement and practice, in order to determine their anti-competitive impact, and the policy adopted by the Commission towards each type.

Types of agreement/practice and competition policy towards them

The various types of agreement and practice may be classified into

(1) vertical agreements between firms in successive stages of production or distribution of goods or services;

(2) horizontal agreements, between companies in the same stage of producing, and/or distributing goods and services;

(3) concerted practices between firms, i.e. co-ordinated market behaviour not founded on explicit agreements;

(4) exclusive rights – patents, trademarks, copyrights, knowhow, etc. – creating monopoly positions on the basis of agreements;

(5) various particular forms of co-operation, having as their main goal trading practices not normally in direct conflict with competition rules, but which may indirectly affect them, such as fairs and exhibitions, joint publicity, use of common labels, etc.

Vertical agreements

Exclusive dealing has occupied a prominent place in EEC competition policy from the outset. Such agreements may stimulate market penetration, but they may also create obstacles to market integration if the dealer is granted territorial protection, i.e. parallel imports from dealers outside the protected territory are prevented because the manufacturer will not supply dealers without an export prohibition, and the protected dealer has no right to sell in another exclusive dealer's territory. The aim of such exclusive dealing agreements is of course to split up markets, practise price discrimination and reap maximum profits by means of pricing according to the competitive situation in each of the divided submarkets. The Commission, aiming for equalisation of prices throughout the Common Market, has therefore stood out against these practices. Exclusive dealing is only objectionable however if agreements between independent trading partners contain such export prohibitions, and in December 1962 it was announced that exclusive agency contracts made with dependent commercial agents, who were assisting their principals to penetrate markets, do not come under Article 85(1). The decisive test for independence is whether the agent assumes the risk arising from the transactions. In the leading case, Grundig/Consten of 1964 (with a ruling from the Court of Justice in 1966) it was found that price levels in France and West Germany differed by between 20 per cent and 50 per cent because Grundig, a German electrotechnical manufacturer, had not only given Consten, a French dealer, exclusive dealing rights in France, but had also prohibited its non-French dealers from exporting to France. In this case, as in other exclusive dealership cases, the Commission initially took the view that exclusive dealership contracts relating to branded products, which give rise to consumer preferences, constituted an infringement of Article 85(1). But the Court took a more subtle position, referring to the economic circumstances of the case such as the nature and quantities of the products concerned, market shares of distributor and supplier, and the existence of a network of similar contracts and protective clauses against parallel imports. In the STM/MBU case (1966) the Court ruled on a question posed by the Cour d'Appel of Paris, that a simple exclusive dealership (like the one granted by Maschinenbau Ulm to Société Technique Minière) was not an infringement of Article 85. In accordance with the view that the legality of an agreement depends partly on its significance, an unimportant exclusive contract, but one which is liable to be imitated on a mass scale, which would create barriers to entry into the market for foreign producers (the case of Brasserie Haecht I, 1967 has already been referred to) was found illegal by the Court. Thus an exclusive dealership contract containing territorial protection (Völk/Vervaecke, 1969) was upheld because the matter was so unimportant.

In the meantime, the Commission had reached its conclusion. It issued a block exemption, authorising bilateral agreements for exclusive dealing which satisfied certain conditions laid down in Regulation 67/67/EEC, especially that stipulating that parallel imports shall not be prevented. Thus export prohibitions, *de facto* or *de jure*, are not allowed and in recent years the Commission has succeeded in removing most of them. Of the 30 000 cases concerning exclusive dealing arrangements initially notified, 4500 of which contained export prohibitions, only 1500 were still pending at the beginning of 1972.[10]

The Court ruling of STM/MBU was also interpreted to mean that territorial protection may be allowed on a temporary basis to enable a firm to penetrate a new market. The Trans-Ocean Marine Paint Association Decision of 1967 (renewed in 1972) under which a group of smaller European paint manufacturers with a limited market share were allowed to co-operate to the extent of dividing markets between them, confirmed this principle. Thus, in the light of these rulings the legality of the geographical separation of markets by exclusive dealing agreements seems to depend on whether the restriction on competition is discernible, or is indispensable for creating new competition.

But nobody can make much out of this limited retreat from an unqualified, absolute prohibition of parallel imports connected with exclusive dealing arrangements. The WEA-Filipacchi Music S.A. in Paris was fined heavily in 1972 because it had forbidden its exclusive dealers in France to export light music records to Germany, thus maintaining a price differential of 50 per cent between these markets. The company pointed out that it had only a small share of the overall record market, but the Commission argued that pop music is no substitute for Beethoven or Mozart. Also the company had exclusive contracts with the stars working solely for this firm. As everybody knows these people are unique. Similarly, Pittsburgh Corning Europe, selling cellular glass from Belgium throughout the Common Market by means of concessionaires tried to prevent parallel imports into West Germany, where prices were maintained some 40 per cent higher than in Benelux, by means of according substantial rebates to Benelux dealers who did not export this insulating material. The company was fined 100 000 units of account.

Neglect of the competition laws is no longer tolerated.

When Deutsche Philips removed all export prohibitions from its agreements covering the EEC countries, except those concerning electric razors, it was fined 60 000 units of account in 1973. The Dutch parent company had warned its subsidiaries to take action in 1969, so the Commission's action is understandable.

The Commission has been very strict against collective exclusive dealing agreements concluded between groups of manufacturers/ importers and distributors. Starting in 1963 with a recommendation to a Belgian tile manufacturers' and traders' association, the Commission has always refused exemption on the grounds that such agreements seal off national markets and thereby restrain or regulate community trade more than other types. Also aggregated rebate cartels of all types have found no grace. If producers in a member state grant buyers in that state rebates related to total purchases made during a particular period, buyers will have an incentive to make all their purchases from domestic producers. Foreign sellers are barred from access to distribution chains even if they offer more favourable terms. The impact of such cartels depends on the market shares of producers/importers and distributors, but as a rule they tend to cover a large number of national firms. In its *Third Report on Competition Policy* the Commission says that many

Common Market firms are members of such cartels.[11] The Belgian hot water boilers and geysers agreement concluded between three producers and two importers having more than 70 per cent of total sales on the market, imposed aggregated rebates on these suppliers to be given on all (not only their own) deliveries to associated dealers. As these distributors bought 94 per cent of their requirements with the cartel members and had 75 per cent of national sales, this erected a barrier to the entry of foreign suppliers. Foreign suppliers, desiring to penetrate the Belgian market, had to wean associated distributors by similar rebates, which were in their case particularly burdensome because of their low (initial) market shares. Such entrance premia are typically required for homogeneous products and are higher the lower the proportion of the annual sales of a foreign supplier accounted for by the distributor.

Two other types of vertical agreements must finally be mentioned, namely resale price maintenance and selective distribution. Individual resale price maintenance falls outside the EEC competition policy rules, provided buyers remain free to purchase wherever they want. This, of course, is a deadly provision for it undermines the national resale price maintenance system, as the German record and photographic producers have discovered. Low priced records, films and photographic equipment simply came into the national market by circulating through France and Benelux and some dealers are said to have become millionaires in the process.

Selective distribution was dealt with in the Omega (November 1970) and Kodak (July 1970) cases. Manufacturers appoint only a limited number of dealers selling high quality wares for each area depending on estimated demand. They make them sign standard sales agreements providing *inter alia* for costly after-sales service and guarantees. In return the dealer is given protection against others who might reduce his sales. Such agreements may be exempted, on condition that the price equalising force of parallel imports is allowed to work. The Commission argued in the Omega case that exemption could be given because the Swiss Omega watch is a quality-branded article. Production and demand for such a watch were severely restricted by the high price. Extending distribution to a great many retailers, the Commission said, would have reduced sales per dealer to a few items and would have hampered service and sales activities. This argument is debatable however, for it rests on the high price, which may have remained high because of the selective distribution system.

Horizontal agreements

The main types of cartel agreements in the classical sense are price, market sharing and quota cartels, and joint sales agencies or syndicates. They may be grouped according to their stature as purely national or international cartel agreements. The latter are so flatly in conflict with the prohibition of Article 85(1) that there is no chance of their being legally valid and they can only survive by failing to notify the Commission of their agreement. If such a cartel is subsequently detected it will be heavily fined unless it can silently dissolve. Table 2 gives a survey of EEC policy with respect to horizontal agreements and practices up to the end of 1973. The agreements and practices have been divided into five groups: (i) those relating to price fixing and the stipulation of other sales conditions to be observed by producers or exporters; (ii) those concerning outright export bans or delivery refusals; (iii) those where quotas, import or export levels or delivery agreements were agreed upon; (iv) agreements and practices containing investment prohibitions or bans on participation in foreign companies, and finally (v) joint sales agencies or syndicates. The last column indicates how the Commission dealt with these agreements: whether they were approved and obtained a negative clearance, often after intervention by the Commission (N.C. and I. cases), or whether they could not be exempted (N.A. cases): in some further cases, it is known that agreements were subsequently dissolved by the parties concerned.

It follows from Table 2 that of 32 cases which came up for examination, only two got a negative clearance, namely Alliance Machine Outils and SAFCO; both were associations of small French producers, not able to restrain competition in the Common Market because of their limited market share, the wide range of products competing in both quality and price and (in the first case) the possibility for association members to fix their selling prices (Alliance was a joint marketing agency set up by firms which already specialised in the production of different lines). On the other hand, SAFCO was the first syndicate granted a negative clearance without the attachment of conditions.

The rest of the cases were either dissolved, amended (conditions, withdrawals of particular clauses, etc.) or not accepted at all and sometimes fined. The heavy preponderance of price and quantity restrictions in this sample of cartels is clear: there were 15 price agreements or concerted practices, and 18 quantity restrictions. The majority of these were not found acceptable and had to be withdrawn or amended. Only a small grouping like VVVF was twice given a negative clearing after some amendment, while other groupings like ASPA were only acceptable after the 'teeth' of the agreement had been drawn out (namely the clauses concerning the obligation of members

Table 2. *Horizontal cartel agreements or practices, 1964–73 (not including specialisation agreements)*

	P	B	Q	I	S	
VVVF	x	—	—	—	—	I. 1965, 1969
Cleaning products	—	x	—	—	—	Dissolved 1966
Construction equipment	—	x	x	—	—	Dissolved 1967
Semi-finished metallic products	—	x	—	—	—	Dissolved 1967
Laminated steel agencies, West Germany	—	—	—	—	x	I. 1967
Cobelaz	—	—	—	—	x	I. 1968
Alliance Machine Outils	—	—	—	—	x	N.C. 1963
International Cables	x	x	—	x	—	Dissolved 1969
Quinine	x	x	—	—	—	N.A. 1969
Dyestuffs	x	—	—	—	—	N.A. 1969
SEIFA	—	—	—	—	x	I. 1969
Sheet glass	x	—	x	—	—	N.A. 1970
Noordwyks Cement agreement	x	—	—	—	—	Dissolved 1970
ASPA	x	—	x	—	—	I. 1970
Julien/Van Katwijk	—	x	x	—	—	Dissolved 1970
German scrap iron	x	—	x	—	—	N.A. 1970
SUPEXIE	—	—	—	—	x	I. 1970
Belgaphos	—	—	—	—	x	Dissolved 1970
NCH	x	—	—	—	x	N.A. 1971
VCH	x	—	—	—	—	N.A. 1971
CIM France	—	—	—	—	x	I. 1971
SAFCO	—	—	—	—	x	N.C. 1971
CRN	—	—	x	x	—	N.A. 1972
Cimbel	x	—	x	—	—	N.A. 1972
Polyester fibres	—	—	—	x	—	N.A. 1972
Gisa	x	—	x	—	—	N.A. 1972
Laminated steel agencies, West Germany	—	—	—	—	x	N.A. 1972
Asybel	x	—	—	—	x	Dissolved 1973
NVCP	—	x	—	—	x	I. 1973
Sugar	x	x	x	—	—	N.A. 1973
SCPA–Kali und Salz	x	—	x	—	x	N.A. 1973
Kali und Salz	—	—	—	—	x	N.A. 1973
Total 32	15	8	10	3	14	

SOURCE: based on the Commission's three competition policy reports.
P = Price fixing and alignment of sales conditions; B = import or export ban or delivery refusals; Q = quotas, frozen import or export levels or delivery agreements; I = investment or participation bans; S = joint sales agency or syndicate.
N.A. = Not accepted by the Commission for exemption or fined.
N.C. = Approved but given negative clearance by the Commission.
I. = Adapted after intervention by the Commission.
'Dissolved' means that the agreement was ended after intervention.

to fix resale prices, boycotting and control by an office). The evidence therefore bears out the statement made in the Commission's first report on competition policy, that market sharing agreements, price-fixing and quantity restrictions cannot be exempted at all.[12] This general rule also holds for purely national cartels with an influence on trade flows, as such cartels may easily raise 'thresholds' against intra-EEC trade, by means of international price or output alignments, or through the connection of horizontal agreements with vertical cartels (e.g. collective exclusive dealing contracts or aggregated rebate systems).

Joint sales agencies seem to have met a different response. Of 14 cases, two got immediate negative clearance, six were adapted and accepted, and six were found unacceptable and had to dissolve. Nearly all these syndicates operated in the raw materials sectors: laminated steel, fertilisers, cement, sulphuric acid, i.e. homogeneous products where price cutting may be fierce. Such syndicates try to restrain price competition by means of their exclusive sales policy, the allocation of delivery quotas among producers and the fixing of uniform prices and other terms of sales. Initially the European cartel authorities (the Federal Cartel Office in Germany and the EEC Commission) were rather favourably inclined towards the syndicates. In 1966 the German steel syndicates were approved and in 1968–70, Cobelaz, SEIFA and SUPEXIE (all fertiliser syndicates) were exempted, although in each case adaptations were required, e.g. fertiliser syndicates were compelled to withdraw arrangements restricting sales in Community countries other than their own. But in imposing this condition the Commission took a rather formalistic position: could it be expected that such heavy cartels would henceforth behave like competitive angels? Sales syndicates are set up by members who have dismantled their own sales organisations, so that individual export activities are not likely, and in any case not very aggressive. Moreover, other member countries had their syndicates too and a confrontation between the individual exporter and another member state's syndicate could scarcely be expected to result in competition. Also, several national syndicates had international co-operative agreements. On top of this, the syndicates' behaviour was not very encouraging. They often encouraged the alignment of prices at the highest level of costs and did not demonstrate much flexibility in adapting to demand changes.

One of the West German steel syndicates threatened to eliminate by price discrimination a small outsider who could only be saved by an appeal to Brussels. German research has shown that the cement and fertiliser syndicates which were authorised did not achieve worthwhile cost reductions from rationalisation (rarely more than five per cent on an ex-works price) and did not benefit the consumer.[13] Such developments, plus a barrage of criticism of the aforementioned syndicate decisions have probably prompted the Commission to change its attitude: in the *First Report on Competition Policy* a critical tone is clearly voiced; in the *Third Report*, a less formal opinion is apparent in that the Commission notes that, by means of mergers and otherwise, the number of syndicate members was often sharply reduced, whereas its arrangements had become more flexible: competitive restraints can evidently be achieved in other ways. Consequently, the decisions taken in 1972 and 1973 with respect to syndicates were negative: the laminated steel groupings were ordered to dissolve, Asybel, the sulphuric acid sales agency of the Belgian non-ferrous metals producers and the Belgian–German kalium-salt syndicates were likewise stopped.

Thus the rule with respect to heavy cartel agreements is now clear: horizontal cartels will only be allowed in those exceptional cases where their market share is unimportant.

Specialisation agreements between small and medium-sized firms are more favourably looked upon. On 20 December 1972 a block exemption regulation was issued for such agreements, on the grounds that they improve production (by securing economies of scale and rationalisation) and strengthen the competitive position of small companies. If effective competition is not jeopardised, the specialisation agreements will have beneficial effects, it was argued. Two conditions were therefore laid down in the exemption regulation: (1) the market share of the participating firms should not exceed 10 per cent (for this purpose the market is defined as the national market) and (2) total turnover of all firms involved should not exceed 150 million units of account. Specialisation is allowed only in the manufacture of goods. Experience of distribution and service trades was considered too limited for the granting of block exemptions, but exemptions may nevertheless be granted in individual cases. Specialisation agreements as covered by the block exemption may include reciprocal obligations not to produce certain items, but the commitment can only refer to the nature and not to the quantity of the goods produced. In such reciprocal agreements, mutual competition may be excluded; commitments to delivery, to exclusive supply and distribution may be made, but parallel imports may not be curbed. Also, price regulations restraining competition will not be approved. In general, restrictions functionally related to increasing specialisation are accepted, but those in excess of this are frowned upon.

Concerted practices

An important area of the 'new' competition policy is the field of concerted practices. Collusion without agreement may be expected to increase when cartel agreements are forbidden. A celebrated initial case was the Dyestuffs Manufacturers' price collusion in the years 1964–7. In two ensuing cases, Pittsburgh Corning Europe and the Sugar pro-

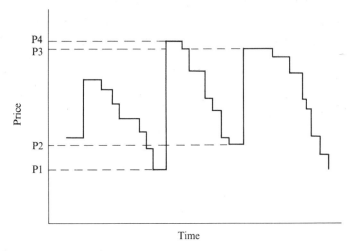

Fig. 1. Pricing in the dyestuffs market.

ducers, concerted practices were also in evidence; the former concerned price discrimination between the German and Benelux markets, operated by the exclusive agents of PCE in Benelux who aligned their export prices to those prevailing in the West German market. The second case related to concerted market sharing; the Commission reproached the sugar manufacturers for respecting each other's markets, by means of export limitations, export price alignments, and pressure on traders to follow these policies. The concept of concerted practices emerges most clearly in the dyestuffs case. In 1964, some ten producers sent telexes to their subsidiaries at almost exactly the same time, telling them to raise the prices of particular dyestuffs by a uniform rate of 15 per cent in Italy and in Benelux. In January 1965 the increase was applied to West Germany. For other dyestuffs, a general round of price increases amounting to 10 per cent took place on the same day.

In the third year (August 1967) there was a meeting of dyestuff manufacturers in Basle, Switzerland, where one of them announced his intention of raising prices by eight per cent on the 18 October 1967. The other firms reacted by stating that the proposal would be considered in their Head Offices. At the end of August 1967 Geigy informed its agents and customers in several countries that prices would be raised. Other companies followed in September.

The accused companies defended themselves by stating that the parallel action was not concerted, but was based on the 'compelling force' of the prevailing oligopolistic situation. In other words, the argument was that the companies could not have behaved otherwise because of the structure of the market. Economists will recognise the argument of the kinked demand oligopoly model. Price cuts were made secretly and price rises were announced beforehand, thereby increasing market transparency with respect to price in order to protect the initiating firm's market share (see Fig. 1). The defence claimed that a firm which abstained from raising its price could not have improved its market position because its competitors would have withdrawn their announced increases and the profitability of all would have been impaired. However, both the Commission and the Court pointed out that concertation of action had been in evidence: in 1964 telex messages, in similar terms had stipulated equal price increases at exactly the same time. In 1965 and 1967 the facts were also against the manufacturers' contention, and indicated, according to the Court 'a gradual progressive co-operation between the firms concerned'. After the experience of 1964, when announcements and increases coincided, behaviour in later years was based on a time interval between them in order to give the firms a chance to observe reactions and behave accordingly. This, it was concluded, constituted concerted action as such behaviour was intended to eliminate the uncertainty of market actions regarding percentage, date and place of the price increases and products affected. The joint actions were therefore unlawful; they exchanged the risks of competition and the uncertainty of spontaneous action for certainty about future behaviour. In this sense, the Court held, concerted action differed from sheer parallelism. Concerted behaviour can therefore be deduced from direct or circumstantial evidence, relating to number and size of firms, the market (growth and size), behaviour, etc.[14] The debate therefore turns on the contention that an oligopolistic market structure compels firms to behave anti-competitively, as economic theory is supposed to teach. However, the theory depends on a number of assumptions and qualifications which may not apply to real-life cases. The most important qualification of the structure–behaviour theory relates perhaps to its static nature. In a dynamic situation the theory cannot offer support for so-called 'market compulsion' (Marktzwang).[15] In the dyestuff's case there were several factors promoting at least intermittently competitive behaviour, such as the interchangeability of the standard colours, the different cost structure of manufacturers and the growing overall demand for dyestuffs. These account for the stepwise price declines which occurred (Fig. 1). Other factors, such as the small part of the price of aniline colours in the final price of the product of the buying company, the technical adaptation of the product to the needs of each individual buyers and the splitting up of the Common Market by the main companies make for parallel behaviour. When profitability has been sufficiently impaired by price 'chiselling', the companies revert to concerted action.

Though the companies' behaviour is understandable, it cannot be excused. The law requires competition, not collusion. And the law is right, not only from a legal point of view, but also from the point of view of economic sense. If collusion were tolerated there would be a tendency (i) to freeze the underlying market structures with all that this implies, and (ii) for the formation of stricter cartels as experience with information agreements indicates.

Open price systems

Some information agreements have recently been condemned. In the Dutch cement traders case (October 1972) the Court upheld the Commission's prohibition of a system of indicative prices practised by the cement traders, because this tended to eliminate uncertainty about competitors' price policies.

In another case, the Dutch cartridge cartel, a dozen suppliers and 150 dealers operated a reciprocal exclusive trading system as well as a collective obligation on the dealers to maintain minimum prices. Both were condemned in accordance with earlier decisions. The distinguishing feature of the cartridge cartel was the open price system which obliged suppliers to register their individually fixed prices with a suppliers committee, which circulated the information. This, the Commission held, hampers competition by reducing individual price flexibility and discouraging collective price changes.

The most interesting case of an information agreement relates to the European glass packages manufacturers. This case was decided on 15 May 1974. A group of 26 producers in West Germany, Benelux, France and Italy operated a 'fair competition rules' agreement supervised by the International Fair Trade Practices Rules Administration (IFTRA) at Liechtenstein. The rules stipulated that sales at below cost price meant to undermine competitors or to establish a monopoly, systematic sales below a competitors' price, discrimination, the granting of special advantages, tying agreements, loss-leader selling and the spreading of misleading information were 'unfair'. Manufacturers therefore had to inform each other immediately about price changes, while foreign competitors were obliged to align their price quotations for exports to those of the 'natural price leader' in the national markets.

The price leader was whichever national manufacturer raised his price first after an increase in costs. The market structure characterising this sector of homogeneous glass packages (bottles, jars and flasks) facilitated the open-price system and was as follows:

The leading German firm, a subsidiary of Owens-Illinois from the US, had some 40 per cent of the market and sales of DM 435 million. The two leading French firms, Saint Gobain and BSN, are international companies and either controlled the leading Benelux and Italian com-

Table 3. *Structure of the European glass packages market*

	Number of producers	Degree of concentration*	Controlled by or liaisons with firms in area
1. W. Germany	13	4 had 88%	—
2. Belgium	3	2 had 100%	4
3. The Netherlands	1	1 had more than 90%	4
4. France	5	2 had 90–100%	—
5. Italy	4	3 had 40%	4
Total	26		

* Of total market in bottles, demijohns, jars and flasks.
N.B. The table is based on information given to IFTRA verified by the Commission.

panies or had important financial holdings in them. Control over the Italian market was rather weak and Italian participation was ended in 1971. In the other countries the IFTRA rules were applied by some eight large and 20 small manufacturers.

In recent years demand has grown relatively fast because of the shift by consumers towards disposable bottles, and the development of the market for glass packages in the pharmaceutical, cosmetic and food industries. National or individual productive capacity was sometimes insufficient to cope with this growth in demand and trade flows within the Common Market increased. The market position of the Dutch United Glassworks was particularly threatened by such flows.

Increased uncertainty during the 1960s led to the establishment of national information bureaux for the designation of producers to centralise all information concerning price lists, rebates and conditions. Such information was exchanged nationally and internationally and facilitated the detection of price cutters. A further step was the introduction of an internationally applicable scheme for cost price calculations in the second half of the sixties. This calculation scheme was used by participants in bottle-making and in some flask manufacturing. A system of carriage-paid customers delivery prices was also operated in order to counter the growing tendency of bottlers to shop around for the lowest ex-works price. The whole system was supervised by the IFTRA and held together by the threat of a fine for trespassers of at least 30 per cent of sales in the sector where the infringement occurred. Naturally, the Commission held the system illegal and pointed out that such an 'information agreement', ostensibly meant to promote fair competition, did in fact eliminate price competition because the firm who is informed about its competitors' behaviour 'knows exactly the present and future behaviour of the said competitors and therefore can adapt its own price policy for exports to those markets' (nos. 43 and 44 of the Commission's Decision).

Elimination of uncertainty is considered equivalent to the elimination of competition.

Industrial and commercial property rights

Rights to industrial and commercial property, such as trademarks, patents, copyrights, etc., and the licences which can be given for such rights, are limited to the national states in which they are issued. Such rights, which may have greater or less economic value, depending on the circumstances, represent a legally exclusive right within a particular country. The resulting separation of markets may permit the owners of such rights, who are mostly firms, to pursue an oligopolistic or monopolistic price policy both within and between national territories. An unrestricted use of such rights would tend to hamper or even eliminate altogether the free flow of trade made possible by the opening of the Common Market. On the other hand, by giving priority to the principle of free internationl trade, such exclusive rights might lose much or all of their economic value. How has this conflict been resolved?

In a series of rulings by the Court of Justice the matter has been clarified sufficiently, at least from an economic point of view, to give the following summary:

(i) In the Grundig–Consten case (1966), the sole dealership of Consten in France for the products of Grundig was also supported by the trademark G(rundig) INT(ernational). The mark GINT had been chosen by Grundig because it had found out in Holland that its trademark Grundig could not protect it from parallel imports deriving ultimately from its own production in West Germany. The Court ruled in this case that the trademark agreement, accompanying the sole distributorship agreement constituted an infringement of competition, because Consten used the GINT mark to prevent parallel imports into France.

(ii) In the Parke-Davis case (1968), a Dutch Court wanted to know whether a patent issued in The Netherlands for a pharmaceutical product could be upheld against imports from independent firms in Italy, where there is no patent protection for such products, and whether the answer would depend on the price differential between the two countries. The Court ruled that the exercise of the patent right with this aim did not infringe on Articles 85 and 86 and moreover, that the price differential did not matter. As the law of industrial property rights within the Community was not yet harmonised, and differences continued to exist between countries, some restriction on the freedom of intra-Community trade might result from the existence of such rights.

3

(iii) In the Sirena case (1971) the issue was different. Before the Second World War an American firm granted the exclusive right to its trademark to an Italian firm for Italy and a German firm for Germany. The Italian firm complained about imports with the same trademark coming from West Germany and sought to stop these. It was told that its behaviour was in conflict with the prohibition of Article 85. Licence agreements between firms or with third parties may not be used to stop parallel imports. Note that whereas in Grundig/Consten the abuse of the trademark (viz the achievement of competitive restraint) was condemned, in the Sirena case the effect of market closure, resulting from the existence of parallel licences, was held to be contrary to the rules of competition.

(iv) In the case of Deutsche Grammophon Gesellschaft (DGG), 1971, a joint subsidiary of Philips (Holland) and Siemens (Germany) producing and selling records in EEC countries, the Court ruled that DGG had no right to invoke the German copyright law in order to stop parallel imports. DGG had sold records to its subsidiary Polydor SA in France under an exclusive licence. Now, DGG exercised resale price maintenance in West Germany, but Polydor was unable to do so in France, as the practice is forbidden in that country. The price differential for records in the two countries was used by a Hamburg dealer to sell DGG records in Germany below the fixed resale price. Polydor, the subsidiary, then cut off sales to the Hamburg dealer, but the latter was able to get supplies from a Hamburg wholesaler, who bought the records from a Swiss firm supplied by Polydor France. And so the circuit was closed again. When the European Court denied recourse to paragraph 85 of the German copyright law, a lower Hamburg court refused DGG the right to stop cheap record imports. As a result, resale price maintenance in Germany crumbled and record prices fell.

(v) The last case in this field which I would like to mention is Kaffee H.A.G. (1974). Due to post-war expropriation of the trademark H.A.G., a Belgian company Van Zuylen became the distributor of this type of decaffeinated coffee for Belgium and Luxembourg on behalf of the Belgian producer who had bought both the producing company and the trademark H.A.G. from the sequestrator. Encouraged by the former rulings of the Court in the cases of Sirena and Deutsche Grammophon, the German firm Kaffee H.A.G., originator of the trademark and pre-war owner of the Belgian subsidiary H.A.G./Belgique, to which the trademark was assigned, started selling this coffee in Belgium. The Luxembourg Court then posed the question to the European Court whether a trademark infringement suit would be barred by EEC law and the Court replied affirmatively. The important economic implications of these rulings seem to be as follows:

First, that no firm can use industrial property rights to restrain competition. In case of conflict, the competition rules prevail over nationally granted property rights. If a problem arises, the first thing to settle should be the possible infringement of Article 85(1).

Second, if no such infringement is ascertainable, it has to be decided whether there is a conflict with other Treaty rules. This might be the case with Article 36, which leaves open the possibility of deviation from unrestricted free trade inside the Community by means of an appeal on industrial and commercial property rights *inter alia*. Such restraints may not, however, be used to discriminate or to secretly hamper competition. This means that the existence of property rights will have to be distinguished from their use and the use will have to be considered case by case.

Third, property rights are viewed functionally, i.e. the scope of patents, trademarks, copyrights, etc. is restricted to their fundamental purpose. In the case of patents for example, no tying agreements are allowed; the function of a trademark is to inform and guarantee the consumer of the origin and quality of the good.

Fourth, it makes a difference whether the owner or licencee(s) of a property right circulate the goods inside the Common Market (DGG or Sirena), or whether independent firms sell the protected good on the owner's or licencee's market. In the latter case the protection given by the property right will be honoured; in the former the owner is not obliged to grant an unlimited number of licences, but on the other hand he is not entitled to restrain competition if and when he gives licences to other firms.[16]

In view of the importance of the subject – the majority of the remaining agreements registered under Regulation 17 and of those newly registered since the new member states joined relate to patent and trademark or licensing agreements – the EEC Commission has set up a special unit on industrial property rights. This unit will have to test such agreements for their effects on the allocation of production and separation of markets.[17]

Conclusion

One of the most important questions from the economist's point of view relates to the impact of competition policy. It is, at the same time, one of the most difficult to answer, because of a lack of sufficient information. The following opinions are therefore tentative and are meant to stimulate further research rather than to take up definite positions.

Many of the important horizontal cartels which have been dealt with were between firms producing goods in inelastic demand and static markets. This indicates one of the necessary conditions for the operation of a successful cartel. If firms find themselves in a stagnating market they have an incentive to restrict supply and price competition. Moreover, there must be some kind of entry barriers to prevent alternative sources of supply from having an effect. These may comprise economies of scale (as in cement, glass packages, fertilisers), long-term supply contracts (as in sugar), technical requirements (as in dyestuffs), product differentiation (as in Trans-Ocean Marine Paints) or the monopolisation of resources (as in quinine). Successful horizontal cartels (i.e. those that have a long existence and an appreciable influence) therefore require a combination of factors which is not at all usual, but is confined to particular sectors and circumstances. It is hardly surprising that the early cartels in the electric lamp industry were not lasting or influential, as technical revolutions in lamp-making undermined their effectiveness. But when conditions had stabilised during the thirties, the Phoebus agreements could regulate the market behaviour of the main firms.[18] I therefore do not believe that the cartel agreements that really matter are an all-embracing phenomenon in the economy. They prevail only where conditions are suitable. To ascertain such circumstances and to weigh their importance will be a major task of future competition policy. Surface indications of the existence of cartels or concerted practices relate to price flexibility, international comparisons of price levels and the timing of price changes by different producers. The EEC deserves credit for having lived up to Adam Smith's requirement that the law ought to do nothing to facilitate conspirational assemblies;[19] indeed, it has by now clearly established that it does not even tolerate them. By stressing the role of free competition in the process of market integration, the responsible authorities have let it be known that Europe is no longer the classic home of cartels. And both the Court and the Commission have displayed a remarkable insight into the question of what competition really is: rivalry under conditions of uncertainty.

After the sugar cartel was broken up, the main Dutch firm expressed its opinion that the profitability of the firms in the sugar industry would be impaired. It therefore proposed a merger to the other firm – from which a monopoly would have resulted – in order to 'rationalise industry'. The impact of competition policy is clear.

Likewise, competition policy has contributed greatly to the crumbling of resale price maintenance in many sectors, and the few vertical price links that remain are under great strain. Again, the sheer existence of competition policy has restrained a number of both EEC and non-EEC firms (e.g. American companies) from taking part in cartel agreements and has thus created a 'third force' in favour of competition.

Finally, competition policy should be given credit for its major achievement: the doors have remained open for new competitors to enter established national and foreign markets. The appeal of Korf to

Brussels when the steel syndicate threatened to eliminate him was sufficient to make the syndicate's barons see reason.

On the debit side, two points and a question mark should be registered. First, the Commission has been too lenient in the past with sales syndicates, particularly in view of the sectors and products concerned. This may now be remedied, but the Commission should be urged to take a strongly negative view of such organisations. They really belong with the most obnoxious cartel agreements and constitute, moreover, a 'breeding ground' for mergers.

Second, the question may be posed whether cartel policy is not too formal and cumbersome. To some extent this is bound up with the Treaty, its institutions and the whole administrative apparatus. The purely legal approach is unmistakable. Fortunately, the Court of Justice has often cut through the wilderness of legal argumentation provided mainly by independent lawyers, which often seemed to have the effect of making the Commission unsure of its case.

Finally, the question mark. Why is it that so many cartel decisions have related to Benelux (and to a lesser extent West German) firms, whereas French and Italian firms have been involved in (comparatively) few cases?

Notes

1 H. W. de Jong, 'Industrial structure and the price problem: experience within the European Economic Community'. In J. M. Blair (ed.), *The Roots of Inflation. The International Crisis* (Burt Franklin & Co. Inc.: New York, 1975), pp. 165–211.

2 EEC Commission, *Second Report on Competition Policy* (Brussels, April 1973), p. 141ff. From 1961–9, member country firms established 2300 subsidiaries in the EEC, while third-country firms founded 3546 subsidiaries. See *Bulletin of the European Communities* (1970), p. 30.

3 H. W. de Jong (see note (1) above), Table 11.

4 In 1968 for the first time the figure for US subsidiaries and financial participations (422) fell below the number of intra-EEC ventures (565). For the 1959–66 period there were nearly 700 trans-national ventures in the EEC, of which 40 per cent were wholly owned subsidiaries and 35 per cent jointly owned subsidiaries. See W. Feld, 'Political aspects of transnational business collaboration in the Common Market'. In M. Hodges (ed.), *European Integration, Selected Readings* (Penguin Books Ltd: Middlesex, 1972), Tables 1–4, p. 425ff.

5 According to Regulation 17, the Commission has exclusive power to apply the exemptions stipulated in Article 85(3), whereas the member states may execute Articles 85(1) and 86 directly (Article 9). Nothing has come of these national privileges, however.

6 F. M. Scherer has, I think rightly, pointed out that this secrecy hampers the development of an adequate competition policy. Secrecy undermines public confidence, makes it difficult to correct errors of the past and prevents the creation of an intellectual infrastructure. It is not perchance, he notes, that US and British economists have led researches in the field of

industrial organisation. 'In short, many decisions are taken in Brussels which influence the welfare of European consumers; but there is no possibility for interested scientists or civilians to test them in order to determine independently whether they were the right ones.' See F. M. Scherer, *Europäische Fusionskontrollpolitik, Die Rule of Reason und die Regel der Verschwiegenheit. IIM Paper*, series no. I/73–36 (Berlin, 1973) (also in *Wirtschaft und Wettbewerb*, **24** (1973), pp. 81–90).

7 Surveys from a legal point of view can be found in: W. Alexander, *The EEC Rules of Competition* (Kluwer Harrap Handbooks: London, 1973); E. J. Mestmäcker, *Europäisches Wettbewerbsrecht* (Verlag C. H. Beck: München, 1974); Europa Institute, University of Leiden, *European Competition Policy, Essays of the Leiden Working Group on Cartel Problems* (Leiden, 1973).

8 In the Grundig/Consten Case of 1966, the Court of Justice held that the advantages resulting from the restrictions should be at least sufficient to compensate for the disadvantages flowing from the lessening of competition and that such advantages should be of an objective economic nature, not to be confused with private interests.

9 See E. J. Mestmäcker, *Europäisches Wettbewerbsrecht* (see note (7) above), pp. 5 and 180–4.

10 EEC Commission, *First Report on Competition Policy* (Brussels, April 1972), p. 57.

11 EEC Commission, *Third Report on Competition Policy* (Brussels, May 1974), para. 54.

12 EEC Commission, *First Report on Competition Policy* (see note (10) above), paras. 1–3.

13 See F. Segelmann, 'Wettbewerb und Rationalierung unter Berücksichtigung der Syndikate und Spezialisierungskartelle'. In *Zehn Jahre Bundeskartellamt* (C. Heymanns Verlag K.G.: Köln, 1968), pp. 137–61.

14 See H. W. de Jong, 'The economics of concerted practices (collusion)'. In Europa Institute, University of Leiden, *European Competition Policy* (see note (7) above), pp. 92–4.

15 H. W. de Jong, *ibid.*, pp. 95–6.

16 E. J. Mestmäcker, *Europäisches Wettbewerbsrecht* (see note (7) above), p. 474.

17 EEC Commission, *Third Report on Competition Policy* (see note (11) above), para. 13.

18 W. Meinhold, Das internationale Glühlampenkartell. In W. Barnikel, *Theorie und Praxis der Kartelle* (Wissenschaftliche Buchgesellschaft: Darmstadt, 1972).

19 A. Smith, *The Wealth of Nations* (Everyman's Edition, Dent: London, 1910; Reprint 1947), vol. I, Book I, chapter 10, part 2, p. 117.

COMMENT

J.B.HEATH

A large number of interesting and important issues were raised by Professor de Jong in chapter 2; I would like to discuss three of them in particular, and to ask a few questions.

Objectives of competition policy

The paper defines the primary objective as being 'effective, rivalrous competition under conditions of uncertainty'. This appears to assume that competition is desired for its own sake. In fact, of course, within the EEC, competition policy is at the heart of industrial policy, and is seen as the instrument whereby the economies of member states will be brought into a state of integration, such that through rationalisation and specialisation in their economies, member states will never again contemplate fighting each other in open conflict. Perhaps this is what is meant by 'effective' competition. In the UK, however, competition policies have been seen more clearly as intermediate objectives designed to achieve such ultimate objectives as low production costs, low margins between price and cost, product and process innovation, the mobility of resources between companies and between sectors of the economy, and fair trading between buyer and seller, as well as fair competition as between one seller and another. To a large extent these objectives have been spelt out in the 1973 Fair Trading Act.

Thus it seems to me that competition policies in the Common Market have objectives which are between those in the USA where competition appears to be desired for its own sake and is a fundamental part of their political philosophy, and those in the United Kingdom where objectives are specified in rather more detail and which relate to fairly specific economic ends. But in the evolution of competition policies within the EEC, the trend would appear to be towards attitudes adopted in the UK, in which situations are looked at in some detail in relation to their specific economic effects.

The objective of competition policy refers also to 'rivalrous competition under conditions of uncertainty', and the creation of uncertainty is seen as being the circumstance from which competition derives its effectiveness. This is not spelt out in the paper, but presumably it is uncertainty about future profit and about future cash flow, arising from the activities of rival enterprises, that has most impact on a company in leading it to try to reduce that degree of uncertainty, through cost reduction, product improvement and in other 'efficient' ways (but not including uncertainty reduction through the formation of restrictive agreements or through mergers that would significantly increase the degree of concentration).

But the effectiveness of increased uncertainty due to competition must surely depend upon the abilities of the companies concerned to respond in socially efficient ways. If senior executives do not know how to improve their companies, if they are lacking in management expertise, then only the extreme penalty of being forced out of business would raise the average level of productivity (and large companies are seldom forced into liquidation, even in the present highly disadvantageous situation). Likewise, companies must have the necessary information that would enable them to respond in socially efficient ways to competitive pressures, and again a management information system that does not supply the necessary information may result in inappropriate responses.

It seems to me that where these conditions are not present, or where there are major cultural differences between competitors, such that responses to competitive situations may be unpredictable, as between the Dutch and Italian firms mentioned in chapter 2, then it is difficult to see how this kind of uncertainty would lead to an efficient allocation of resources. If companies pursue different objectives and have fundamentally different ways of going about things, it is easy to see that competition between them may lead to the kind of uncertainty that would not have socially efficient results. Furthermore, if there is a lack of market information, as may often arise in sealed bid tendering situations, or where sellers find it difficult to ascertain at what prices rival sellers are making deals, uncertainty is likely to be high but socially efficient results may not be forthcoming.

Can there be too much uncertainty? This rather begs the question 'too much for what?', but I believe that too much uncertainty can drive managers into making short-run – and possibly short-sighted – decisions, and if prolonged can cause mental breakdown and may drive away good managers who see easier tasks elsewhere.

A related point is that both in the UK and in the USA the frontiers of restrictive agreement policies were reached once companies started engaging in information agreements. These are agreements to exchange information, often about prices, but also about other matters, which do not involve specific agreements about, for example, the prices to be charged. In the UK such agreements are now registrable under the 1973 Fair Trading Act, although it seems unlikely that any cases involving information agreements will emerge before the Restrictive Trade Practices Court; while in the USA the test of whether such an agreement was restrictive or not was considered to be its *intent*. If the intent was held to be restrictive, then *per se* the agreement would be declared illegal; but if the intent were to make good a deficiency in market information that was inherent in the competitive situation, then such an agreement may not be considered restrictive. This emphasises once again the role of market information in achieving a socially effective competitive environment, and it is a consideration that appears to be missing from the preceding chapter.

Exclusions

The above points lead on directly to the second area I would like to discuss. While some of the exclusions from the general declaration of prohibition under Article 85 relate quite specifically to economic and commercial matters, as spelt out in 85(3), and in these respects go further than does the legislation in either the UK or the USA, in other respects the EEC Commission is going down a different route that may have certain disadvantages.

In particular, it has introduced decisions based upon quantitative insubstantiality. Thus, as Professor de Jong mentions, if the market share is less than five per cent in the territory where an agreement is effective, or where the aggregate turnover of the participating firms is less than 15 million units of account (20 million units of account for companies in the distributive sector) the infringement is considered insignificant. (In the UK, under the 1956 Restrictive Trade Practices Act, agreements which are 'of no substantial economic significance' may be removed from the register, but no specification of what this means is provided.) While blanket exemption may be a practical necessity, engaging in cartel activities is a state of mind that the authorities would not wish to encourage. Indeed, it should be an objective of the authorities to make it unthinkable that companies would engage in cartel activities. By providing clear-cut exemptions, there may be some encouragement for enterprises that would fall in this category to form cartels, and to maintain themselves in such a state that the legality of their agreements would not be jeopardised. This would surely be undesirable.

Co-ordination of investment

My third point is that evidently the co-ordination of investment to avoid over-capacity is regarded as a prohibited agreement (the Cimbel and the Polyester Fibre cases were mentioned in the preceding chapter).

Yet there is a real problem here for management in situations where the minimum economic size of the plant is much larger than the market prospectively could absorb, and where several companies wish to expand capacity. Not only is it a problem for managers, but if one of the objectives of competition policy is to achieve an efficient allocation of resources, then a lack of co-ordination in investment in such circumstances may well result in substantial surplus capacity and an inefficient use of resources. There is no easy answer.

One role performed by the British Island Steel Federation (prior to nationalisation) was to publicise plans for steel works expansion made by individual enterprises, so as to reduce the likelihood that several companies would simultaneously build large plants, thus creating in aggregate far too much capacity. More recently, however, the problem has been acute in the chemical industry, especially in relation to ethylene plants.

It is perhaps worth noting that in the USA Pan Am and TWA have been permitted by the regulatory authorities to discuss route rationalisation so as to diminish the degree of competition in circumstances where both airlines possessed substantial surplus capacity, although it should be added that the Civil Aeronautics Board are supervising closely the agreements that result, and have not been prepared to accept the initial proposals made by the companies.

While not suggesting that the decision in the Cimbel and Polyester Fibre cases were wrong, I can envisage some situations where an efficient allocation of resources could only be achieved by some agreement between the enterprises concerned.

To conclude, let me ask four questions. First, reference is made to an 'Advisory Committee on Restrictive Practices and Monopolies': how are its members appointed; what are its terms of reference? In the UK ordinarily an Advisory Committee that was statutorily required to give an opinion would also be required to publish that opinion, and perhaps the body receiving that opinion would be obliged to accept it, unless they had good reason, openly stated, for differing. It is surely undesirable that the advice of this Committee on particular cases should remain unpublished, and that general information about it should be so obscure.

Second, the number of informal applications of cartel policy is extremely large – the paper mentions 34000 cases cleared without formal decision. Perhaps this figure is deceptively large, but one would like to know something more of the procedures by which these clearances are made, and whether a monitoring of subsequent action is undertaken.

Third, could something more be said about the 'review procedure' that led to the cases mentioned in chapter 2 coming up for examination? By what criteria were these cases chosen from among the 37000 agreements notified to the Commission by 1963/4?

Finally, reference is made to the relatively few French and Italian firms that have been subject to cartel decisions by the EEC Commission. How does the Commission set about the task of identifying such agreements that may contravene Article 85? Is there an investigation department? What is the role of national authorities in this regard?

3
EEC competition policy towards mergers

K. MARKERT

EEC policy towards mergers is characterised by two main goals. The first is to remove artificial obstacles, mainly resulting from differing national systems of company law and taxation, to mergers between firms situated in different member states with the aim in particular of enabling small and medium-sized firms to adapt themselves to the larger dimensions of the Common Market. The second is to prevent undue concentration as a danger to the system of undistorted competition which the EEC Treaty in Article 3(f) describes as one of the fundamental aims of the Community. These two goals and the relationship between them can best be seen in the Commission's memorandum *Concentration of Enterprises in the Common Market*,[1] where both are extensively discussed. This chapter will only deal with the second aspect of EEC merger policy.

The development of merger control in the EEC
In its earlier stages discussion centred on the question of whether, and if so to what extent, the competition rules of the EEC Treaty (Articles 85 and 86) are applicable to mergers. In contrast to the competition law of the ECSC Treaty (Article 66), these rules do not expressly deal with mergers. To clarify the situation under the EEC Treaty the Commission in 1963 asked two groups of professors for their opinion. The first group, by a majority of three to one, affirmed the applicability of Article 85 to mergers which are the result of agreements between firms that remain legally distinct and which have the effect of appreciably restricting competition.[2] The second group came to the conclusion that a merger can in certain circumstances constitute an abusive exploitation of a dominant position and thus be prohibited by Article 86. While stating that Article 86 does not necessarily apply when the objective of a merger is to acquire or reinforce a dominant position, the group favoured the application of Article 86 to mergers 'whose direct object is the improper exploitation of the dominant position thus obtained or if the concentration is the result of an abuse of a dominant position.'[3]

The Commission rejected the opinion of the first group, but adopted that of the second and concluded that, 'where a dominant enterprise strengthens its position through concentration to the point where, in violation of the concept on which the Treaty, and particularly Article 86(*b*), is based, it thereby creates a monopolistic situation which prevents competition from functioning, to the detriment of consumers, suppliers, and dealers ',[4] this is a violation of Article 86. The Commission recognised, however, that this would in practice be applicable 'only in rare, exceptional cases '.

The only merger case so far tried on the basis of this concept is the Continental Can case. Although the European Court reversed the Commission's ruling that the acquisition by Europemballage Corporation, a subsidiary of the Continental Can Company, New York, of about 80 per cent of the shares of the Dutch firm Thomassen & Drijver–Verblifa N.V. was a violation of Article 86,[5] it expressly confirmed the Commission's general premise that Article 86 was applicable to mergers. Taking into account the spirit, meaning and terms of Article 86 in the system and objectives of the Treaty as a whole, the Court noted that the latter is based on regulations to ensure that competition is not distorted or eliminated in the Common Market. It observed that the prohibition of cartels laid down in Article 85 would be meaningless if Article 86 allowed these practices to be lawful if they took place within a concentration of enterprises. Such a contradiction would undermine the rules of competition in such a way as to compromise the effective working of the Common Market. The Court accordingly decided that there was abuse when 'an enterprise in a dominant position strengthened this position to the point where the degree of domination thus achieved hampered competition to an appreciable extent, i.e. would leave only enterprises whose actions depended on the dominant enterprise '.[6]

Parallel to the Commission's attempt to develop Article 86 into an instrument of merger control, plans to enact special provisions to deal with mergers gained momentum. The first important step in this direction was the Resolution of the European Parliament of 7 June 1971 demanding 'that for concentrations which exceed a certain share of the market or a certain size there should be prior notification; such concentrations should be regarded as authorised only if the Commission does not raise any objection within a time-limit yet to be fixed '.[7] The Paris Summit Conference of 19–21 October 1972 considered 'the formulation of measures to ensure that mergers affecting firms established in the Community are in harmony with the economic and social aims of the Community, and the maintenance of fair competition as much within the Common Market as in external markets in conformity with the rules laid down by the treaties '[8] to be necessary.

Obviously encouraged by the Continental Can judgement of the European Court, the Commission in July 1973 submitted to the Council a proposal for a Council regulation based on Articles 87 and 235 which provides for a detailed system of merger control.[9] It would empower the Commission to prohibit mergers involving combined assets of 200 million units of account or 25 per cent of a market where the merger in question creates or strengthens the ability of the parties 'to hinder effective competition in the Common Market or in a substantial part thereof' and to exempt such anti-competitive mergers in particular cases where this is 'indispensable to the attainment of an objective which is given priority treatment in the common interest of the Community' (Article 1). It further provides for a compulsory system of advance notification for large mergers involving combined assets of 1 billion units of account unless the acquired firm has assets of less than 30 million units of account.

The Commission's proposal has already been considered and, subject to minor amendments, approved by the European Parliament.[10] The Social and Economic Council has also given its approval.[11] At present the proposal is under consideration by a special working party of experts from the member states as a preliminary to the Council's decision.

The following discussion will focus on the Commission's proposed regulation. In the explanatory memorandum to this proposal a brief description of the development of concentration in the Common Market is given. According to the Commission 'in some cases the process of concentration has already gone so far that as few as four suppliers are left in the Community'.[12] This makes it clear that the demand for the power to deal, on a Community level, with the anti-competitive effects of mergers is not only a theoretical demand for completion of the Community's anti-trust system, but is also justified by urgent competition policy needs. Article 86, even as widely interpreted as in the Continental Can judgement of the European Court, cannot be regarded as sufficient to meet this demand because it can reach only those mergers where the acquiring firm already has a dominant position on the market. In other words it can only be used when the horse has already bolted from the stable. Besides, the directly applicable prohibition of Article 86 and the sanctions of Regulation 17 are not very appropriate to merger cases.

The regulation proposed by the Commission is to be based on Articles 87 and 235 of the Treaty. The reference to Article 235 is necessary because the powers provided by the proposed regulation, which apply to mergers regardless of whether the acquiring firm had a dominant position before the merger, clearly go beyond the mere 'implementation of the principles laid down in Articles 85 and 86' within the meaning of Article 87.

The Commission, in a comprehensive note to the Legal Affairs Committee, has explained how these two Articles supply a sufficient legal basis for the proposed regulation.[13] For the purpose of the present paper it is not necessary to go into further detail.

The proposed EEC merger regulation

This part of the chapter will discuss the main points raised by the Commission's proposed Regulation, namely (1) the standard by which 'good' and 'bad' mergers are to be distinguished; (2) the question of quantitative criteria as a requirement for the applicability of the control; (3) the question of pre-merger notification and approval; (4) the definition of 'merger'; (5) the territorial scope of the proposed control; (6) the ability to enforce the law; (7) the relationship to Articles 85 and 86; and (8) the relationship between EEC merger control and the national control systems in the member states. On each point a brief description of what the Commission proposes will be given and where appropriate, reference will be made to the merger control systems of the European Coal and Steel Community (ECSC) and the Federal Republic of Germany, both of which served as models for the proposed EEC Regulation. There will then be a discussion of, in particular, the points of actual or possible controversy. The views expressed are strictly personal and are naturally influenced by the author's direct involvement in the application of the German merger control law.

The standard of judgement

The criterion used in Article 1(1) of the Commission's proposal for taking action against mergers is that the participating firms, as a result of the merger, 'acquire or enhance the power to hinder effective competition in the Common Market or in a substantial part thereof' and that the merger 'may affect trade between Member States'. However, under Article 1(3) an exemption can be given to a merger covered by Article 1(1), if the merger is 'indispensable to the attainment of an objective which is given priority treatment in the common interest of the Community'.

The meaning of 'power to hinder effective competition' is not defined in the proposal by objective criteria such as market share or size. Article 1(1) merely states that this power 'shall be appraised by reference in particular to the extent to which suppliers and consumers have the possibility of choice, to the economic and financial power of the undertakings concerned, to the structure of the markets affected, and to supply and demand trends for the relevant goods or services'. In the Commission's explanatory memorandum it is pointed out that the Court of Justice in the Continental Can judgement referred particularly to the concept of 'preserving effective competition' in order to describe the objective of the competition rules in the EEC Treaty and that this concept 'can thus be taken as a basic criterion for appraising compatibility with the Common Market'.[14] The memorandum then continues by saying that a merger 'may be incompatible with the Common Market by virtue of the share of the market held or of the special availability of technical knowledge, raw materials or capital. The absolute size of the undertakings concerned as well as their links with suppliers, resellers or undertakings of third countries must be considered. Further, the ability of other suppliers to compete and their conduct, the structure of demand and supply, the barriers to entry to the market, the rate of technical progress, the growth of the relevant sector and of actual or potential international competition and competition from substitute products must all be considered.'[15]

As to the exemption clause of Article 1(3) the memorandum points out that this clause 'makes it possible to take account of certain necessities of industrial, technological, social and regional policy applied at Community level. In the same way integration into an important group sometimes becomes indispensable to secure the viability of an undertaking situated in an area which is economically underdeveloped or declining, and where employment problems are particularly grave.'[16]

The formula in Article 1(1) is identical with language used in Article 66, para. 2, of the ECSC Treaty ('power...to prevent the maintenance of effective competition in a substantial part of the market for such products'). It is therefore appropriate for the interpretation of Article 1(1) to consider cases dealt with under Article 66, para. 2. The 'case law' relating to this provision is summarised as follows in the OECD report *Market Power and the Law*: 'In the ECSC the primary concern of the High Authority (now the E.C. Commission) and of the Court of Justice in applying Article 66 of the ECSC Treaty was not so much, as is the case in the United States, the prevention of probable adverse effects on competition as the actual maintenance of effective competition in order to ensure the achievement of the fundamental aims of Article 2 of the Treaty. In pursuing this goal the High Authority in its merger decisions has in particular seen to it that the oligopolistic market conditions largely prevailing in the coal and steel fields are not changed by mergers in such a way that there would be no longer a large number of independent suppliers, none of which has a substantially stronger market position than his competitors. This concern with maintaining "balanced" market structures may be seen particularly from the Thyssen/Phoenix Rheinrohr and Hoesch/Hoogovens decisions and the decisions concerning the German steel syndicates. Considering that the "balance" in these cases was maintained the High Authority has not opposed further concentration in markets with an already significant oligopolistic character.'[17]

The OECD report also points out that Article 66, para. 2, has the same approach as US merger law, namely that 'in the United States and in the ECSC a merger which has anti-competitive effects, as specified in the law, can normally not be justified by beneficial economic effects (e.g. economies of scale) or other reasons'.[18] The system of Article 66 is thus based on a pure competition criterion that does not permit trade-offs between the anti-competitive effects of the merger and beneficial effects of some other kind, such as increased efficiency as a result of larger plant or firm size.

In contrast to Article 66, para. 2, Article 1(3) of the EEC proposal provides a limited trade-off system for exemptions from the competition criterion of Article 1(1). In this respect the proposal parallels the German system which also uses, as its basic rule, a competition test with provision to grant exemptions if 'the anti-competitive effects of the merger are outweighed by advantages connected with the economy in general or if the merger is justified by the overriding interest of the public'. The exceptional character of this trade-off clause in Germany is underlined by the fact that its application requires a special authorisation by the Economics Minister and can be given only after the Federal Cartel Office has formally prohibited the merger because of its anti-competitive effects. The Minister cannot question the findings of the Federal Cartel Office but merely outweigh them by policy considerations for which he takes the full political responsibility.

Neither Article 66, para. 2, of the ECSC Treaty nor Article 1 of the EEC proposal expressly provide for trade-offs between the effects on competition in different markets as does German law. Under Section 24(1) of the German law a merger, even if it creates or strengthens a market dominating position, cannot be prohibited if 'the participating firms can show that the merger also causes improvements of competitive conditions and that such improvements outweigh the disadvantages of the market dominating position'. This clause was designed to deal with situations where a merger of firms that are actual or potential competitors on several different product or geographic markets (markets A and B) leads to a market dominating position on market A but strengthens competition on market B. Under Article 1 of the EEC proposal the prohibition of such a merger could only be avoided by application of the general trade-off clause requiring an overriding 'common interest of the Community'.

In my view the Commission's basic approach of using a competition criterion as the basic rule with a limited public interest trade-off clause is preferable to a general trade-off system. It is doubtful whether a theoretically convincing case for such a general cost–benefit approach can be made, given that no objective standard for weighing anti-competitive effects against 'positive' effects of some other kind exists, that such effects are not normally more than mere expectations about future developments, and even where they are reasonably foreseeable, they may be offset by 'X-inefficiencies' as a result of the merged firm no longer being exposed to strong competitive pressure from outside.[19] More important, however, are the practical considerations against a general cost–benefit system. During the relatively short examination period that is usually available to a control agency, particularly with a pre-merger clarification system, it is not normally feasible to make a reasonable attempt to assess the non-competitive benefits of each merger, at least if one is not prepared to accept a market analysis and trade-off neither of which is based on thoroughly researched facts.

Whether the competition criterion of the EEC proposal is in itself satisfactory is more difficult to say. As a general guideline the maintenance of effective competition in individual markets is indispensable to a competitive economic system. The Commission is therefore right not to propose a standard which would only reach those monopolistic mergers which virtually eliminate competition from the market. As can be seen from the application of Article 66, para. 2, of the ECSC Treaty, the proposed test can also take account of market situations where, even though there are only relatively few firms, active competition prevails.

What is doubtful, however, is whether the standard used in Article 1(1) of the Commission's proposal is sufficiently practicable. To determine whether competition on the market is 'effective' means a test of conduct that usually requires detailed information about the competitive behaviour of the firms in the market over a period of time. Experience of a similar pure conduct test in Germany suggests that the control authority will normally not be able to find the necessary facts within a short period of time. The German conduct test was therefore supplemented last year by structural criteria, i.e. the market position of a firm in relation to its competitors and its market share. Experience with the use of these criteria shows that they have considerably reduced the difficulty of obtaining the relevant information. The US merger control practice is also largely based on market-share criteria.[20]

The ECSC experience does not disprove the need for more specific criteria. Merger control there essentially involves only one industry (steel) so that it is usually possible to use data available from prior cases. Of course, as the US example shows, structural criteria can be developed in the course of time by 'case law'. But if the need for such criteria is already obvious when the legislation is under consideration, there is no reason not to put them into the statutes. There is all the more reason for doing so, since the vague formula of Article 1(1) of the EEC proposal calls for more specificity anyway.

As for the trade-off clause of Article 1(3), it is in my view acceptable as a narrowly interpreted exception to the competition criterion. One should, however, point to the danger that the broad language of the clause covers almost anything considered by the Commission to be 'in the common interest of the Community' so that the exception could easily become the rule. One can only hope that public opinion will keep this risk within reasonable limits. After an experimental period of a few years this whole problem might have to be thoroughly reconsidered.

Quantitative criteria for mergers to come under the system

In Article 1(2) the proposal provides that to come under the control established by the regulation a merger must be of a certain minimum size in terms of aggregate turnover per year (200 million units of account) or market share (more than 25 per cent in any member state). Only if neither criterion is met is the merger outside the scope of the proposed regulation. In the Commission's explanatory memorandum it is said that mergers below this ceiling 'are not such as to prevent effective competition in the Common Market or in a part of it'.

The Commission's explanation suggests that Article 1(2) merely has the clarifying function of indicating which mergers would not come under Article 1(1). It is indeed hardly conceivable that a firm whose market share as a result of a merger does not exceed 25 per cent can acquire 'the power to hinder effective competition'. The Commission's view does not, however, take sufficient account of the situation in which the merged firm is part of a group of non-competitive oligopolists with a high aggregate market share. In such a case the Commission's argument would only be acceptable if the words 'concerned by the concentration' could be interpreted as including the shares of the other oligopolists although they are not included in the merger.

The real question, however, is not, as the Commission suggests, to specify those mergers which because they obviously have no anti-competitive effects, would not come under the control standard anyhow. It is rather to establish minimum quantitative criteria to limit the cases to be examined to a reasonable number in the interests of the workability of the system. From this point of view, it does not appear that Article 1(2) of the proposal will sufficiently reduce the number of examinable cases. Since substitute products are to be included and the market share of more than 25 per cent relates to any member state, relatively small mergers would be above the minimum size.

In German law the minimum criteria are 500 million marks aggregate turnover or 50 million marks turnover of the acquired firm. Even so, during the first year of application of the law, about 120 mergers were covered. In this connection it should be noted that, due to the rule that the turnover of all affiliated firms shall be included in calculating the relevant turnover and market-share figures – a rule which the proposed Regulation also contains (Article 5) – relatively unimportant transactions, such as small joint ventures of medium-sized firms, are above the minimum turnover.

Even though at present no comparable figures are available on a Community level, one can reasonably conclude that the proposed minimum criterion of 200 million units of account would itself reach several hundred mergers a year. It is true that not every merger above this size in the Community 'may affect trade between member states', but in view of the wide interpretation of this term in cases under Articles 85 and 86, it cannot be expected that the EEC regulation will cover only a small minority of the mergers in the Community which meet the size criterion.

For this reason the 25 per cent market share criterion should be deleted. Since, under Article 20 of the proposed Regulation, Article 86 remains applicable to any mergers not covered by the Regulation, mergers below 200 million units of account aggregate turnover would not be totally immune from EEC competition law.

Pre-notification and advance approval

The EEC proposal is a combination of ex-ante notification and approval and ex-post control. Under Article 4 mergers involving firms with an aggregate annual turnover of one billion units of account or more must be notified in advance, unless the acquired firm has an annual turnover of less than 30 million units of account. Other merger proposals may also be notified to the Commission on a voluntary basis. In both cases, if the merger has been duly notified to the Commission, the Commission has a maximum of three months to decide whether to commence proceedings – Article 6(2) – and a maximum of nine months after the commencement of proceedings to decide whether to prohibit the merger (Article 17(1)). If no notification is made, no time-limits for the commencement of proceedings and prohibition decisions are provided.

Where notification is compulsory, the merger may not be 'put into effect' during the first three months after it has been duly notified, unless the Commission expressly gives the 'green light' by informing the parties that proceedings will not be commenced (Article 7(1)). If the Commission decides to commence proceedings, the automatic stand-still ends, but the Commission may, by a decision, order the suspension of the merger (Article 7(1)). In this respect the proposed regulation resembles Section 74 of the British Fair Trading Act 1973. The stand-still under Article 7(1) can also be ordered in cases where notification is not obligatory and the merger has not yet been put into effect.

In the preamble to the proposed regulation the compulsory pre-notification of large mergers is explained by a need 'to ensure effective supervision'. The reason stated in the explanatory memorandum for the voluntary pre-notification of other mergers is 'to give interested undertakings the chance to benefit from the procedural regulations from Article 6 onwards'. It is further indicated that about 300 firms in the Community are covered by the one billion units of account turnover criterion, but that this does not give a complete picture of notifiable mergers since mergers of firms which individually are below that ceiling may reach or pass it as a result of their merger.

A similar combination of advance and ex-post control to that proposed by the Commission now applies in Germany. Ex-ante examination is compulsory for large mergers, i.e. those involving at least two firms with an annual turnover of one billion marks. During the first year of the new law 33 such mergers took place. German law also allows other mergers to be notified in advance on a voluntary basis. The time-limits for the control authority in cases of pre-notification are considerably shorter than those in the EEC proposal – one month to commence proceedings and four months from notification to issue a prohibition order. On the other hand, the ECSC system is based entirely on compulsory examination of mergers before they take place.

The pros and cons of a compulsory system of examination *ex ante* were extensively discussed in Germany in connection with the passing of the new merger law. The main argument in favour of such a system was that if mergers can be put into effect before they have been examined, at least in a preliminary manner, by the control authority, the difficulty of undoing a merger which is later prohibited, particularly where companies have been dissolved or assets of merging firms amalgamated, might be so enormous that implementation of the prohibition will be virtually impossible and the authority, foreseeing these difficulties, will tend to avoid a prohibition order which it would otherwise have made. It was feared that for this reason a system of ex-post control, even if it provides that the control authority can issue 'stand-still' orders while still examining the case, would be less effective.

After a year of experience with the German pre-notification system there is no empirical proof that 'good' mergers have been prevented by the necessity of prior notification to the Federal Cartel Office. This experience shows that the parties to a merger normally consider it to be in their own interest to inform the control authority in advance and to find out whether the merger is likely to be challenged. This can be seen from the fact that pre-notification was compulsory in only 33 of the 50 notified mergers. Experience also shows that in cases which do not raise serious questions of market dominance the 'green light' can be given within a few days or weeks. Of the 50 cases pre-notified during last year, 28 did not extend beyond the one month period during which the Federal Cartel Office must decide whether to commence a thorough investigation.

Of course a 'critical' merger may be held up for several months even though it may eventually turn out to be a 'good' merger. But such mergers may also be delayed in an ex-post control system as a result of a stand-still order while the examination is pending. Under German practice the parties are allowed to make binding agreements and perform transactions during the three months after notification subject to the condition that the merger obtains approval by the control authority. ECSC practice has apparently developed a similar rule. Thus in the Thyssen/Rheinstahl case Thyssen, by charging a group of banks to act as trustee, was able to make a takeover bid to the shareholders of Rheinstahl, even though the authorisation by the Commission under Article 66 was only given nine months later.[21]

All this demonstrates that a pre-notification system along the lines proposed by the Commission is not an unreasonable burden on merger candidates. The automatic stand-still under the proposed Regulation only lasts until the Commission decides whether to commence proceedings and is limited to three months from notification. Of course the reasonableness of the burden will greatly depend on whether the Commission usually takes most of the time allowed or reacts more quickly.

In the light of experience with the one-month period in Germany it should be possible to reduce the three-month period proposed by the Commission to two months. This seems feasible since during that period only a preliminary examination of the merger is required and the decision to commence proceedings does not have to be made formally by the Commission but could be delegated to the Commissioner responsible for competition policy or to the Director General for Competition. On the other hand, such a formal decision is necessary under Article 9(2) of the proposed Regulation if the Commission wishes to impose a stand-still after proceedings have been commenced. Since such formal decisions usually take a long time, this requirement should be dropped.

The definition of 'merger'

Mergers as covered by the EEC proposal are defined in Article 1(1) and in Article 2. Article 1(1) covers 'any transaction which has the direct or indirect effect of bringing about a concentration between undertakings or groups of undertakings'. Article 2(1) specifies that concentrations within the meaning of Article 1(1) are those 'whereby a person or an undertaking or a group of persons or undertakings acquires control of one or several enterprises'. Article 2(2) defines control as being 'constituted by rights or contracts which, either separately or jointly, and having regard to the considerations of fact or law involved, make it possible to determine how an undertaking shall operate'. It further lists a number of examples of such 'rights or contracts', starting from ownership of all or part of the assets of an undertaking and ending with 'contracts of an undertaking concerning the whole or an important part of supplies or outlets where the duration of these contracts or the quantities to which they relate exceed what is usual in commercial contracts dealing with those matters'. Article 2(3) specifies the persons to be considered as acquiring control including trustees. Finally, Article 2(4) excludes from the definition of control the acquisition of shares by banks where this is done 'upon the formation of an undertaking or increase of its capital...with a view to selling them on the market', provided that the bank does not use the voting rights in respect of the shares acquired.

As the Commission points out in its explanatory memorandum, the definition of merger in the proposed regulation is largely inspired by the ECSC decision no. 24/54 of 6 May 1954 which 'has shown its value over nearly 20 years of practical application, during which more than 200 individual decisions were taken'. This tendency of the Commission to rely primarily on legal concepts with which it is familiar and which it has applied successfully for a long time is understandable. On the other hand, there is no reason why possible clarifications and improvements in the legal texts should not be made.

In my opinion the following clarifications are necessary:

(*a*) What proportion of the shares of another firm is to be considered as constituting control? In German law the share is 25 per cent.

(*b*) Under what conditions is the acquisition of part of the assets of another firm to be considered as constituting control? In German law the acquisition of a substantial part is necessary, but the term 'substantial' has already given rise to legal controversies resulting in court proceedings.

(*c*) Joint ventures are not separately defined. Is the Commission anticipating that joint ventures are to be treated as under ECSC law including the 'group effect' concept?

(*d*) What is the definition of a 'group of persons or undertakings' within the meaning of Article 2(1)?

(*e*) Are further merger transactions among firms between which 'concentration' already exists to be regarded as separate mergers? For example, if a firm already owns 40 per cent of the shares of another firm and is regarded as controlling that firm, is the acquisition of the majority or all of the shares of the controlled firm a separate merger? German law provides that such further merger transactions are separate mergers unless they do not result in 'a substantial increase of the existing interlock'.

(*f*) The banks clause of Article 2(4) as proposed by the Commission is not suitable for rescue operations by banks taking over the shares of 'sick' firms with a view to finding another buyer. In German law the banks clause is wider, since it covers acquisitions by banks not only in connection with the formation of an enterprise or the increase of its capital but also 'otherwise within the framework of their business'.

Territorial scope

The proposed regulation applies to mergers between firms 'at least one of which is established in the common market'. This means that purely national mergers of firms established in the same member state are covered if the merger in question may affect trade between member states. On the other hand, mergers of firms established in third countries (foreign mergers) are excluded regardless whether such mergers have effects on intra-Community trade.

It is sensible for the Commission's proposal not to exclude national mergers *per se*. Such an exclusion would be inconsistent with the basic idea of the competition rules of the Treaty as interpreted by the European Court. If national cartels and abuse of dominant position in a national market which may affect intra-Community trade do fall under Articles 85 and 86,[22] there is no reason to treat mergers differently. Of course, as previously stated, the inclusion of national mergers is an important point to consider in connection with the minimum quantitative criteria. That the applicability of the proposed regulation to national mergers increases the possible overlap between Community and national merger control is no reason to limit its coverage to international mergers. Such overlaps are only part of the general problem of the relationship between Community and national competition law and must be considered in that context.

The per-se exclusion of foreign mergers from the coverage of the proposed Regulation is acceptable for practical reasons, although it is not in line with the practice regarding Articles 85 and 86.[23] Even if such a merger had serious effects on intra-Community trade, for example where the only two competing importers of a product not manufactured in the Community merge, it is impossible in practice for the Community authorities to prevent such a merger. Community law should, however, remain applicable where a foreign merger involves firms established in the Common Market, for example if two foreign firms merge one or both having subsidiaries in the EEC.

In German law a special clause provides that a merger of parent firms is to be regarded at the same time as a merger between their subsidiaries. This clause is intended to ensure that mergers of foreign firms abroad can be reached in so far as these firms have domestic subsidiaries. It is not clear from ECSC practice whether ECSC subsidiaries of foreign firms are covered by Community law if there is a merger between their parent firms. If ECSC practice does not provide a clear positive answer to this question, a clause as in the German law should be added to the Commission's proposal.

Ability to enforce the regulation

The proposed regulation is based on the same enforcement system as applies in other areas of competition law, i.e. the Commission acts at the same time as investigator, prosecutor and decision-maker. Although the investigation is done by the Directorate General for Competition, final decisions prohibiting certain practices or granting exemptions are taken by the Commission itself. The Commission's procedure follows the general pattern of administrative law enforcement in continental Europe. The proceedings are not adversary, but the parties have a right to a hearing before a decision is made and can challenge the decision before the Court of Justice. The member states are only indirectly involved in this process, they have to be consulted through a Consultative Committee before final decisions are taken. The opinions of this Committee are not binding on the Commission, but the member states have the right to challenge the Commission's decision before the Court of Justice for violation of the Treaty or implementing regulations or for abuse of discretionary power (Article 173(1), EEC Treaty).

The working of the system in practice has been thoroughly analysed recently by a UK observer with inside experience.[24] It is a strictly hierarchical system with numerous steps in the ladder which make it extremely time-consuming and discourages teamwork and initiative by those civil servants who actually deal with the cases (the *rapporteurs*). As the British observer points out, 'the technicalities of the journey of approval that the decision must make are highly frustrating to the civil servants'. For instance, a *rapporteur* asks a representative of a firm for an appointment by telephone, the written confirmation of the date to the visitor will only be drafted by the *rapporteur*, and must then be approved by the Advisor and finally signed by the Director (who has the lowest grade to which the right of signature has been delegated). They find the procedure so burdensome that consequently from time to time they tend to take short cuts in the interest of a speedier conclusion although running the risk of hierarchical disfavour. There have been, for example, policy disputes between Directorates A and B which have prolonged cases for two to three years. Each time and from whatever level an objection to a draft is raised, the objector sends a note to the *rapporteur* and the *rapporteur* must revise the draft and send it up the complete ladder again, without skipping any rung. Statistics have been prepared in the Commission which show that each individual case contains at least fifty to seventy transmissions of drafts and notes. This number can easily attain the figure of 150. Each transmission takes up to half a day to pass from one office to another through the internal postal system, so that 150 transmissions involve a loss of seventy-five working days. In addition to these mechanical difficulties, many civil servants consider that they are burdened by inadequate office and research facilities, which limit them still further.

Under the circumstances just described, one cannot be confident that the proposed enforcement system will be able to deal effectively with the administrative problems of merger control and in particular of a pre-notification system. Without a properly equipped and organised administrative machinery the proposed merger control risks becoming a bureaucratic farce which would discredit the name of competition and place an unnecessary burden on merger candidates. As long as no substantial improvement of the situation is in sight, the proposed Regulation does not seem ready for adoption.

One important step towards improving the situation would be the setting up of a separate office for the enforcement of competition law. Such an office was envisaged in Article 3 of the Decision by the representatives of the Governments of the member states relating to the provisional installation of certain institutions and services of the Communities of 8 April 1965.[25] Experience in the UK and in Germany suggests that such a separate enforcement agency is essential for the efficient, speedy administration of competition law. A separate competition law enforcement agency in the EEC could be limited to examining the competitive aspects of mergers and other restrictive practices, while the Commission would retain the power to grant exemptions for reasons of public policy.

No improvement in the situation can be expected from giving the member states enforcement powers of their own, similar to the powers provided in Article 9(3) of Regulation 17 for cases arising under Articles 85(1) and 86. Experience with Article 9(3) of Regulation 17 shows that it has had virtually no practical effect. To include a similar rule in the proposed merger Regulation would also raise serious problems as to the uniform application of Community law and the proper administration of the exemption clause in Article 1(3).

Likewise, more direct involvement of the national governments in the Commission's decision-making process, particularly in the form of the right to veto Commission decisions or to appeal to the Council, would not accelerate the procedure but delay it. Of course national governments may have a vital interest in how particular mergers are treated by the Commission under the proposed Regulation. The normal situation of this kind will be that a national government favours a merger for national policy reasons whereas the Commission intends to prohibit it. In such cases the national governments have sufficient ways in which to present their views to the Commission and to appeal to the Court of Justice.

The fact that the Commission (or perhaps eventually a separate agency for competition law) both investigates and decides cases in accordance with the general practice of continental administrative law does not appear to raise serious questions of equity, as long as the 'accused' firms are given the opportunity to present their views on the matters of 'complaint' during the administrative stage of the proceedings and have a right to appeal to an independent court if the decision goes against them. The present system does not seem to have serious deficiencies in this respect. This does not mean of course that the system could not be improved. For example, more opportunity could be given to 'accused' parties to inspect the Commission's evidence before the decision is taken. There is also scope to improve the judicial review system, for example by instituting a lower court with wider review powers as to the evidence presented by the Commission. It should not be the rule that, as one British observer[26] noted, 'the Court sits in silence, there is no dialogue with the parties, there is no effort to test points of fact or points of law by confrontation of parties, the hearing of witnesses is not a regular feature of the Court'.

Relationship to Articles 85 and 86

Article 20 of the proposed Regulation provides that 'concentrations covered by this Regulation' shall not be subject to Regulations 17 and 1017 which relate to Articles 85 and 86. The purpose of Article 20, as indicated in the Commission's explanatory memorandum, is to ensure that mergers 'caught by the proposed Regulation' are considered under this regulation only, even though in a particular case the merger may also violate Article 86 by the standards of the Continental Can judgement.

The meaning of the expression 'concentrations covered by this Regulation' is not entirely clear. It may be interpreted as referring generally to all transactions listed in Article 2 in so far as they affect trade between member states. A narrower interpretation would be that such transactions are 'covered by this Regulation' only if the aggregate turnover of the parties is at least 200 million units of account or they have a market share of more than 25 per cent. Finally, the term 'covered by this Regulation' can be understood as meaning only those mergers which are prohibited under Article 1(1) because of their anti-competitive effects. The most sensible interpretation is undoubtedly the second, for it would make no sense to exclude from Regulation 17 mergers that are not even examinable under the proposed Regulation. On the other hand whether Regulation 17 is applicable should be clear from the beginning rather than only when the Commission has ascertained, after an examination that may last up to one year, that the merger has no anti-competitive effects as required by Article 1(1).

If Article 20 is interpreted in this manner, this would mean that the Commission retains its power to challenge, under Article 86 and Regulations 17 and 1017, mergers of firms with an aggregate annual turnover of less than 200 million units of account. On the other hand, mergers covered by the proposed Regulation would not be entirely outside the scope of Article 86, since Regulations 17 and 1017 do not affect the private law consequences of Article 86 (nullity, right of affected persons to ask for an injunction or sue for damages). Private persons might therefore bring the merger in front of the ordinary courts for violation of Article 86 even though it has been approved under the merger regulation. It is true that in view of the narrow scope of Article 86 as applied to mergers this is rather unlikely to happen. But in the interest of legal security it might be preferable to exclude any applicability of Article 86 to mergers covered by the Regulation. In this case a special reference to Regulations 17 and 1017 would no longer be necessary.

Article 20 of the proposed Regulation also touches upon the relationship between merger law and the rules laid down in Article 85 on restrictive agreements and concerted actions (cartel law). Here the problem is of much greater practical relevance, since Article 85(1) covers any appreciably restrictive agreement or concerted practice and many mergers, particularly the formation of joint ventures, involve agreements between independent firms which have restrictive effects on their competitive behaviour. If such 'agreed' mergers where the acting firms retain their independence after the merger are also considered to come under Article 85, they could become lawful only if, in addition to the 'green light' under merger law, an exemption is granted under Article 85(3). However, Article 20 of the proposed Regulation, by rendering Regulation 17 inapplicable to 'concentrations' covered by the merger regulation, prevents the Commission from granting such exemptions. This suggests that the Commission's opinion underlying Article 20 is that 'concentrations' covered by merger law cannot also fall under Article 85.

The view that there is a clear distinction between mergers and cartels was taken in the Commission's Concentration Memorandum of 1965 where it is pointed out that 'it is not possible to apply Article 85 to agreements whose purpose is the acquisition of total or partial ownership of enterprises or the reorganisation of the ownership of enterprises (merger, acquisition of holdings, purchase of part of the assets). If, after the concentration process, several independent enterprises continue to exist (e.g. in the case of joint ventures), it will be necessary to examine carefully whether, apart from changes in ownership, the participating enterprises did not enter into agreements or concerted practices within the meaning of Article 85, paragraph 1. Furthermore, Article 85, paragraph 1, continues to be applicable if the agreement has as its purpose no permanent change in ownership but a co-ordination of the market behaviour of enterprises that remain economically independent. In such cases, the reasons that militate against an application of Article 85 to concentrations do not exist. The situation in such cases is actually that of a cartel, and not that of a reorganisation of ownership.'[27] The Commission thus considered the 'change in ownership' as the basic factor to distinguish mergers from cartels, but did not entirely exclude the possibility that certain mergers may come within the scope of Article 85. Further indications as to which types of mergers these might be were, however, not given.

In any case, the Commission's reasoning is not convincing. Undoubtedly many modern merger transactions, such as the establishment of joint ventures and arrangements as in the case of Agfa/Gevaert, are not primarily characterised by 'changes in ownership'. In fact, most of the transactions listed in Article 2(2) of the proposed Regulation involve no such changes at all, but are purely contractual arrangements. It is therefore obviously not possible to consider the 'change in ownership' as in general relevant to distinguish mergers from cartels covered by Article 85.[28]

In ECSC practice the question of possible overlaps between Articles 65 and 66 in merger cases has been considered in several joint venture cases. Until 1962 the establishment of a new firm by several existing firms was not regarded as a merger but the contrary view has been taken since the SIDMAR decision of 25 April 1962.[29] In this case the underlying agreement of the parent firms was not regarded as a cartel falling under Article 65. It was recognised that, as a result of this agreement, competition between the parents in the field of activity of the joint venture (flat steel products) was restricted, because 'it is clear that if the controlling enterprises and the enterprise controlled make the same or similar products, group control automatically ends by limiting competition with regard to these products among all the enterprises concerned. Thus in the exercise of joint control, as when fixing the prices of the products of the controlled enterprise, the controlling firms will inevitably consider their own prices for the same or similar products and reach agreement among themselves on all prices (group effect).' It was said, however, that this 'inherent' restriction resulting from the 'group effect' should 'rather be assessed at the time of the concentration so that authorisation may if necessary be refused when the consequences of the concentration and of the group effect no longer comply with the criteria for authorisation under Article 66'.

This distinction in ECSC practice between the 'inherent' restrictive effects of a joint venture agreement to be considered solely in the context of merger law and other restrictive agreements falling under

Article 65 can be seen more clearly from a later decision by the High Authority also concerning the SIDMAR joint venture.[30] At issue was an agreement to set up a joint sales organisation for the products manufactured by SIDMAR and two of the parent firms. This was considered to be a cartel agreement falling under Article 65 on the following grounds: 'When the SIDMAR joint venture was authorised, this meant that those concerned might co-ordinate their business activities in SIDMAR's field, even outside the joint subsidiary itself, and restrain competition between themselves. Although this "group effect" was authorised, however, the parties were still at liberty to proceed with such co-ordination or not, as they wished. Now it is this liberty to remain competitors between themselves that has been abandoned in the new agreements, in which they contract to follow a specified line of conduct towards one another.'

The Commission's decision in the Henkel/Colgate case[31] appears to show a different approach from that of the ECSC cases. In this case the Commission considered an agreement between two manufacturers of household detergents to set up a joint research company in Switzerland as an agreement falling under Article 85, even though the parent firms remained free to conduct research individually. In the opinion of the Commission it was sufficient that 'for factual reasons' such individual research was unlikely and therefore competition in research restricted.

If Article 20 of the proposed Regulation were adopted in its present form, it is uncertain whether the Commission could still consider such cases under Article 85. As a result, the Commission might lose its power to impose conditions as in the Henkel/Colgate case, because joint ventures of the Henkel/Colgate type are normally unlikely to create or enhance the 'power to hinder effective competition', in which case there is no legal basis for prohibiting the joint venture. On the other hand, the second SIDMAR decision shows that clear cases of evasion of the cartel prohibition by joint venture agreements can be prevented. However, the distinction between inherent and 'express' restrictions in such cases is artificial and might open the way to more refined methods of evasion.

Undoubtedly the question of the relationship between merger law and cartel law is a complex problem that requires greater elaboration than can be expressed by such formulae as 'change in ownership' or 'inherent restrictions'. What seems certain, however, is that overlaps between the two laws cannot be excluded *per se*. Since Article 20 of the proposed Regulation is apparently based on this wrong premise and might therefore obstruct the development of sensible, pragmatic solutions by administrative and court practice, it should be deleted in so far as it refers to Article 85.

Relationship to national merger laws

At present, only two member states, Germany and the UK, have a national system of merger control as a part of competition policy. In two other member states, Ireland and the Netherlands, legislation providing such control is currently under consideration. The number of mergers per year considered in Germany and in the United Kingdom is more than 100 in each country. In view of the customary wide interpretation of the formula 'may affect trade between member states' it may be assumed that a substantial number of these cases would also be covered by the proposed EEC Regulation. The adoption of this Regulation is therefore likely to lead to frequent overlaps between national and Community merger law.

The general situation as regards the relationship of national to Community competition law is that both laws apply concurrently, but, according to the Court of Justice, the application of national competition law in a particular case may not 'prejudice the full and uniform application of Community law or the effect of measures taken to implement it'.[32] This means that inter-state mergers to be lawful must conform with both laws. A merger prohibited by EEC law would thus be illegal regardless of whether it has obtained approval under national law. In this respect Community law has absolute priority. In the opposite case, where an exemption is given under EEC law (Article 1(3) of the proposed Regulation), but national law calls for a prohibition of the merger, the prevailing view is that such a prohibition would be in conflict with EEC law. There is, however, no obligation on the national authorities to suspend their national law proceedings until the Commission has terminated its Community law proceedings.

In consequence of this legal situation a merger between a British and a German firm with a combined turnover of more than 200 million units of account would normally require examination under three different merger laws. Likewise, many national mergers in Germany or in the UK would require two different proceedings. Such double or triple control already exists in the fields of coal and steel in cases where merging coal or steel firms are also active in markets not covered by the ECSC Treaty.[33] Although it has not appeared that this causes insurmountable difficulties for parties to the mergers, it must be admitted that this situation, at least in the long run, is not ideal.

One possible solution to this problem would be to automatically exempt from national law all mergers which come within the scope of EEC law. It could be argued in favour of this solution that if the Commission finds that the merger is hindering effective competition, it will either prohibit it or grant an exemption under Article 1(3). In both cases this decision would have priority over a contrary national decision. If, on the other hand, the Commission finds that the merger does not result in the power to hinder effective competition in any member state being a substantial part of the Common Market the preconditions for prohibiting the merger under national law would not be fulfilled anyway.

The practicability of such a system would, however, require generally agreed objective criteria on the basis of which it can be rapidly determined whether a merger 'may affect trade between member states' and thus falls within the scope of EEC law. It would further require that the EEC control standard as interpreted by the Commission is not significantly less strict than the standards of national law and that the Commission has the administrative facilities to conduct a thorough investigation in all critical cases. Since none of these requirements is definitely met at present, it is unrealistic to expect that Germany and the UK would agree to the general priority of Community merger control.

Under these circumstances less far-reaching solutions with more emphasis on practical than on legal aspects must be developed. Such a solution would be an arrangement between the Community and the member states concerned providing that in cases of overlap of Community and national merger control both sides will agree in each case on an ad-hoc basis whether the Commission or the competent national authority will take the case. It could further be provided that the Commission has a right of priority under certain conditions, for example if the activities of the merging firms are primarily in trade between member states or in all cases of cross-border mergers. Of course such ad-hoc agreements would have to be made within very short time-limits. Further, provision in the merger laws would have to be made as to the legal consequences of an agreement that a particular case is not to be dealt with under the law concerned. It is obvious that the development of pragmatic solutions of this kind would be an experiment and one should not underestimate the difficulties of finding formulae acceptable to all sides.

Conclusions

By far the most important current issue in EEC competition policy towards mergers is the proposed Regulation on merger control. This proposal is an immediate result of the Court of Justice's judgement in the Continental Can case in which it stressed the need to supplement the laws against cartels by laws against anti-competitive mergers. Rather than content itself with attempting to implement the inherently limited potential of Article 86 as an instrument of merger control, the Commission is seeking wider powers better fitted to the particular problems of merger control. In view of the high degree of concentration already reached in a number of important industries in the Common Market and the continuing wave of mergers such powers are necessary in the interest of an active competition policy.

The discussion in this paper has focused on a limited number of competition policy questions raised by the Commission's proposal, including those which seem to be central and controversial. The conclusion of this discussion is that the basic elements of the proposal – the competition criterion with only a limited trade-off clause, the limitation of control to mergers fulfilling certain quantitative criteria relating to minimum size and the obligatory pre-notification system for very large mergers – are acceptable, but that a substantial number of details still require thorough consideration and revision.

With regard to the particular questions discussed in this paper the following suggestions are made:

(*a*) The competition criterion in Article 1(1) should be specified in structural terms to make the proposed control easier to apply.

(*b*) The market-share criterion in Article 1(2) should be deleted so that only mergers involving an aggregate annual turnover of 200 million units of account or more are covered.

(*c*) It should be possible to shorten the time-limit within which the Commission must decide whether to commence proceedings under Article 6(2) from three months to two months. Further, the procedure provided in Article 7(2) for stand-still orders should be simplified.

(*d*) The definition of merger in Article 2 requires to be clarified and made more specific in a number of respects, particularly with regard to the acquisition of capital interests and assets. Also, the scope of the clause relating to acquisition of shares by banks appears too narrow.

(*e*) Provision should be made for foreign mergers to be covered by the proposed Regulation in so far as affiliated firms established in the Common Market are involved.

(*f*) The establishment of a separate competition law enforcement agency and of an intermediary appeal court with full powers of review, including over the facts found by the control authority, should be considered.

(*g*) Article 20 concerning the relationship between the proposed merger Regulation and Articles 85 and 86 needs careful reconsideration. It should be replaced by a text merely dealing with the applicability of Article 86. The question of the applicability of Article 85 in merger cases should be decided by case law.

(*h*) The full concurrent applicability of Community and national merger control should be modified by special rules. The time has not yet come to accept that all mergers covered by the proposed Regulation are exempt from the national merger control laws of the member states, but it seems possible to adopt pragmatic arrangements with a view to avoiding unnecessary double or triple control.

Of course the proposed Regulation raises many more questions than have been discussed in this paper. Some can be found in the statements of the European Parliament and the Economic and Social Committee. An important practical point not discussed is the inclusion of affiliated firms in computing market-share and turnover figures. Also, a large number of questions connected with the practical operation of a pre-notification system have not been touched, mainly because they are to be dealt with in a later implementing regulation. These points will be particularly important since under Article 6(2) the three-month period for the Commission's decision on whether to open proceedings begins only when a complete notification has been made.

Laws are of value only to the extent that appropriate means to enforce them are made available. Therefore the administrative and procedural problems raised by the proposed Regulation are perhaps even more important than the points of substantive law. Considering the present organisation of the Community's competition law enforcement machinery and how it operates these problems seem to be the 'Achilles heel' of the whole system. Substantial improvements and assurances in this respect are necessary before one can whole-heartedly advocate the adoption of the Commission's proposal.

Notes

1 Doc. Sec. (65) 3500, 1 December 1965, *The Problem of Concentration in the Common Market* (hereinafter cited as *Concentration Memorandum*).

2 *Concentration Memorandum*, part III, para. 3.

3 *Ibid.*, para. 4.

4 *Ibid.*, paras. 5–27.

5 Decision of 21 December 1971, *Official Journal* no. L7 (8 January 1972), p. 25.

6 Judgement of 21 February 1973, case 6/72, *Recueil de la jurisprudence de la cour* XIX (1973), p. 215 (hereinafter cited as *Recueil*). The Court reversed the Commission's decision on the grounds that the relevant market had not been adequately defined. The Court indicated that 'in order to be regarded as constituting a separate market, the products in question must be distinguished not only by the mere fact that they are used for the packaging of certain products, but also by the special characteristics of production making them suitable specifically for the purpose'.

7 *Official Journal* no. C66 (1 July 1971), p. 19. This resolution is based on a report of the Economic Committee of the European Parliament, Doc. EP no. 197 (2 February 1970) (the *Berkhouwer Report*).

8 *Communiqué of the Paris Summit Conference*, point 7.

9 *Proposal for a regulation (EEC) of the Council on the Control of Concentration between Undertakings*, Doc. COM(73) 1210 final (18 July 1973), *Official Journal* no. C92 (31 October 1973), p. 1.

10 *Official Journal* no. C23 (8 March 1974), p. 19. The debate in the European Parliament is summarised in the *Bulletin of the European Communities* 1/1974, no. 2403, and 2/1974, no. 2419.

11 *Official Journal* no. C88 (26 July 1974), p. 19.
12 Doc. COM(73) 1210 final, p. 5. Further data are given in the EEC Commission, *Third Report on Competition Policy* (Brussels, May 1974), paras. 130–60.
13 Doc. EP 35.343 (12 December 1973). The European Parliament accepted the Commission's argument in its resolution on the Commission's proposal.
14 Doc. COM(73) 1210 final, p. 8.
15 *Ibid.*
16 *Ibid.*, p. 10.
17 OECD, *Market Power and the Law* (Paris, 1970), para. 204.
18 *Ibid.*, para. 205.
19 See M. A. Crew and C. K. Rowley: 'Anti-trust policy: the application of rules'. *Moorgate and Wall Street* (Autumn 1971), pp. 19–34. I share the general tendency of the views expressed by these authors.
20 See OECD, *Market Power and the Law* (1970), para. 126–60.
21 Decision of 20 December 1973, *Official Journal* no. L84 (28 March 1974), p. 36.
22 For application of Community competition policy to national cartels see judgement of Court of Justice of 17 October 1972, case 8/72, *Recueil* XVIII (1972), p. 977 (VCH). For application to abuse of national dominant positions see judgement of Court of Justice of 27 March 1974, case 127/73 *Recueil* XX (1974), p. 51 (SABAM).
23 See Court of Justice, judgement of 25 February 1971, case 22/71, *Recueil* XVII (1971), p. 949 (Béguélin), in which the Court decided according to the 'effects' doctrine. In the dyestuffs case the Commission adhered to this doctrine but the European Court left the question open since in its view the agreement had been implemented inside the Community. See Commission's decision of 24 July 1969, *Official Journal* no. L195 (7 August 1969), p. 11; and Court of justice, judgements of 14 July 1972, cases 48/69, 52/59 and 53/69, *Recueil* XVIII (1972), pp. 619, 787 and 845.
24 F. Graupner, 'Commission decision making on competition questions.' *Common Market Law Review* 10 (1973), pp. 291–305.
25 *Bulletin of the European Coal and Steel Community* no. 56, part III, pp. 65–73. See also K. Holderbaum: 'Chancen für eine Europäische Kartellbehörde', *Europarecht* 2 (1967), p. 116.
26 *Financial Times European Newsletter* (July 1973), p. 6.
27 *Concentration Memorandum*, part III, para. 58.
28 For an elaborate discussion of this problem see E. J. Mestmäcker, *Europäisches Wettbewerbsrecht* (München, 1974), paras. 30 IV and 33.
29 Summary in OECD *Guide to Legislation on Restrictive Business Practices*, vol. VI, section 3, no. 10. SIDMAR was set up as a joint venture of four steel firms in Belgium, France and Luxembourg for the production of certain flat steel products.
30 Decision of 16 March 1967; see *Ibid.*, vol. 6, section 3, no. 28.
31 Decision of 23 December 1971; see *Official Journal* no. L14 (18 January 1972), p. 14.
32 For details see K. Markert, ' Some legal or administrative problems of the co-existence of Community and national competition law in the EEC'. *Common Market Law Review* 11 (1974), pp. 92–104.
33 One example is the merger between Thyssen and Rheinstahl which was examined both by the Commission and by the West German Federal Cartel Office (see note (21) above).

COMMENT

T. BARNA

Dr Markert gives a clear and useful account of the developments that led the EEC Commission to formulate legislation on mergers, which constitute a distinct area within the field of competition policy.

Developments in the UK were somewhat similar inasmuch as legislation on monopolies and restrictive practices has been introduced in 1948 but provision to deal with mergers as such has not been made until the Act of 1965. In fact experience with the operation of mergers legislation is limited as the Labour Government of 1964–70 made few references to the Monopolies and Mergers Commission. Most of the significant mergers of the great merger movement of the late sixties have been agreed by the Government without reference to the Commission. It is worth pointing out that although the Act of 1973 gives great powers to the Director General of Fair Trading, as regards mergers his role is only advisory. The right to refer mergers to the Commission is reserved for political decision. The fact that merger activity has been extremely low in 1973–4 is due to economic and financial conditions rather than to changes in legislation and administration.

The philosophy on which EEC policy has been based follows closely, as Dr Markert points out, that of West Germany. The Hallstadt doctrine may be illustrated by quoting from the introduction to the *First Report on Competition Policy*:

> Competition is the best stimulant of economic activity since it guarantees the widest possible freedom of action to all. An active competition policy...makes it easier for the supply and demand structures continually to adjust to technological development. Through the interplay of decentralised decision-making machinery, competition enables enterprises continuously to improve their efficiency...competition policy is an essential means for satisfying to a great extent the individual and collective needs of our society,...competition policy...encourages the

best possible use of productive resources for the greatest
possible benefit of the economy as a whole and for the
benefit, in particular, of the consumer.

By contrast, UK legislation puts emphasis not on competition as an
inherently desirable objective but on 'the public interest'; this is a
vaguer but a much wider objective. Section 84(1) of the Fair Trading
Act, 1973, directs the Commission to 'take into account all matters
which appear to them in the particular circumstances to be relevant'.
Having said this, it lists by way of example several matters which
are relevant including the desirability of 'maintaining and promoting
effective competition'.

In spite of differences in philosophy between the EEC and the UK,
I believe that in the practical application of mergers legislation these
differences are more apparent than real. I certainly agree with Dr
Markert that it is not possible to apply cost–benefit techniques to judge
the desirability of mergers.

Perhaps we should ask why we are concerned with mergers, as
distinct from quotations of industrial concentration and monopoly
power; the general public is suspicious of mergers and in many
instances probably rightly so. First, the objectives of some mergers are
predatory, short-term considerations, such as capital gain for an individual or group, rather than the better utilisation of resources. Second,
in some mergers personal factors play an important role rather than
objective economic conditions.

Personal factors must of course be taken into account. In some cases
a merger may be part of 'empire building' which is unlikely to bring
economic benefits. In other cases a businessman who has become old,
and has failed to provide his own succession, may wish to sell out; it
is rather difficult to prohibit a merger in this instance without risking
the possible closing down of a firm.

On specific points, I agree with Dr Markert on the usefulness of prior
notification. It is difficult to unscramble mergers once they have become
effective. Moreover, the attitude of those administering legislation is
also likely to be influenced towards a more lenient view if it is a
question of dissolving a merger which has taken place.

I am convinced that merger investigations can be completed in a
matter of months. There is no need to collect all possible detailed facts;
if the merger has been well thought out, the salient facts should be
readily available, and in any event one cannot collect statistics on the
future. The judgement on a merger, and its possible future effects, is
necessarily subjective and a lengthy enquiry may not lead to a better
judgement.

Merger activity is a one-way traffic – there are practically no instances of voluntary un-merging. I would therefore advocate the investigation of large companies (as against monopoly in individual products) to see whether or not they ought to be split up.

In conclusion it should be emphasised that the policing of mergers, whether by the EEC or the UK Government, does not extend to the whole economy. All governments actively encourage mergers in certain sectors and in this there is a possible source of conflict between the EEC and national governments.

4
British merger policy

M. A. UTTON

In a recent influential article Williamson[1] has argued for a major change in American policy towards mergers. In essence he suggested that mergers should be judged on their net effects (benefits weighed against costs) rather than purely on their effect on competition as at present. He concluded that any policy that does not basically use this trade-off approach 'fails to meet a basic test of economic rationality'. EEC policy so far seems to lean towards the American approach, examining mergers for tendencies to reduce competition, while the British approach has been broadly to examine both costs and benefits.

The central section of this chapter uses the merger reports of the Monopolies Commission to discuss whether a more explicit and formal adoption of 'cost–benefit' analysis in this area is likely to produce a more effective policy and one which might commend itself to the EEC. The conclusion is rather sceptical on this issue. The first part gives a brief introduction to the framework of British policy and in the final section some suggestions are made for policy modification.[2]

In order to put the comments on British policy into proper perspective it is useful to refer briefly to some recent statistics which reflect changes in industrial structure and the overall effects of mergers. First, there is the rather startling rise in the share of the 100 largest firms in manufacturing-sector net output from 21 per cent in 1949 to 31 per cent in 1958 and 46 per cent in 1970. The share of the 10 largest plants in this sector has remained roughly unchanged at about 11–12 per cent.[3] Second, the publication of five-firm product concentration ratios for manufacturing in 1968 suggests that concentration has on average risen from about 59 per cent in 1963 to about 65 per cent in 1968.[4] This follows similar increases recorded for comparable product sets between 1935 and 1951, 1951 and 1958, as well as 1958 and 1963.[5] More directly important for the problem of competition policy is the growing significance of very highly concentrated products, i.e. those where the largest five firms account for 80 per cent or more of total UK output. For a comparable set of 301 product groups between 1963 and 1968 these heavily concentrated groups increased their proportion of total sales from 33 per cent to 39 per cent. Indeed by 1968 product groups accounting for three-quarters of the sample sales had five-firm concentration ratios of 50 per cent or above, and those accounting for half of the sales had ratios of at least 70 per cent. Third, since the early 1960s the volume and importance of merger activity has increased substantially, reaching a peak in 1968 (when the value of acquisitions more than doubled from the previous year) and again in 1972. The evidence also suggests that even before the peak of merger activity had been reached, mergers were playing an important part in increasing concentration levels both in the aggregate and in individual product groups.[6,7] Analysis of the late 1960s and early 1970s would probably show an even more important role for mergers. Finally, the evidence on the *effects* of mergers on firms.' performance, although subject to a large number of limitations which should not be underestimated, has generally suggested that the internal effect on the firm was either more or less neutral or actually adverse.[8,9,10] Where market power was increased at the same time as merger the net social effect may frequently have been negative.

Professor Galbraith apparently believes that all competition policies tend merely to lead up blind alleys,[11] and that figures like those quoted above show conclusively that past efforts in this direction have so clearly failed that future efforts are also bound to be ineffective. The contrary view is that background information like that quoted above merely underlines the urgent task that competition policy in general and merger policy in particular have in helping to avoid undesirable changes in industrial structure which may lead to poorer economic performance.

The framework and approach of British merger policy

British policy towards competition and monopoly entered a new phase in 1973 with the passage of the Fair Trading Act which created the position of Director General of Fair Trading with overall responsibility for co-ordinating policy on competition and consumer affairs through the new Office of Fair Trading. However, the position as far as *mergers* are concerned remained largely as set down in the 1965 Monopolies and Mergers Act. Before 1965 there was no permanent machinery in Britain for investigating mergers in the private sector of industry. Several reports by the Monopolies Commission (MC) had commented adversely on the acquisition policies of firms dominant in their industries[12,13,14] but it was the increase in merger activity in the 1960s which aroused considerable public debate[15] which culminated in the Monopolies and Mergers Act of 1965. The Act empowered the Department of Trade and Industry (or in its previous guise, the Board of Trade) to refer certain mergers to the MC which was then to report on whether the merger operated or might be expected to operate against the public interest. The MC in its report can make recommendations that the merger should be allowed (with or without undertakings about its future market conduct). The MC must normally make its report within six months of the reference, although in certain circumstances the time period may be extended to nine months.

The Department of Prices and Consumer Protection (hereafter the ministry responsible for mergers policy is referred to as the Department) may now refer a merger or merger proposal to the MC where (*a*) it creates or increases a market share of one-quarter or more, and/or (*b*) where the assets to be taken over exceed £5 million.[16] The Department retains complete discretion over which mergers satisfying the above criteria should be referred, and it also received in the 1965 Act considerably increased powers of direct intervention in the private industrial sector. Thus it may prohibit mergers, regulate the conditions under which a merger might subsequently operate and order the dissolution of a merger. If necessary the Department can also make an order to hold up a proposed merger while the MC is making its investigation. In all of the references made so far the Department has accepted the recommendations of the MC, although in all but one of those cases where the Commission concluded that the merger should *not* proceed the merger proposals have been abandoned by the parties concerned without the Department having to use its considerable powers.

All mergers of size are scrutinised initially by a Mergers Panel of members of the Department, with the Director General of Fair Trading as chairman, to decide whether or not a reference to the MC is justified. In a special publication in 1969 the (former) Board of Trade set out at some length the multifarious questions on the market power, efficiency, balance of payments, regional and redundancy implications of a proposed merger that the Panel weighs up (normally in a space of two or three weeks) before making its decision.[17] In view of the complexity of the subject revealed by the catalogue of questions and by the actual reports of the MC one can only wonder at the energy and nerves of the Panel members who can resolve such an important public policy issue with comparatively little information and in such a short time.[18]

The scale of operations undertaken by the Panel may be judged from part (*a*) of Table 1 which gives the number of industrial, commercial and financial mergers scrutinised between August 1965 and June 1973.

A total of 798 merger proposals had been considered by the panel at the rate of about eight per month to mid 1973. In 35 per cent (281) of the cases examined a market share of at least one-third was

Table 1. *Mergers considered by the Mergers Panel (1965–73 part):*
(a) by the statutory criteria; (b) by the type of integration

	Number	Per cent	Value (£ million)	Per cent
(*a*) *Criteria*				
Size of assets	517	65	14295	80
Monopoly only*	193	24	370	2
Both	88	11	3173	18
Total	798	100	17838	100
(*b*) *Type*				
Horizontal	622	78	12739	71
Vertical	43	5	887	5
Diversified	133	17	4212	24
Total	798	100	17838	100

* Before the Fair Trading Act, 1973, the 'Monopoly Criterion' referred to a market share of one-third or more.

SOURCE: J. D. Gribbin, 'The operation of the Mergers Panel since 1965'. *Trade and Industry* **14** (1974), no. 3, pp. 20–3.

involved, although these amounted to only some 20 per cent by value. Part (*b*) of the table suggests that the most common type of merger scrutinised was horizontal. They accounted for 78 per cent of the total, although it was also noted that diversified mergers had been more important in the last three to four years.

In a further analysis of 239 of the cases where a legal monopoly was created or strengthened just over half resulted in market shares of 50 per cent or more. Many of these, of course, may have involved quite small and insignificant markets, but in many other more important cases sizeable market shares must have been created after just the preliminary screening by the Panel. For in the eight years following the 1965 Act only 20 mergers were referred to the MC, excluding newspaper mergers. This amounts to something over two per cent of all mergers coming within the 1965 Act.[19] Of these, 15 did not take place: seven were abandoned before the MC's report, six were dropped following an unfavourable report and two were dropped despite a favourable finding by the MC. The remaining five mergers were subsequently completed.

Set beside the data on the recent changes in industrial structure and indeed beside the volume of important mergers qualifying under the Act, the number of references to and reports by the MC seems remarkably small. The issue of how more mergers might be referred to the MC is taken up again on p. 117 below. We consider now whether the completed merger reports give much ground for confidence in a future policy specifically framed to weigh the costs of mergers in the form of increased market power against the benefits from scale economies and savings.

The merger reports of the Monopolies Commission

In the 1973 Fair Trading Act the MC is given more direct guidance about how to interpret 'the public interest' than in the 1965 Act where it was exhorted to 'take into account all matters which appear in the particular circumstances to be relevant'. In the 1973 Act there is a strong emphasis on competition. Thus the MC is urged among other things to have regard to the desirability of (*a*) maintaining and promoting competition, (*b*) promoting through competition reductions of costs and the development and use of new techniques and new products and facilitating entry of new competitors into existing markets, (*c*) maintaining and promoting competitive activity in markets outside the UK on the part of producers of goods, as well as (*d*) maintaining and promoting the interests of consumers and (*e*) maintaining and promoting a balanced distribution of industry and employment in the UK. Nevertheless the MC still has a free hand in deciding in each case whether or not a merger is likely to operate *against* the public interest. This negative requirement has come in for a good deal of criticism on the grounds that it has sometimes affected both the quality of the evidence put before it and the balance of its judgement. Thus, for example, where the MC seemed uneasy about the outcome of a merger and yet did not recommend its dissolution, there is a feeling that if it had been necessary to show *net benefits* from the mergers the MC would have inevitably reached a different conclusion.[20] But it made it plain in one case that 'it is not our function...to say whether the merger may be expected to be positively in the public interest'.[21] And again more recently: 'Even if the merger resulted in no benefits, or no substantial benefits of the kind claimed for it, it does not follow that it would necessarily be against the public interest.'[22]

On the other hand, in its 'General observations on mergers' the MC took a more positive view of how the public interest might be determined in merger cases: 'In horizontal and vertical mergers the gains likely to flow from increases in efficiency may be found great enough to offset some losses resulting from an impairment of competition and the merger may accordingly be regarded as compatible with the public interest. Conversely, in conglomerate mergers, losses in efficiency may in some cases be found sufficiently likely and substantial, even in the absence of anti-competitive consequences, to cause the merger to be regarded as contrary to the public interest.'[23] This view was reiterated when the MC examined the proposed merger between British Sidac Ltd and Transparent Paper Ltd. Before recommending that a merger could proceed the MC had to be satisfied that 'any disadvantage involved is at least balanced by advantages of other kinds that would result from the merger'.[24] No substantial modification to this approach of the MC in its evaluation of the public interest would be needed to bring it into line with that suggested by Williamson.

Formally two crucial elements in Williamson's 'naive trade-off' model for assessing the static welfare effects of large mergers are the pre-merger level of market power and the post-merger percentage lowering of costs. We consider first the way the MC has handled the issue of market power and then the evidence it has received on estimated cost savings. It is also clear, however, that if the income redistribution effects associated with increases in market power are regarded as unfavourable then the valuation of net benefits may be significantly affected. The attitude of the MC to the distributional effects of mergers is then considered together with its attitude to the timing of mergers (compared to internal expansion) and post-merger efficiency.

Market definition and market power

It is clear that before a detailed assessment can be made of the extent to which a merger will enable a firm persistently to maintain prices above their long run competitive levels 'the market' must be clearly delimited. In theory, products may be considered as exchanged in the 'same market' where their cross-price elasticities of demand are 'high'. Similarly, firms may be in competition with each other where their cross-price elasticities of supply are 'high'. In practice just where these cross-elasticities cease to be 'high' and hence where the market boundary occurs is a matter for judgement based on detailed knowledge of the industries in which the firms operate.

In a number of mergers considered by the MC, judgement of what constituted the relevant market was of central importance for the final recommendations.[25] For the most part the MC has been criticised for putting too narrow an interpretation on the market and consequently overstating the market power effect.[26,27] Thus in the proposed merger between Ross Group Ltd and Associated Fisheries Ltd (*Ross*)[28,29] the MC placed special emphasis on the combined group's share of cod landed at Humber ports. On this basis the share was 54 per cent, although Humber cod constituted only 70 per cent of total UK cod supplies. On the wider basis the combined group would have had a share of about 38 per cent of total UK cod supplies. If the whole of the market for fish was treated as one then the group would have supplied less than 20 per cent of the total for the UK. For reasons not properly spelt out the MC was therefore satisfied not only that the market for fish fell 'into distinct sections by reference to types of fish and class of customer' but that the mainstay of the trade, cod, should be further sub-divided between Humber landings and supplies at other ports.

Similarly, in the United Drapery Stores Ltd and Montague Burton Ltd (*Burton*) report the MC considered the relevant market to be not that for all men's wear or men's outer wear but that for complete men's suits. 'Moreover within the market for men's suits we think it right to pay particular attention to the cheaper ranges, that is the market for suits selling to the public at prices up to about £20.'[30] By defining the market in this way the combined group would have supplied about 36 per cent of the total. Again, the MC gives very little by way of explanation as to *why* it decided to give this part of the market special consideration.

On the other hand in the Thorn Electrical Industries Ltd and Radio Rentals Ltd (*Thorn*) case the MC was careful to point out why it laid special emphasis on the market share defined in a particular way. The combined group would 'at the stage at which television sets are supplied to the public', supply only something over 20 per cent, but its share of the trade in specialist television rentals (i.e. sets obtained through outlets specialising in renting) would be close on 50 per cent. Not only was the rental sector very highly developed in the UK but it was 'to some extent a market which is insulated against competition from retail sale'.[31] The MC was satisfied that the public believed that reliable service was more important than small price differences and that service would be more dependable if the servicer owned the set and particularly if he specialised in this activity on a large scale. These factors, the MC concluded, would if anything be reinforced as the market for colour television sets developed and as a result would put 'a large, and possibly a predominant, share of the supply of colour sets in the hands of renters for many years to come'. Hence the MC felt justified in separating the specialist rental market from the much wider market of total supplies of television sets to the public.

In two further cases involving producers' goods the MC spent considerable time in deciding whether the market should be interpreted narrowly, in which case the acquired firms had an important share, or on a much wider basis with the acquired companies' products forming only a small fraction of the whole market. The British Insulated Callender's Cables Ltd and Pyrotenax Ltd (*BICC*) report had to determine whether mineral insulated cable was distinct enough in costs and use to constitute a separate market. If it was, then the market share of the combined group would be about 90 per cent. If, however, the product was correctly regarded simply as one of *many* alternative cables, then the merger company would have a little over one-third of the market. It is evident from its discussion that MC questioned the large number of interested parties very closely about the degree of substitutability between mineral insulated and other types of cable. While it concluded that the 'competition of alternative cable systems sets a ceiling to mineral insulated cable prices', it was also satisfied 'that there is a field in which mineral insulated cable has such an advantage, either because of its technical merits or because of its low installed cost, that the effect of competition from other systems is greatly reduced'. It therefore regarded the narrow interpretation of the market as important for most of its analysis.[32]

Rather similar characteristics arose in the British Sidac Ltd and Transparent Paper Ltd (*Sidac*) case where the MC had to decide how close other packaging materials, especially polypropylene, were as substitutes for the cellulosic film produced by the two companies involved in the merger. While commenting on the US anti-trust case in which Du Pont was accused of monopolising the cellophane trade the MC defined its view on product competition: 'For two products to be in effective competition with one another, they must be broadly in the same price category and sufficiently interchangeable in use for the relative demand for the two products to be sensitive to changes in their relative prices.' In view of this definition the MC considered that to interpret the market as including *all* flexible packaging materials (as in the Du Pont case) was much too wide and would include materials such as paper and aluminium foil which could not be regarded as effective competitors of cellulosic film. It is clear, however, throughout its conclusions in this report that the MC, while recognising that cellulosic film would continue to have special uses, thought that it would be increasingly subject to strong competition from *plastic* film. Hence the combined group's share of 46 per cent in total UK supplies of cellulosic film overstated its real market share.

The above references to five of the MC reports illustrate the complexity of establishing the 'market' or 'markets' in particular merger cases. Where the MC can hear the views of large numbers of specialist customers (buying producers' goods) its own judgements about market boundaries are probably better informed. The above quotation from the *Sidac* report shows that the MC does think, albeit in a rather cumbersome fashion, in terms of cross-price elasticities of demand when attempting to define the market. It is plain, however, that this concept is not used in any precise sense by the MC in making its analysis. One of the MC's most tenacious critics has faulted two of the earlier reports for not actually using data on cross-price elasticities. Thus in an article peppered with invective and quotations from *The Times* newspaper, Rowley argued that in the *Ross* case the narrow interpretation of the cod market 'at the minimum...should have been tested by reference to the magnitude of cross-elasticity of demand between cod and other fish and non-fish products'. And again in connection with *Burton*: 'No attempt was made at measuring the cross elasticity of demand either between "cheap" and expensive suits, or between cheap suits and equivalent non-suit clothing.'[33] He does not enlarge on how the MC, already subject to a fairly severe time constraint, could cope with the subtle statistical and econometric problems which would have to be overcome in estimating cross-price elasticities of demand. Even given that some estimate could be made it would only form one part of the evidence that the MC would have to weigh in reaching its conclusion about the proper definition of the market. For the most part it would still have to rely on its judgement based on the evidence of customers, other competing companies, etc. On balance it seems unlikely that the resources required to make estimates of cross-price elasticities would yield a 'net return' to the enquiry.

The examples from the MC reports also highlight the central import-ance of market definition to the issue of market power. Thus in *Ross* the share of the combined firm was taken as 54 per cent rather than 38 per cent, in *Thorn* as 50 per cent rather than 20 per cent and in *BICC* as 90 per cent rather than 33 per cent. But the market definition is only the first, substantial, step in the complex analysis of market power. For a given level of concentration in the market, the extent to which prices can be persistently raised above the competitive level will depend crucially on actual and potential competition at home and abroad, the rate of growth of demand and the level of buyer concentration. Just as it is generally recognised that a concentration index is merely a first indication about the likelihood of market power, so the MC in its merger reports has treated the market shares of the merging firms simply as a starting point for its analysis of the competitive pressures in the market.

The merger enquiries of the MC, mostly in concentrated oligopoly or near monopoly industries, have usually shown fairly clearly the competitive pressures (or lack of them) in the industry prior to the proposed merger. Thus in *Burton* the MC was convinced that competi-tion at the retail level for men's cheap suits had not only kept prices down (United Drapery Stores said that its cheapest range had not changed in price or quality for ten years) but also maintained high efficiency levels in production. Competition between the two largest groups, Burton and UDS, had played a large part in this performance which was also helped by easy entry to the industry and the large number of other competitors. In the Guest, Keen and Nettlefolds Ltd and Birfield Ltd[33] (*GKN*) case, on the other hand, the MC was unable to decide whether GKN's entrance to the propeller shaft trade in 1960 (so that Birfield's monopoly of the product was ended) had kept prices down or not. It was influenced in this judgement by Birfield's policy of raising prices as soon as GKN entered the market (a policy not usually predicted for a monopolist but possibly explicable in terms of a failed limit price strategy). But there was also evidence of general price stability and some price falls after 1960 and the profitability of this product for both companies remained low.[34]

In a case rather similar in some respects, *BICC*, the entry of a larger company ending the monopoly of a smaller one did produce effective price competition. Just prior to *BICC*'s entry Pyrotenax reduced its list prices and although subsequently list prices of the two companies remained close together the MC was convinced that active competition in net prices remained. Pyrotenax, for example, said that it had had to increase discounts to counter competition from BICC, and there was evidence that customers were changing their supplier in order to obtain better terms. Indices of prices for different types of cables further suggested that the price of mineral-insulated cable had been kept down by competition between the two producers rather than as a result of competition from other cables, as BICC and Pyrotenax claimed.

In the *Thorn* case the MC considered that there was 'strong competition' among manufacturers in a highly concentrated industry where the largest four producers accounted for about 80 per cent of the market. Possibly more important was the intensification of competition that would arise, with or without the proposed merger, from imports. These had been restricted in the past by quota, tariff and technical impediments. More controversial was the MC's judgement in this case on the form and extent of competition at the rental end of the market. The majority report concluded that price competition was of little importance amongst renters and cited the persistence of a considerable spread in the monthly rental charges quoted by competing companies. In a persuasive note of dissent, however, Barna argued that the level of rental charges was substantially influenced by competition between the biggest groups of specialist renters and the evidence from Radio Rentals that he quoted tended to confirm this view.

In *Sidac* the MC considered that 'competition in this industry is somewhat muted'. The market shares of the three largest companies had remained stable over a considerable period and the industry operated an aggregated rebate scheme which although far from completely effective suggested 'some willingness to live and let live'. Nevertheless the evidence also suggested that although Transparent Paper (the company to be acquired) was probably not the lowest cost producer its average *net* prices were lower than its two larger competitors and consequently their price policy was constrained in those areas of the market where Transparent Paper was active. Indeed the stated purpose of British Sidac in its merger bid was to raise the prices of Transparent Paper. Not unexpectedly the MC concluded that if 'the desired increase in prices cannot be obtained without eliminating

Transparent Paper, then the competition of Transparent Paper must be thought to have a significant effect on price'.

If the competitive pressures described in the five cases above have been effective in restraining prices then this should show up in the profitability figures of the companies. A 'low' ratio of profit to sales would indicate that average prices were roughly in line with average costs and similarly for profit–asset ratios (assuming in the case of comparisons between companies or industries that capital-turnover ratios are equal). In *Burton* and *GKN* the profitability record was low enough to confirm the evidence of competition and suggest a low level of market power. Broadly speaking the same applied to *Sidac* and *Thorn* where profitability, although higher, was nevertheless close to the average for manufacturing industry.[35] Only in *BICC* where the average profitability of the two main suppliers was well above that for manufacturing industry generally was there some evidence of significant market power, although even in this case the entry of BICC into the UK market had tended to depress profitability once it was established.

Two main points stand out from the MC's examination of pre-merger market power. First, the problem of market definition remains formidable. Case histories from American anti-trust actions as well as from the British merger cases (and indeed the difficulties in the Continental Can case) suggest that this problem is unlikely to be easily resolved. Formal estimates of cross-elasticities of demand might assist in some cases, if the time constraint could be met, but in the last analysis the responsible body, whether a Monopolies Commission or a Court will have to use its judgement based on all the available evidence. There is some evidence for the view that the MC has been overcautious and seen the relevant market too narrowly. Second, the cases which have come before the MC have usually been clearly oligopolistic. But there were frequently signs that active competition between the firms directly involved in the proposed merger had restrained prices and profits with the implication that this source of restraint would be eliminated if the merger took place.

Cost savings

The central element to be weighed against increased market power in a trade-off calculation is the level of cost reduction that would be achieved by merger. After his examination of some of the earlier MC merger reports Sutherland concluded that 'the economies, where they are quantified at all, are strikingly small, even as promises'.[36] We examine some of the estimates in more detail below but we may note at this point that formally, in Williamson's simple static model, quite modest reductions in cost (of the order of five per cent or less) are sufficient to offset substantial price increases (e.g. if elasticity of demand is 1 and the pre-merger market power index as high as 1.05, a 20 per cent price increase following merger would be offset by a cost reduction of just over three per cent[37]). But this trade-off is based on the (explicit) assumption that a transfer of consumer surplus to producers' surplus in the form of a monopoly profit following the merger should continue to be counted entirely as a 'benefit'. Although this procedure follows customary cost–benefit analysis there are considerable doubts as to whether it is the most useful formulation in competition policy. This point is taken up in more detail on p. 112.

In fact, out of 13 merger reports involving firms in manufacturing industry, estimates of prospective cost savings have been quantified to a greater or lesser extent in eight. In *Burton* the MC did not ask for detailed estimates from the companies but looked closely at the possibilities for cost savings. It concluded, however, that there was 'no scope for significant economies of scale resulting from the merger'. Generally in the remaining cases the companies have given broad indications of where and how they expect cost savings to arise after the merger without forecasting their extent. Perhaps the most extreme case in this respect was *GKN* which quoted the White Paper on the Industrial Reorganisation Corporation urging the need for 'more concentration and rationalisation, to promote the greater efficiency and international competitiveness of British industry', yet 'was not able to make any present estimate of the cost savings that might be achieved, but...was convinced that they would be "real and substantial"'. The MC was considerably less sanguine and concluded that the prospect of saving costs in the production and supply of propeller shafts had played no great part in bringing about the merger.

It must be recognised, however, that since the measurement of scale economies is acknowledged to be difficult, *a fortiori* the forecast of *prospective* economies is likely to remain an extremely hazardous task. The problems are probably worse where the merger is contested, as in *Rank* and The Dental Manufacturing Co. Ltd or the Dentists' Supply Co. of New York and The Amalgamated Dental Co. Ltd[38] (*Dental*), or where the acquired company is an unenthusiastic partner in the merger, as in *Sidac*, or Davy International and the British Rollmakers Corporation[39] (*Davy*). In *Sidac*, Transparent Paper said that it regarded its acquisition by another British cellulosic film manufacturer as the least attractive of 'six broad categories of possibility' because of 'the negative characteristics of horizontal mergers with implications of retrenchment and rationalisation'. As a result, throughout the report the influence of Transparent Paper, like Banquo's ghost at the feast, casts a shadow over the aspirations of British Sidac. Except where the companies have already merged (which brings its own drawbacks), forecast cost savings have to be made with neither company having detailed knowledge of the internal affairs of the other.[40] The *fact* of reference to the MC and the real possibility of its rejection of the merger almost certainly inhibits close collaboration in preparing estimates of savings in cost.

The MC received evidence on forecast savings in *production* in six cases, *Ross*, *Thorn*, *BICC*, *Sidac*, *Dental* and *Davy*. In all cases the MC was very sceptical either at the size of the expected savings or of their ever seeing the light of day. In *Ross*, for example, where about 60 per cent of the total anticipated savings were to come from merging the trawling activities of the two companies, the MC argued that the scope for savings in this area was very limited because 'the operational unit' remained the trawler and the companies already operated the two largest fleets in the UK, both of which were well organised. Although the MC acknowledged that Associated Fisheries were the most efficient trawler operators they could not accept that the combined fleet would achieve a daily earnings level of two per cent higher than the present daily earnings level of Associated, even if the Ross Group's efficiency was raised to that of Associated, a possibility which in any case the MC doubted.

Similarly in *Dental* where Dental Manufacturing Co. forecast that about 61 per cent of estimated savings would be in manufacturing cost the MC considered they should be regarded as 'targets rather than as firmly established figures'. In this case, however, it is fair to add that the company concerned had taken the trouble to give a detailed breakdown of how it expected the production and other economies to arise only to have them summarily dismissed without any discussion by the MC as 'targets'. If the trade-off issue was to hold the centre of the stage in the MC enquiries it is likely that the estimated cost savings would be given more serious consideration than in this case.

In *Thorn* the scope for saving in production seemed more firmly established. Forecast production economies amounted to five per cent of total manufacturing cost and the majority of the MC accepted that 'production capacity would be likely to show significant cost savings as compared with the present performance of the two units'.[41] But even here not only did the majority feel that possibilities for savings in overheads through product standardisation were 'speculative' in view of the long-term fluctuations in demand but Professor Barna in a note of dissent cast doubt on the very notion of scale economies in production. He described television manufacture as an assembly industry using little fixed capital and argued that Radio Rentals whose output was much smaller, was about as profitable as Thorn, while GEC, also with a smaller market share, 'is much more profitable'.[42] He did not therefore anticipate any production benefits from the merger.

The whole of the *production* saving forecast in *Sidac* (which was largely concerned with cutting down on waste of materials) was being put into effect in any case by Transparent Paper and as a consequence the MC discounted it entirely in its final judgement. The most substantial quantified saving anticipated in *BICC* was a reduction in input prices (especially copper tubes) if Pyrotenax was supplied from BICC's own mill. Strictly speaking, therefore, the saving was not a production economy so much as a financial saving from vertical integration, but it is convenient to mention it here.[43] But again the MC considered it possible that some of the savings might be made by Pyrotenax alone either by seeking another source of supply for its tube requirements or by building its own mill. In fact the information thrown up by the MC report on the relative costs of copper tubes to BICC from its own recently established mill on the one hand and to Pyrotenax who purchased from Yorkshire Imperial Metals (a subsidiary of ICI) on the other, seems quite sufficient to have provoked Pyrotenax into building its own mill if it had remained independent. BICC said that it could supply Pyrotenax from its own mill at a price of £57 per ton which included a £12 per ton profit for the mill subsidiary. In comparison Pyrotenax had been paying Yorkshire Imperial Metals £135 per ton. Even allowing for the latter's lower level of efficiency, as its plant was older than BICC's, the prices paid by Pyrotenax seem to have borne little relation to costs. Yet as the MC pointed out, despite the input cost disadvantage Pyrotenax was more profitable than BICC.

In general, in that area where empirical studies of economies of scale have found themselves on fairly firm ground, namely production, the evidence in merger reports has so far been unconvincing and the estimated savings very small. The largest prospective economy in production was the five per cent in *Thorn* but in other cases the figures were much lower than this, for example, about three per cent in *Dental* and something over one per cent in *Ross*. The data thus far do not hold out a very promising prospect for an incorporation into the MC's enquiries of a more formal trade-off approach in which estimated cost savings would play a central part.

It is generally acknowledged that the difficulties of measuring *firm* scale economies in areas such as marketing and distribution, administration, and research and development, are considerably greater than those arising in the plant. Estimates of *prospective* savings after merger are thus likely to be exceedingly tenuous. These problems are reflected in those MC reports where quantified forecasts of savings have been made. The MC's usual comment on the acquiring firm's attempts to put a figure to the anticipated savings has been that they are exaggerated or speculative. Thus in *Sidac* where an annual saving of £50 000 'on administration, selling and other expenses' was claimed, the MC viewed this as a 'somewhat speculative net figure' and gave it no attention in its final recommendations. In *Ross* where a detailed breakdown of savings in fish merchanting and distribution was given by the acquiring company the MC conceded that there was probably some scope for efficiency increases by cutting out duplication but it considered that both companies were large enough already to take full advantage of mechanisation in what was a labour-intensive industry. As a consequence it considered the estimated savings (amounting to about 1.0 per cent reduction in costs) over-stated. Although in this case the MC did not comment on each item of expected savings separately it did give some explanation of why it considered the estimates too high. In *Dental*, on the other hand, where a similar detailed estimate is given, the MC appears to have paid little attention to it (see above p. 107).

Marketing economies of different kinds were anticipated in *Unilever* and in Beecham Group Ltd and Glaxo Group Ltd, or The Boots Company Ltd and Glaxo Group Ltd (*Glaxo*).[44] Although the expected savings were quantified in both cases there was little in the report or in the MC's comments on which to form a balanced view of their likelihood. Thus in *Unilever* it was claimed that by the aggregation of the two companies' advertising and public relations expenditures increased discounts amounting to between two to three per cent of Allied Breweries' total expenditure on these items would be obtained. The MC does not discuss whether this is a realistic estimate or whether the saving would be a purely private one for the merged firms or amount to savings in real resources. In fact no further direct reference to the estimate is made in the report. In *Glaxo* the forecast marketing economies were judged to be exaggerated but to have some substance, yet there is little discussion of how wide of the mark Beecham's claim of an annual saving of £1.25 million from pooling the companies' world marketing resources was thought to be.

In only two of the six cases where some quantified estimate of firm economies was made it is clear that the MC gave it due weight in its final analysis, these were *Thorn* and *BICC*. It is notable in both cases that a detailed discussion of how the economies were likely to arise was provided by the companies concerned. In *Thorn*, for example, savings were expected in accounting and general administration, and in servicing and distribution of television sets. Radio Rentals was able to point to the economies which had resulted from an earlier merger involving similar operations. The MC took this into account in their final assessment and with only slight reservations accepted that 'a case has been made out for at any rate a substantial part of these estimates. If a saving of, say, 6 to 8 per cent were achieved this would be beneficial'. In a rather similar vein the MC accepted the estimates of the savings in input prices in *BICC* (although it went on to consider whether similar savings could be made if Pyrotenax built its copper tube mill without merging with BICC).

Table 2. *Quantified estimates of cost savings in eight merger cases in manufacturing industry* examined by the Monopolies Commission*

Case (short title) and year	Estimated cost reduction in:			Importance for final recommend-ation†	Recommen-ation‡
	Production (%)	Other (%)	Total		
Ross (1966)	1.5–1.8	1.0–1.2	2.5–3.0%	Little	N
Dental (1966)	3	2	5%	None	A
BICC (1967)	0.5	3.5	4%	Much	A
Thorn (1968)	5	6–8	5+6–8%§	Much	A
Unilever (1969)	—	2–3	2–3%	None	A
Sidac (1970)	—	—	£0.34 m p.a.	None	N
Glaxo (1972)	—	—	£1.25 m p.a.	None	N
Davy (1974)	—	—	£0.15 m	None	N

* In the remaining five manufacturing industry cases no quantified estimate given, these were: BMC, GKN, Burton, Rank and Match.

† Classified in 3 ways: none, little, much.

‡ Merger A = not likely to operate or N = likely to operate against the public interest.

§ Estimates for manufacture and distribution kept separate.

It is convenient to summarise the information on quantified estimates of savings in tabular form (see Table 2). Thus no estimates were made in five manufacturing cases and in a further five no particular attention was paid to the estimates by the MC in its final judgement. On the other hand it can be argued that in one case where no quantified estimate was made, namely *Burton*, the MC nevertheless made a detailed examination of the possibilities for increases in efficiency by comparing the relative productivities of the two companies.

If the MC had been using the formal trade-off approach, prospective cost savings would have had to play a much greater part both in the evidence of the acquiring firm and in the final deliberations of the MC. As Sutherland has argued, this would probably improve the quality of the data presented by firms to the MC and the detailed argument lying behind them. It might also serve to dispel the idea that firms enter lightly into mergers involving very large investments without a full appraisal of the (private) economic costs and benefits. Of course where firms formerly had undertaken mergers without a detailed appraisal, the knowledge that an MC investigation would require one, may in itself serve to improve the private assessment made by individual companies.[45]

Evaluation would nevertheless remain very difficult and the completed reports do not give much reason to expect that 'the tools for assessing these effects can be expected progressively to be refined'.[46] While appreciating the problems, the MC would have to become more sensitive to the details of estimates (than it was, say, in *Dental*) and more persistent (than in, say, *GKN, Unilever* or *Glaxo*) if the trade-off approach were formally adopted.

Further complications

It is quite possible for a merger which shows positive net benefit using Williamson's 'naive trade-off model' nevertheless to show a net detriment if the model is complicated by considering the timing of the merger or the adverse effects of post-merger market power, including in particular, a deterioration in the internal efficiency of the firms concerned.

The MC has only to decide whether or not the referred merger is likely to operate *against* the public interest. For the most part, therefore, it has naturally concentrated specifically on the effects of the acquired company ceasing to have an independent existence. This emphasis probably diverts the attention of the MC away from consideration of the alternative possibility of internal expansion by the acquiring firm whereby it could attain the same objectives without undesirable effects on market power. Thus even though it may not be possible immediately to achieve economies through internal expansion, the discounted value of such benefits may well be greater than the discounted value of *net* benefits (economies minus dead weight loss) attained by merger. Strictly speaking it is not sufficient to show simply that economies would occur by merger, but that the net gains would be maximised by merger rather than by internal expansion. As Williamson points out this argument loses its force where the market is static or declining since the market power effects will occur here anyway, and the internal expansion route merely delays and may upset the market adjustment.

While focusing on the time stream of benefits and costs of a merger it is nevertheless recognised that a formal application of these principles may place too large a burden on the anti-trust authorities and may lead them more and more to assume the 'managerial' role of recommending the timing of mergers.[47] Without going this far, a good case can be made for ensuring that the regulatory body examines the possibilities for internal expansion as an alternative to merger.

Although in all three conglomerate merger cases the MC dismissed the probability of the acquiring firm being a potential entrant (i.e. by new investment) to the industry of the acquired firm, in most horizontal cases there was often no direct consideration of internal expansion. The closest the MC has so far come to consideration of alternatives was probably in *Sidac, BICC* and *Thorn*. In *Sidac* 85 per cent of the estimated economies of the merger were to result from reduction in the waste of materials at the 'acquired' company's plant. But it was clear from Transparent Paper's evidence that these economies would be achieved without the merger and therefore the MC discounted them entirely in its final assessment. In *BICC* the MC considered that 'at least some of the (expected) savings might have been secured by other means'. The greater part of the savings in input costs would have been achieved if Pyrotenax had established its own copper tube mill as BICC had done. However, in this case the MC did not pursue the implications of the argument, for example, that this could have led to a price reduction of 3.8 per cent while avoiding adverse market power effects and it did not affect the final recommendation in favour of the merger. Similarly in a revealing passage in *Thorn* the MC suggested that the expected production economies may not necessarily be a function of merger: 'the assumption is that the difference between Baird's and Thorn's current prime costs is a measure of the savings to be achieved in Baird's factors as a result of the merger. We doubt whether this assumption is valid since Baird is in course of expanding and might well be capable of achieving at least some part of the savings which are envisaged if it were to remain independent of any other manufacturer; since expansion in component making appears to have lagged somewhat beind expansion in assembly, it might well, for instance, be able in the near future to reduce the cost of its components by making more of its own.' But this did not shake the view of the majority of the MC that the merger of the companies' production capacity would yield significant economies.

What is missing, however, in these and other merger cases is a clear examination of internal expansion as an alternative to merger. This would involve not only an assessment of what proportion of the prospective 'merger economies' could be achieved internally but also how long the time lag would be before they actually occurred.

In Williamson's original article, in addition to the qualification he made to the simple trade-off model by considering the timing of mergers and the possible alternative of internal expansion he also discussed the effect on income distribution and post-merger internal efficiency. Both of these are mentioned briefly in the following paragraphs. On the first point Williamson recognised that it may be necessary in important merger cases to treat the transfer of surplus from consumers to producers as a detriment. This goes against the stream of most cost–benefit analysis where income transfers are treated as neutral and income redistribution regarded as the province of the central government in its taxation and transfer payments policies. Williamson suggested that in merger cases there may be good social reasons for treating an income transfer as a detriment. Recent British experience perhaps bears out the view that large mergers which imply a transfer from consumers to producers may lead to social discontent and in its turn to inefficiencies. It is also evident that if a negative weighting is given to income transfers, then some mergers which on pure resource allocation grounds yield a net benefit, would fail on an overall appraisal.

The MC has not systematically explored the possible effects and distribution of post-merger profits. Sutherland, for example, commented that the MC makes very little reference to the effect that the merger might be expected to have on profits: 'Presumably the effect on their profits is a major incentive for companies to merge; but the MC does not in general press companies to quantify that effect'.[48] In fact in only three of the manufacturing industry mergers, *Ross*, *BICC* and *Sidac*, has the issue of post-merger profitability received much consideration.

In *Ross* it was envisaged that the estimated cost savings would be retained in order to improve on poor profitability and thus make the industry more attractive to outside funds and eventually less reliant on subsidy. Ross estimated that the combined group's return on capital would increase by about 1.6 per cent, an amount unlikely to have affected to any extent the final outcome of the report. The forecast increase in profits in *BICC* was more important. The MC estimated that, if the prospective savings were retained as profit, the rate of return for Pyrotenax would increase from 32 per cent to 42 per cent and for BICC from 23 per cent to 28 per cent. As Sutherland has pointed out, however, by using the pre-merger book value of Pyrotenax assets to calculate the rates of return on capital, rather than the value at which the assets stood under the terms of BICC's offer, the estimated profitability increase for the acquired company was grossly over-stated. In fact using the appropriate asset valuation gives a rate of return (15 per cent) less than half the rate earned by Pyrotenax prior to the merger.

Perhaps more important in the present context is the interpretation put upon the high rate of return that BICC might be expected to enjoy as a result of the merger. Rather than seeing any danger in high profitability after the merger which increased BICC's market share from 45 per cent to about 90 per cent, the MC actually relied on it to produce beneficial results since 'BICC will have a strong interest in promoting mineral insulated cable as long as it continues to yield satisfactory profits'. The prospective returns were high even compared with other monopoly enquiries of the MC and the argument used in this case would seem to be a general defence for any abnormal level of profit earned by a dominant firm.

In *Sidac* the emphasis was rather different. Here the acquiring company relied on its enhanced market position after merger to raise prices by about five per cent in order to increase profitability which it argued would be in the public interest. The expected increase in profitability from this source would have put about 1.8 per cent on the profit–sales ratio.[49] Not unsurprisingly the MC had no difficulty in rejecting the merger. It was confident that Transparent Paper had had a competitive influence on prices in the past and it did not consider that 'the public interest demands that British Sidac should make higher levels of profit in this rather static market so as to be able to finance expansion'.

It is difficult to reconcile the treatment of expected profits in *BICC* and *Sidac*. While rejecting the idea in *Sidac* that reduced competition should be traded for increased profitability, in *BICC* where if anything the reduction in existing competition was likely to be more severe, the MC regarded increased profitability as wholly beneficial.[50] Furthermore, in none of the cases did the MC see the possibilities for increased profits as a possible danger to the efficiency of the company concerned.

This brings us to the second point. Just as income transfers in large mergers may be weighed negatively for social reasons it seems equally plausible to argue on economic grounds that they may help to generate inefficiency within the merged firms. If their post-merger market position allows them to earn abnormal profits this may mean that prospective economies are not in fact realised. 'Economies which are available in theory but, by reason of market power, are not sustainable are inadmissible.'[51]

The MC has considered the effect on post-merger *competition* in all cases, including the conglomerate mergers. In five of the six manufacturing mergers which it ultimately considered would operate *against* the public interest the adverse effect on competition played a major part in forming its judgement.[52] Yet its main emphasis has been on the post-merger opportunities for raising prices rather than on maintaining low costs. Apart from some references to the immediate post-merger difficulties of co-ordination which may affect efficiency (e.g. *Dental*, *Unilever* and the special problems that British Match may have in assimilating Wilkinson Sword), the MC has only rarely touched on the issue of possible losses in efficiency due to increased market power. Probably the best example occurred in *Burton* where the MC commented that 'there have been great efforts to increase efficiency in the factories and to absorb rising costs, especially wage costs...Both Burton and UDS have achieved impressive results in these respects. We have no doubt that this progress has been stimulated by the keen price competition between retailers, and we think that it is most important in the public interest that this competition should be preserved both as a spur to efficiency and as a safeguard to the general public.' In a case having many features in common with *Burton* the dissenting view of Professor Barna was that an independent Radio Rentals had provided a similar spur to Thorn Electrical.

In *Glaxo* the decision turned on the implications of the merger for the effectiveness of research and development (R & D) in the industry. The Beecham Group argued that their acquisition of Glaxo would improve the innovative performance of the firm in the pharmaceutical industry. In the event the MC satisfied itself that existing UK pharmaceutical companies were large enough to achieve all necessary economies in R & D and that the removal of one of the few remaining British-owned independent centres of research in the pharmaceutical industry would impair the 'industry's overall prospects of success in finding and developing new products'[53] which would affect the productivity of the resources employed. Thus while it was satisfied that the industry as a whole would remain competitive if either of the mergers proceeded, the MC felt that the *British*-owned part of the industry required competition between a number of independent centres of R & D to ensure its future innovative performance.

In one of the cases where the increase in market share was most pronounced, *BICC*, the MC considered in some detail the possible adverse effects on prices and continuity of supplies, for example, but did *not* examine directly the implications for efficiency. Existing competition would be practically eliminated and the MC anticipated 'substantial barriers to entry' for other firms. Under these circumstances the MC went so far as to conclude that 'the most satisfactory safeguard for the public interest would undoubtedly be the continuance of competition between two producers of comparable stature' before recommending, five pages later, that the merger would *not* operate against the public interest. In *BICC* there was not even the safeguard of powerful customers to which the MC pinned its hopes in the other case where very large market shares were created. Thus in *GKN* the MC was satisfied that 'the bargaining power of the buyers in this case is sufficient to ensure that the merged company will always be under the strongest pressure to keep its costs and its profit margins as low as possible'. But in this case it is at least arguable that buyer power would be sufficient to keep costs down since *all* car manufacturers would purchase their supplies from GKN and were unlikely, in the MC's view, to rely on imports. The buying power of the large customers might, therefore, trim profit margins for GKN but have little effect on their cost levels.

The evidence on internal inefficiency is, to say the least, flimsy and it is not yet possible to form more than a general impression of its quantitative significance. It is hardly surprising, therefore, that the MC has not directly paid much attention to it in its merger enquiries. Yet its importance may be many times greater than the dead-weight welfare loss due to increased market power and thus may be more than sufficient to turn what appears on a naive analysis to be a positive net gain from merger into a large potential net loss. A first step towards meeting this difficulty may therefore be for the MC to pay close attention to the pre-merger efficiency of the firms involved (along the lines of the *Burton* enquiry, although not necessarily using the same productivity measures) in order to make a reasonable prediction of the post-merger effect on efficiency once competition has been reduced.

The direction and scope of future merger policy

The MC has so far had to report on something over two per cent of all mergers falling within the scope of the 1973 Fair Trading Act. There are some grounds for thinking that more large mergers should be examined than is presently possible under the screening procedure of the Mergers Panel in the Department, especially if, as recent studies suggest, mergers involving the largest firms are now a more important source of change in industrial structure than in previous periods.

One approach to investigation and control requires a detailed trade-off of the net benefits of a merger. The cases in manufacturing industry so far examined by the MC were discussed in order to find out whether a more specific cost-benefit approach was feasible for the UK. Three areas of special importance in this approach were identified and examined in some detail. (i) Market definition and pre-merger market power. It was clear that the 'market' definition remains a very difficult problem but there was also evidence from the MC reports that competition was frequently very active amongst the firms involved in the proposed mergers. (ii) Estimated cost savings through merger. Two points stood out on this question: first, the MC did not always require estimates to be made and, second, if made they were generally small (i.e. under five per cent). Some of the estimates were, even so, rather unconvincing but to some extent this may have been the fault of the MC in that it did not always appear to give them the detailed scrutiny they deserved nor allow them an important place in their final judgement. A formal trade-off analysis would bring such estimates to the centre of the stage and thereby not only improve the quality of the data submitted but also possibly the internal analysis that potential acquirers undertake as a matter of course. (iii) Complications of the simple trade-off analysis by such factors as the timing of mergers and effects on excess profit and internal inefficiency. So far the MC has concentrated mainly on the merger proposed rather than possibilities for internal expansion and has not been too anxious to investigate the implications of future profitability.[54] Finally, the present state of knowledge about internal inefficiency makes it doubtful whether the MC could assess very precisely the post-merger impact on efficiency where market power has been increased. Nevertheless at least one of the cases illustrated that a pre-merger assessment of the efficiency of the companies involved is a useful first step.

The central question coming out of this discussion is this: is it possible to expect more mergers of size to be examined by a body like the MC and at the same time to recommend that the degree of detail in the analysis of each case should also be increased substantially, since this is what a strict interpretation of the trade-off approach implies? One school of thought would argue that the costs involved in applying a cost–benefit analysis to all significant mergers would not themselves bring a net benefit in terms of improved quality of the decisions by the regulating authority.[55] Regarding the likely economies as probably slight and the analysis of costs and benefits as intractable, they suggested the outright banning of all mergers which created or strengthened a market share above an acceptable limit (suggested as 50 per cent).

In its extreme form this proposal is more severe than even American policy where the courts may ultimately find in favour of a merger, and indeed such a policy would require fresh legislation and a completely new stance for competition policy in Britain.[56] The following suggestions, in contrast, are broadly compatible with the existing legal framework but point to a more severe approach to mergers than hitherto, in recognition of the high and growing levels of concentration and the so far unconvincing evidence of positive social benefits from large mergers. The main purpose of these suggestions is to ensure that more sizeable mergers are referred, that the quality of merger analysis by firms (and hence the data they can submit to the MC) is improved and that a greater knowledge is gained of the *effects* of mergers.

First, although the British approach has hitherto avoided the idea of 'guidelines' on the American pattern they might usefully be incorporated now into British procedure. Thus where market concentration would as a result of a proposed merger increase by five per cent or more and where the five-firm concentration ratio is already 70 per cent or more (which judging by the 1968 Census of Production might now include about half of manufacturing industry) reference to the MC could be *automatic* just as it is in the case of certain newspaper mergers.[57] Section 84 of the 1973 Act identifies the public interest with (amongst other things) the preservation and promotion of competition and such a guideline can be justified in those terms. It also has the advantage of removing the uncertainty about important mergers which, it has sometimes been argued, impairs business decisions in such cases. Similarly vertical mergers involving the leading firms from two (or more) markets where concentration is 70 per cent or more could automatically be referred. In conglomerate cases this principle could be extended to cover mergers in which the acquirer was amongst the 100 largest and where the acquired firm was a leader in a concentrated industry as defined above. Other mergers coming within the 1973 Act could still be subject to the preliminary screening by the Mergers Panel. Recent experience suggests that something like one-third of the references are abandoned before the MC proceeds far with its investigations. The operation of the guidelines may increase this proportion and help to ensure that only those mergers with fairly clear social benefits would proceed.

This would be further assisted, secondly, by changing the general criterion used by the MC in its investigations. The MC should have to be satisfied that the proposed merger would operate positively in the public interest (rather than as at present, that it would not operate against the public interest). This would place firmly on the shoulders of the firms concerned the burden of demonstrating the probable public benefits of the merger. They would naturally then have a keen interest in ensuring that their estimates were well founded and detailed.

Third, the Office of Fair Trading could, especially in cases referred automatically to the MC, present its assessment of the possible dangers to the public interest. One of the purposes of the 1973 Act was to bring together in one unit, i.e. the Office of Fair Trading, overall responsibility for competition policy. Its expertise could be very usefully employed representing the public before the MC in such merger cases, and thus as one commentator recently put it 'develop a role as an adversary in presenting information to the MC...(and become) a kind of "prosecuting" Registrar'.[58]

Finally, in all mergers that are completed after a favourable report by the MC, information relating to the post-merger benefits should be monitored by the MC as in the case of those firms which have given it an 'undertaking' about their future conduct as the result of an enquiry.

These suggestions would provide for a more aggressive merger policy while still recognising that economies can provide a satisfactory defence, even where the *prima facie* case against the merger seems strong. However, after a number of years (five would seem to be adequate), when experience of this procedure and evidence on the effects of mergers has accumulated, further changes may be necessary. In particular if post-merger economies are shown to be slight or non-existent the case for shedding the trade-off approach altogether would be very strong. Under these circumstances British policy might have to be further modified so that a reduction in competition would be sufficient to find a proposed merger against the public interest. In other words unless the benefits from large mergers clearly show themselves in the near future the British approach should move closer to the American and that which seems likely to develop in the EEC.

Notes

1 O. E. Williamson, 'Economies as an antitrust defense: the welfare trade-offs'. *American Economic Review* **58** (1968), p. 34.

2 Merger policy is here interpreted as part of a more comprehensive competition policy in line with the title of the conference. The activities of the Industrial Reorganisation Corporation, which deserves a separate and full treatment and whose stated purpose was 'promoting industrial efficiency and profitability and assisting the United Kingdom' (see *IRC Report and Accounts, 1970–71* (HMSO, 1971)), are not discussed here.

3 S. J. Prais, 'A new look at industrial concentration', *Oxford Economic Papers* (1974).

4 R. Clarke, 'Market concentration 1958–68'. Unpublished paper, NIESR, 1974.

5 P. E. Hart, M. A. Utton and G. Walshe, *Mergers and Concentration in British Industry* (Cambridge University Press, 1973).

6 *Ibid.*

7 M. A. Utton, 'The effect of mergers on concentration: UK manufacturing industry, 1954–65'. *Journal of Industrial Economics* **20** (1971).

8 J. Kitching, 'Why do mergers miscarry?', *Harvard Business Review* **45** (1967), pp. 84–101.

9 G. D. Newbould, *Management and Merger Activity* (Guthstead: Liverpool, 1970).

10 A. Singh, *Take-overs* (Cambridge University Press, 1971).

11 J. K. Galbraith, *Economics and the Public Purpose* (Andre Deutsch: London, 1974), p. 18.

12 Monopolies and Restrictive Practices Commission, *Report on the Supply and Export of Matches and the Supply of Match-Making Machinery* (HC 161, 1953).

13 Monopolies Commission, *Report on the Supply of Certain Industrial and Medical Gases* (HC 13, 1956).

14 Monopolies Commission, *Report on the Supply of Wallpaper* (HC 59, 1964).

15 For example: P. Hutber, *Wanted – a Monopoly Policy*, Fabian Research paper 219; Conservative Political Centre, *Monopoly and the Public Interest*, publication no. 270 (London, 1963); the Bow Group, *Monopolies and Mergers*, Conservative Political Centre publication no. 270 (London, 1963). Although the 1965 Act was passed by the new Labour government, most of the principles had been set out in the Conservative White paper of the previous year, *Monopolies, Mergers and Restrictive Practices* (Cmnd 2299, 1964).

16 There are special provisions for newspaper mergers.

17 Board of Trade, *Mergers, A Guide to Board of Trade Practice* (HMSO: London, 1969), para. 60.

18 Presumably the Panel has less information available for its scrutiny than the MC has for a full enquiry. Yet the MC itself has complained of being hampered by inadequate data (see its report on the *Rank–De la Rue merger* (see note (23) below), Appendix 4, Annex 4).

19 There have also been some instances where the possibility of a reference to the MC has led the parties to drop a merger proposal and also some where the Department has allowed mergers only after assurances about future market behaviour have been given. See M. D. Beesley, 'Economic

effects of national policies towards mergers and acquisitions' (para. 86). In B. W. Denning (ed.), *Corporate Long Range Planning* (Longmans: London, 1969).

20 This opinion is based particularly on the GKN–Birfield and BICC–Pyrotenax mergers, both of which were complete before the MC finished its report and involved the creation of extremely large market shares for the very large acquiring company. See notes (32) and (34) below and also A. Sutherland, *The Monopolies Commission in Action* (Cambridge University Press, 1969), chapters 8 and 9.

21 Monopolies Commission, *Thomson Newspapers Ltd. and Crusha and Sons Ltd.*, *A Report on the Proposed Merger* (HC 66, 1968).

22 Monopolies Commission, *British Match Corporation and Wilkinson Sword*, *A Report on the Proposed Merger* (Cmnd 5442, 1973).

23 Monopolies Commission, *The Rank Organisation Ltd. and the De La Rue Company Ltd.*, *A Report on the Proposed Acquisition of the De La Rue Company Ltd.* (HC 298, 1968–9).

24 Monopolies Commission, *British Sidac Ltd. and Transparent Paper Ltd.*, *A Report on the Proposed Merger* (HC 154, 1970–1), para. 166.

25 Throughout the remainder of this paper attention is centred on the merger cases from manufacturing industry examined by the MC.

26 J. F. Pickering, 'The Monopolies Commission and High Street mergers', *Scottish Journal of Political Economy* **18** (1971).

27 C. K. Rowley, 'Mergers and public policy in Great Britain'. *Journal of Law and Economics* (1968).

28 Monopolies Commission, *Ross Group Limited and Associated Fisheries Limited*, *A Report on the Proposed Merger* (HC 42, 1966–7).

29 For convenience each MC report is given its full title once in the text and thereafter is cited by an abbreviation which appears in brackets.

30 Monopolies Commission, *United Drapery Stores Ltd. and Montague Burton Ltd.*, *A Report on the Proposed Merger* (Cmnd 3397, 1967), para. 130.

31 Monopolies Commission, *Thorn Electrical Industries Ltd. and Radio Rentals Ltd.*, *A Report on the Proposed Merger* (HC 318, 1967–8), para. 202.

32 Monopolies Commission, *British Insulated Callender's Cables Ltd. and Pyrotenax Ltd.*, *A Report on the Proposed Merger* (HC 490, 1967), paras. 136–39.

33 C. K. Rowley (see note 27 above), pp. 98 and 103.

34 Monopolies Commission, *Guest, Keen and Nettlefolds Ltd. and Birfield Ltd.*, *A Report on the Merger* (Cmnd 3186, 1967).

35 *Sidac* (see note (24) above) para. 168; *Thorn* (see note (31) above) paras. 53 and 82; and Monopolies Commission, *Report on the Supply of Metal Containers* (HC 6, 1970).

36 A. Sutherland, 'The management of mergers policy'. In A. Cairncross (ed.), *The Managed Economy* (Blackwell, 1970), p. 123.

37 O. E. Williamson, 'Economies as an antitrust defence: reply', *American Economic Review* **59** (1969), p. 97.

38 Monopolies Commission, *The Dental Manufacturing Co. Ltd. or The Dentists Supply Co. of New York and The Amalgamated Dental Co. Ltd.*, *A Report on the Proposed Mergers* (HC 147, 1966–7).

39 Monopolies Commission, *Davy International and The British Rollmakers Corporation*, *A Report on the Proposed Merger* (HC 67, 1974).

40 In three cases the merger had been completed before the MC made its report: *BMC*, *GKN*, and *BICC*. Possibly for this reason the latter two cases are amongst the least persuasive of the MC's efforts.

41 In this case, as with *Sidac* and *BICC*, it was likely that the production economies would be achieved even in the absence of merger. This point is developed below (p. 112).

42 It is a little disconcerting that several of the points made in the note of dissent, especially *Thorn*, para. 230, found no place for discussion in the main body of the report, so that the reader is confronted with quite fresh material which appears to conflict with the majority view.

43 The estimated production economy from running the tube mill more efficiently amounted to only three per cent of the total estimated savings compared to about 76 per cent represented by savings on tube prices (*BICC*, para. 109).

44 Monopolies Commission, *Unilever Ltd. and Allied Breweries Ltd.*, *A Report on the Proposed Merger* (HC 297, 1968–9); Monopolies Commission, *Beecham Group Ltd. and Glaxo Group Ltd.; The Boots Company Ltd., and Glaxo Group Ltd., A Report on the Proposed Mergers* (HC 341, 1971–2).

45 In two cases where the MC concluded that the proposed mergers were not likely to operate against the public interest, *Dental* and *Unilever*, the mergers were not pursued. It is possible that the scepticism voiced by the MC about the private advantages may have made the bidding companies reconsider the prospects, cf. Beesley (see note (19) above), p. 36.

46 O. E. Williamson (see note (1) above), p. 34.

47 M. A. Crew and C. K. Rowley, 'Antitrust policy: the application of rules'. *Moorgate and Wall Street*, Autumn 1971.

48 A. Sutherland. *The Monopolies Commission in Action* (Cambridge University Press, 1969), p. 66.

49 Anticipated savings from the merger were almost entirely discounted by the MC, see above p. 108.

50 Following the merger with Transparent Paper, British Sidac would still only have been the second largest company in the industry (see note (24) above), para. 78.

51 O. E. Williamson (see note (1) above), p. 32.

52 The exception was *Rank* where the MC decided that there would be a serious risk to the future performance of De La Rue if the merger proceeded because of opposition from many senior managers whose position was thought to be crucial in view of the special character of De La Rue's bank note and security document business.

53 A report on the pharmaceutical industry by the National Economic Development Office which the MC had consulted in draft came to very different conclusions on this issue. See *Focus on Pharmaceuticals* (NEDO: London, 1972), para. 253.

54 Although this is probably a limitation stemming from the framework established by the monopolies and mergers legislation.

55 M. A. Crew and C. K. Rowley (see note (47) above).

56 Although apparently such instances have been rare enough in recent experience for one judge to conclude that 'The sole consistency that I can find is that in litigation under section 7, the Government always wins' – See B. Wasserstein, 'British merger policy from an American perspective', *Yale Law Journal* **82** (1973), p. 689.

57 The concentration ratio includes the sales of the five largest firms as in the Census of Production.

58 B. Wasserstein (see note (56) above), p. 689.

COMMENT

A. SUTHERLAND

Dr Utton's lucid chapter raised two broad sets of issues for me, the first relating to UK policy; and the second relating to EEC competition policy.

The implications for UK policy

If the case by case appraisal of mergers is to continue here, should there be improvements in the procedure? If the UK has been trying to compare potentially better performance with loss of competitive structure and conduct, has the comparison been carried out in an effective and convincing way? We are not mainly concerned with these matters today, but since Dr Utton makes policy suggestions for the UK, perhaps I can welcome his support for the kinds of suggestions my own investigations led me to at the British Association five years ago.[1] There were three main suggestions:

(1) In order to avoid situations where the Monopolies Commission seemed to be looking mainly for conspicuous detriment rather than for solidly based evidence of benefit, the question in the 1973 Act should be put positively, so that it becomes 'will a qualifying merger be likely to be in the public interest?'. The present formulation leads the Monopolies Commission in a favourable case to conclude that the merger would not be contrary to the public interest. Despite logical arguments about the formal equivalence of the two ways of putting it, that does in practice lead to the onus of proof being in the wrong place – both before the Commission, and, even more significantly, at the prior stage when references to the Commission are being considered. For instance, Sir Geoffrey Howe in November 1973[2] described how the Mergers Panel was able to conclude 'in the vast majority of cases' that 'the merger need not be referred to the Monopolies Commission'. Would that decision *not* to investigate have been quite so frequent if the question had been 'what is the case for saying that this merger need *not* go to the Monopolies Commission for investigation?' rather than 'who thinks this merger needs to go to the Monopolies Commission?'

(2) To avoid reliance on the quick and superficial appraisals inevitable if officials have only a week or two to make recommendations about whether a particular merger should be referred to the Monopolies Commission, there should instead be automatic reference for investigation of all qualifying mergers which also meet the criteria to be specified in published guidelines. It is worth emphasising once more that adopting a system of guidelines for making *references* would *not* turn the UK system into a replica of the US one. There the guidelines define the structural changes which will (almost) automatically be *prevented* by the law. That is quite different from suggesting that all structural changes of a defined kind will automatically be sent to the Monopolies Commission for investigation.

My suggestion was that any merger by a company already in the top 100 of UK companies by size of net assets, or turnover, would be automatically investigated. Dr Utton is now more detailed; his suggestions on pp. 117–18 strike me as a very sensible basis for discussion. However, Dr Utton keeps the size qualification only for conglomerates. I would wish to retain it for all mergers as an alternative to his proposals for referring those horizontal and vertical mergers which increased concentration by specified amounts.

Guidelines of this kind still seem to be necessary to get enough investigations; though it is encouraging to see the potentially radical change which has removed responsibility for making references from the Department of Trade and Industry and transferred it to the Secretary of State for Consumer Affairs. Explicit separation of the role of watchdog from that of sponsor should relieve internal tensions; and should lead to more frequent references. An even better solution would be to give the Director General an initiative in making merger references. Also, perhaps one day the Mergers Panel might have consumer representation?

(3) The final policy recommendation was that, when investigations are undertaken by the Monopolies Commission, then, whether or not one dignifies the performance by calling it cost–benefit analysis, the enquiries should be much more vigorously quantitative. Companies by now know the kind of question to which the Monopolies Commission should require an answer; and should be geared to producing the kinds of defensible forecasts that go into the prospectuses of companies making a Stock Exchange issue, though of course the detail required would be greater than that. The onus, both of evidence and of proof, given the changed question, should of course be firmly on the merging companies. If the parties to the merger are indeed entirely in the dark about the potential effects, then that should be brought out.

Hence, as regards current UK policy, if the UK is to continue as the only adherent to performance tests in dealing with mergers, it is clear that Dr Utton and I would be in close agreement about desirable changes.

Competition policy in the EEC

Here the Commission's proposals for the control of concentration are based on a hypothesis quite different from that underlying UK policy; namely that concentration by merger, when it leads to the power to hinder effective competition, is universally to be prevented, save for Article 1(3). While the structural and conduct criteria to be applied are still too vague, it is clear that a performance test is *not* allowed as a defence to the structural situation, though, appropriately, the structural situation in Article 1(1) is viewed dynamically, and not just statically. Here then the following issues arise:

(1) Has Dr Utton, in his re-examination of the approach made by Professor Williamson, found anything to suggest that this potentially more rigorous EEC approach is misguided?

One should begin by saying in fairness to Professor Williamson that his articles are quite heavily cushioned with qualifying remarks. In particular, he says he is concerned only with 'the occasional case', not with the generality of mergers.[3] Further, he would require the net gain to exceed a clear threshold value before cost reduction should even be considered as a defence; and he would put the burden of proof on the companies.[4] Again, he accepts for the US a continuation of the more or less per-se prohibition of expansion by merger of the biggest corporations.[5, 6] Further, he acknowledges that unacceptable effects on the distribution of incomes (that is, the increase in monopoly profit which is, as Dr Utton remarked, treated as a neutral transfer in Williamson's 'naive trade-off model') may be severe enough for distributional criteria to overrule the efficiency ones. Further, bad distributional effects may alter production conditions and so reduce or reverse any efficiency gains from the merger.

One is tempted to add that in the Williamson model the post-merger situation (lower cost, but higher price and lower output than initially) is not, of course, optimal. The increase in monopoly profit has raised consumers' marginal valuation above social opportunity cost. Provided it can be done without losing the cost reduction, an improvement in social welfare can be secured by any policy which induces or compels the merged companies to reduce price and to increase the quantity sold – ideally up to the point where the new lower average (and marginal) cost curve intersects the old demand curve.

But the major objection to reviving Professor Williamson's argument is of course that he produces no empirical support for his major premise, namely that non-trivial real economies are typical for the kinds of big but not gigantic merger that he was concerned with. Nor does he show that such mergers (which typically leave plants, and their machinery, unchanged), if they do produce real economies, are the only way of getting them. His own work might indeed suggest support for the more familiar conclusions that increasing company size may lead to worsening X-efficiency and to slower progressiveness.

So the EEC need not fear that it is being *irrational* if it decides to continue to ignore performance tests for major mergers.

(2) Does Dr Utton's survey indicate that there has been anything in UK experience with the opposite, performance-based method, to suggest that a basically structural approach would be sacrificing considerable economic benefits? Has the UK reaped more advantages by allowing almost all mergers to proceed, than would have been the case if more of them had been prevented by a structural, per-se approach? The *potential* evidence is of two kinds – that gathered *ex ante* from the few mergers investigated by the Monopolies Commission; and that which might have been gathered *ex post* from follow-up investigations of mergers which have taken place, whether or not they went to the Monopolies Commission.

As to the potential ex-ante evidence, the Monopolies Commission has had only some 25 references out of over 800 qualifying mergers. Over the period 1965–73, some £17800 million of assets were acquired by merger;[7] meanwhile the formal procedure of the Monopolies Commission prevented about £1100 million of assets from being acquired. In assessing the effect of the policy, it would of course be fair to add on to this six per cent effect something for those mergers which were abandoned, rather than forbidden by the Commission; and for mergers not even considered, because of the possibility of a reference. But both the range and the type of merger actively being investigated have not been such as to allow the Monopolies Commission to generate much evidence. As others have remarked, the biggest mergers have singularly not been investigated. For the cases which it *has* investigated, Dr Utton's review does not wish me to revise my 1969 conclusion; as he puts it on p. 108, 'evidence for production economies of scale has so far been unconvincing and the estimates very small'.

But if the UK has been incurious *ex ante*, we have been even less curious *ex post*. Does anyone know whether even the major mergers which have taken place since 1965 have proved to be more profitable than the unmerged companies might have been? Does anyone know whether any private net benefit so obtained has produced equal public benefit, via cost or price performance improvements? Or whether any public benefit obtained by merger could not have been obtained more effectively and fairly by internal expansion; or indeed by alternative policy measures, such as taxes or subsidies; or by direct action by nationalised industries? (Some such conceptually and practically difficult questions such as these will require answers in the EEC framework also, if use of the exemption clause in Article 1(3) is to be reasonably rare.) Hence, I very much support Dr Utton when he urges that there should be serious follow-up investigation by the Monopolies Commission and the Director General of Fair Trading.

Even at the conceptually much easier level of recording what has actually happened, can we now conclude that the gaps in basic accountancy information have been filled? Can even the reasonably assiduous investigator discover from published sources what a company's sales have been, by usefully and narrowly defined product, and what the assets employed and profits have been for those products? (Those questions also of course arise in the EEC framework. Without such regularly published information, policy makers are operating blindfold. Professor de Jong's remarks about secrecy, even in investigated cases, are not encouraging on this aspect.)

In this regard, therefore, I would conclude that British experience does not begin to invalidate the EEC hypothesis. We have no details, *ex post*, of the benefits produced by the large volume of mergers. As for the ex-ante evidence, the details we do have in the handful of investigations by the Monopolies Commission are of, at most, small real benefits. And, looking more broadly for the fruitful outcome of merger activity, we have not been frequently exposed to claims that UK competitiveness, UK growth of productivity, and UK growth of real income per head have markedly improved in the last decade.

(3) Has there been any empirical work to suggest that growth by merger of companies already large and/or dominant produces any better result in other parts of the EEC than seems to be the case in the UK? N. Owen's work does not suggest a positive answer, but that was using data from 1964.[8] Is there perhaps more recent work?

(4) Are the proposed criteria in the EEC proposal for regulating concentration improvable by amendment?

(i) Dr Markert's suggestions here are all very helpful, especially for inserting more specific structural tests of power to hinder competition in Article 1(1). However, I am not convinced by his argument that one should drop the market share criteria for applicability of the regulation on the grounds that any concentrations smaller than 200 million units of account would have little power anyway. Contrary arguments would be that effective control of incipient increases in concentration requires some attention to even modestly sized mergers when they produce a significant market share. Further, the EEC machinery may be required to deal with relatively local monopolies (provided they qualify by affecting inter-member trade) in those countries without national legislation for controlling mergers.

(ii) One should also perhaps ask whether the reference in Article 1(2) to *consumers* is indeed wide enough to include *buyers*, whether or not they are final consumers?

(iii) May one suggest in Article 2 that the now rather narrowly defined concept of 'control' could be supplemented by the less legally precise but more practically useful definition of Section 65.3 of the 1973 Fair Trading Act: which says those 'able, directly or indirectly, to control or materially to influence the policy of' a company can be treated as having control of it. Here there does seem to be scope for a practical test.

(5) Finally, in the EEC context, should we not really be thinking much more seriously about harmonising UK and EEC competition policy? My reactions here were four.

(i) I began by saying that Dr Utton and I were plainly in broad agreement about what should be done to improve the effectiveness of UK policy, if there is to be no change in the policy approach. But my hope would be that the introduction of the EEC proposals, mainly structurally based and without performance tests, would provide an incentive for UK policy to change in that direction, and without waiting for the further five years which Dr Utton proposes. On that point then I would disagree with him.

(ii) However, while the evidence suggests to me that the UK should harmonize with the EEC Commission on the policy approach, in terms of practical administration Whitehall methods look distinctly preferable to the bureaucratic tangles describes by Dr Markert. It was reassuring to hear from Dr Schlieder that Brussels is not really like Byzantium.

(iii) All EEC member states should be urged to adopt the EEC Commission's approach for application in their national legislation. (One is tempted to ask whether it is simply coincidental that we have no French and Italian colleagues with us today?)

(iv) Some duplication of investigations could be avoided if agreement could be reached that, if a national agency ruled against a merger, the EEC would not wish to enquire further. However, if a national agency allows a merger, then the EEC would always conduct an investigation, in order to ensure that each member country was adopting the same standard. For it seems possible that some governments on some occasions might think it advantageous to allow an increasing concentration by merger provided that the outcome was an exploitation of foreign buyers even greater than the exploitation of domestic buyers. Further, of course, if there is no national legislation, then the EEC procedure must in any event handle the burden of making the primary investigation.

Conclusion

Broadly then, my view is that the EEC should not be inspired by the UK experience into changing its proposed policy. Rather the UK should, at least for this aspect of competition policy, be entirely influenced by the EEC example. Finally, both the EEC and the UK should then given prominence to structural criteria not merely in conducting investigations into mergers, but should be prepared to recommend, and carry out, structural remedies, in dealing with existing abusive concentrations.

Notes

1 A. Sutherland, 'The management of mergers policy'. In A. K. Cairncross (ed.), *The Managed Economy* (Basil Blackwell: Oxford, 1970), chapter 7, pp. 106–34.
2 Sir Geoffrey Howe, 'Government policy on mergers'. *Trade and Industry* **13** (1973), no. 5, p. 231.
3 O. E. Williamson, 'Economies as antitrust defense'. *American Economic Review* **58** (1968), p. 18.
4 *Ibid.*, p. 24.
5 *Ibid.*, p. 29.
6 O. E. Williamson, 'Allocative efficiency and the limits of antitrust'. *American Economic Review, Papers and Proceedings* **59** (1969), p. 114.
7 J. D. Gribbin, 'Operation of the mergers panel'. *Trade and Industry* **14** (1974), no. 3, p. 70.
8 N. Owen, *Trade and Industry* (22 March 1973), p. 588.

5

Abuse of dominant position and changing European industrial structure

A. JACQUEMIN

The role given to competition in the Treaty of Rome which established the Common Market, seems to be central. The establishment of competition is apparently considered as indispensable for the achievement of an efficient allocation of economic resources and for ensuring an equitable basis of operations for production.

> Competition is the best stimulant of economic activity since it guarantees the widest possible freedom of action to all. An active competition policy pursued in accordance with the provisions of the Treaties establishing the Communities makes it easier for the supply and demand structures continually to adjust to technological development. Through the interplay of decentralised decision-making machinery, competition enables enterprises continuously to improve their efficiency, which is the *sine qua non* for a steady improvement in living standards and employment prospects within the countries of the Community.[1]

Two aspects must be emphasised.

First, promotion of competition includes control of cartels, dominant firms, state aid to business and the harmonisation of national laws which affect business, including those concerning taxation, industrial property, unfair competition, public contracts, company laws, bankruptcy rules, the characteristics of goods, and the enforcement of decisions in commercial disputes.

> This broad view of competition has evolved because of the differences of economic organisation that are evident in the member states. In one state the production and sale of a given type of goods may be carried on by private enterprises united in a restrictive agreement. In another state the same activity may be carried on without agreement by one or two dominant enterprises. In a third

state a government monopoly may control the field. For the Community to take action against any one of these forms of organisation without equivalent action against the others would be to discriminate between the different states. The Community has consistently emphasised the point that its various forms of action should go forward together in close co-ordination.[2]

Second, that part of the Community's broad competition policy which is explicitly concerned with private restrictions and set forth in Articles 85, 86, 88 and 89 of the Rome Treaty and in regulations pursuant thereto, should be given a wide interpretation appropriate to their function within the system of the Treaty as a whole. 'Articles 85 and 86 are the first mentioned '' common rules '' of the Community...Except for clearly intended limits, these competition rules should be interpreted to reach transactions, whatever their form, which eliminate workable competition without supervening justification founded in the basic goals of Article 2.'[3] These 'basic goals' are as follows: harmonious development of economic activities, continuous and balanced expansion, increased stability, accelerated raising of the standard of living and closer relations between member states.

The emphasis in the Treaty on the necessity of attacking equally all the various forms of action which could restrict European competition and the 'teleological' approach which considers Articles 85 and 86 to be basic rules linked to the Treaty goals have important implications for the interpretation of these provisions. However, it was not until 1971 that the implications for monopoly situations became clear.

The purpose of this paper is to analyse the recent bringing into play of Article 86 and the problems which this has raised for competition policy. The draft regulation on the control of mergers is also discussed. We shall do this by following the traditional 'market structure–market conduct–market performance' distinction used in industrial economics. This methodology is particularly relevant because the anti-trust policies pursued by industrial countries vary mainly in the emphasis laid on the roles of structure, conduct and performance, as criteria for determining the existence of monopoly power or for enforcing remedial measures.

Market structure and dominant position

Article 86 provides that 'to the extent to which trade between any Member States may be affected thereby, action by one or more enterprises to take improper advantage of a dominant position within the Common Market or within a substantial part of it shall be deemed to be incompatible with the Common Market and shall thereby be prohibited'. Article 86 further provides examples of such abusive practices: '(a) the direct or indirect imposition of any inequitable purchase or selling price or of any other inequitable trading conditions; (b) the limitation of production, markets or technical development to the prejudice of consumers; (c) the application to parties of transactions of unequal terms in respect of equivalent supplies, thereby placing them at a competitive disadvantage; (d) the subjecting of the conclusion of a contract to the acceptance by a party of additional supplies which, either by their nature or according to commercial usage, have no connection with the subject of such contract'.

The first and most important aspect is that the establishment of a dominant position is lawful; it is only the abuse of such a position which is condemned. Article 86 does not define a dominant position, even from a legal point of view, and this could be one explanation of its delayed enforcement. According to the Commission's *Memorandum on Concentration,* such a dominant position requires *more* than a situation where there exists some margin of discretion with respect to prices or quantities: otherwise almost every market would contain a firm in a dominant position. It implies the absence of effective competition and the ability of the dominant firm to exert a 'major influence' or control over the decisions of the other economic units by means of an independent strategy.

We think that to determine the existence of such a dominant position, a structural approach is required, in which all the dimensions of market structure are analysed: not just the degree of concentration, but also such factors as the level of barriers to entry, the degree of product differentiation and the growth rate of the industry. Two industries which are identical in terms of some measure of concentration may clearly be different in terms of market growth, product differentiation, and so on, and will need to be treated differently for policy purposes.

In the Continental Can case, the Commission did indeed take into account, not only the market share held by the group but also:

> (a) its technological predominance, particularly through patents and technical know-how;
> (b) the wide range of its output and the geographical spread of its factory and warehouses;
> (c) the availability of the required machinery for production and application of metal containers;
> (d) the possibility of obtaining capital from the international markets.[4]

Thus, the Commission used an overall test integrating various structural features. But the Commission seems to go further in asserting that 'market domination cannot be defined solely in terms of the market share of an enterprise *or of other quantitative elements of a particular market structure.* It is primarily a matter of economic potency, or the ability to exert on the operation of the market an influence that is substantial and also in principle foreseeable for the dominant enterprise.'[5] According to this line of reasoning, the ultimate test of a dominant position is the firm's ability to behave persistently in a manner which would be impossible in a competitive market, and not the structure of the market.

In the Continental Can case, the Commission insisted on the existence of 'independent conduct'. This concept of a separate conduct test of dominant position is much more controversial as is evident from the discussion at the Court level. The plaintiff (Continental Can) argued that 'the existence of such independent conduct – possibly in the form of overpricing, scarcity of the goods, or deterioration of quality – was not proved anywhere in the decision of the Commission'. The defendant replied that it is not true that the proof of dominant position in this case depended on demonstrating the types of 'conduct' mentioned by the plaintiffs, since such types of conduct represent the 'abuse of a dominant position'. But after saying this, the Commission does not define which types of conduct could show the existence of a dominant position without being an abuse.

In fact, either market conduct has a clearly competitive nature and it is not possible to infer the existence of a dominant position, or it has a clearly non-competitive nature and could be an abuse. We shall return to this problem, but we may conclude that once the criterion used to define a dominant position shifts from structure to conduct, the issue becomes most controversial.

Unhappily, even if dominant position is regarded as a structural concept, problems still arise. A basic one, given present-day developments in Europe, is that of defining the relevant market.

The wave of conglomerate mergers[6] makes it difficult to stick to the traditional rule by which one should look at the firm's component parts separately in their respective markets, and the economic analysis of the multi-product firm is far from conclusive. A related aspect is the classic problem of defining the product market. In *United States v. Continental Can Co.* (378 US 441, 1964), Continental Can argued that the purpose of its merger with Hazel–Atlas was to diversify into the glass container field. Contrary to the District Court who held that indeed the case involved a conglomerate merger, the Supreme Court stated that although metal containers and glass containers were separate industries, the inter-industry competition between the manufacturers of these two types of containers brought both metal and glass containers under one combined product market for judging the merger. Let us recall that at the European Court of Justice, Continental Can has on the contrary argued that glass and metal containers do not constitute a separate line of commerce.[7]

In particular it is not yet clear if a diversified firm, by virtue of its multiplicity of geographic and product markets, has a competitive advantage over a single product firm. We can at least agree with the view that such a firm, inasmuch as it already has a dominant position in one product market, has the means to expand its empire into another. In summarising the reasons for finding illegal the acquisition of the Clorox Chemical Company by Procter and Gamble the US Hearing Examiner stated:

> The deciding factor is the ability of Procter and Gamble's conglomerate organisation to shift financial resources and competitive strength through a broad front of different products and markets and its ability to strategically alter the selected point of greatest impact as time, place and market conditions require...The test of conglomerate power is whether a corporation is able to concentrate its competitive efforts at one point by shifting its financial resources and competitive strength from one industry or market to another.[8]

Another argument is that large diversified firms can benefit from reaching a higher echelon in the imperfect capital market. This view can be generalised to all factor markets: firms may wish to grow through the acquisition of other firms, not to expand or diversify output but in order to gain control of scarce factors such as qualified management, funds or patents, markets for which are imperfect or non-existent.

Whatever the economic value of these arguments, the European Authorities have without doubt the power to apply Article 86 to certain types of conglomerates. As we have seen, the Commission has explicitly mentioned that financial power may make a firm dominant. The proposed Regulation on the control of concentration between undertakings[9] confirms this view since 'the power to hinder efficient competition' is defined among other things in terms of the possibility of choice by suppliers and users and of economic and financial strength. Furthermore, this regulation requires the prior notification of mergers to the Commission if the combined turnover of the enterprises concerned is over one billion units of account unless the acquired firm has a turnover of less than 30 million units of account. Hence size *per se* is considered a relevant criterion, so that a large conglomerate without a dominant position in any one product market in the Common Market could come under the regulation.

The other dimension of the market relevant for determining the existence of a dominant position is its *geographical extent*. Article 86 requires a dominant position 'within the Common Market or within a substantial part of it'. As in the GEMA and in the Continental Can decisions one country (e.g. West Germany) can constitute a substantial part of the Common Market. The difficulty arises in determining the extent of the market in which the competitive process is operating in any specific situation. It could be argued, for example, that in general the relevant market should be defined as the whole Common Market, which would mean that national concentration ratios such as those computed in the Commission's Reports on competition policy grossly overstate the extent of real market dominance.

It has even been considered that, as it is essential to enable EEC firms to compete on the world-wide market, it is the international market which is relevant and that restriction of competition in the Common Market should be tolerated in order to improve competitive position at world level. This point of view is at the heart of the possible conflict of objectives between European anti-trust and industrial policies: the latter encourages the creation of 'Eurogiants' able to challenge the American and Japanese giant firms. It is probably true that in some sectors like computers and aerospace, a firm may hold a dominant position over a substantial part of the Common Market but control a very small share of the world-wide market in which it has to compete.

For many products, however, it makes sense to consider the national market to be the relevant one in determining the existence of a dominant position: 'oligopolistic market structure (typical of most manufacturing industries) and a long history of collusive behaviour allow for market segmentation into areas generally coincident with national boundaries'.[10]

Furthermore, barriers to trade are important even between neighbouring countries and these barriers are of the non-tariff variety. 'Those industries which already invite scrutiny because they combine high concentration and entry barriers based on heavily advertised product differentiation (household detergents, brewing, food manufacturing) are precisely those least likely to be affected by reductions in tariffs',[11] given the corresponding low price elasticities.

Market conduct and abuse of a dominant position

As previously stated, it is action by one or more enterprises which takes improper advantage of a dominant position which is condemned in Article 86. The concept of improper advantage or abuse has normally been interpreted widely. 'An improper exploitation of dominant position must be assumed when the dominant firm utilises the opportunities resulting from its dominance to gain advantages it could not gain in the face of practicable and sufficiently effective competition.'[12]

Clear examples of abuse are given in the GEMA case.[13] The GEMA corporation deals with author's rights with regard to musical works and has a virtual monopoly on the German market. GEMA's members were to all intent and purposes tied for life to the society and were prevented from granting the use of their rights to any other society. Furthermore, various forms of discriminatory practice were exercised against citizens of other member states. Among other things, the Commission's decision provided each member of GEMA with the right 'to resign at the end of each year and recover his full rights and to split the rights enjoyed according to country and the different forms of exploitation (e.g. general performing rights, broadcasting rights)...so that each member could choose freely the society to which he would concede his rights, in relation to the royalties'.[14]

In 1973, the Commission examined a case which involved an abusive practice on the part of a buyer.[15] A company, on behalf of six national railways managements, invited tenders for the development and de-livery of passenger carriages. One of the conditions for tendering was a provision giving unrestricted rights to use the designs, documents, patents and other proprietary rights arising from the planning and execution of the contract to the company which had invited the tenders. The Commission took the view that, as the largest customer for the type of carriage which was the subject of the tenders, the prospective buyer held a dominant position in the Common Market, and that the right of unrestricted exploitation in the sole interest of the prospective buyer constituted an abuse. The Commission discontinued the proceedings without decision when the abusive practice was abandoned.

Nevertheless, not all practices are so obviously abusive and it is not always easy so to classify an observed trade practice, even if it is among those mentioned in Article 86. Few trade practices are abusive under all circumstances. Sometimes a given practice is not only compatible with competition but may actually enhance it. For instance, 'the more successful the price discrimination, the greater is the incentive toward increased output. The final result of effective price discrimination might be a total output that falls not far short of the competitive level. Thus monopoly that cannot discriminate may lead to a more serious misallocation of economic resources than one that can.'[16]

Thus, where a dominant position exists, it may sometimes be hard to determine whether a specific practice exploits this position and promotes inefficient performance, or in fact reduces inefficiency to a greater or lesser extent.

It can at least be said that once a dominant firm, defined by a broad set of structural features, exists, whatever its origin there is a very strong probability that there will be some market conduct showing market power and resulting in some form of resources misallocation.

At the limit, the economic rationale of a transaction where one of the parties has a dominant position implies an abuse, in the sense that its position gives it automatic leverage in the transaction, which is not available to a non-dominant firm. It is only by assuming that the firm will not exploit its position and will behave 'as if' there were an effective competition, that the distinction between a dominant position and its abuse holds. But to ensure such 'good' behaviour would require the exercise of much more direct public interference than that usually implied by anti-trust policy. It has indeed been recognised that the focus on abuses of dominant position 'does not mean that the Treaty is necessarily more lenient with respect to concentrated economic power. Experience in Holland and elsewhere indicates that an abuse provision permits price control and other direct regulatory measures which in the United States are rarely invoked, even against regulated utilities.'[17]

This is why it may be argued that it is more important to attack the conduct which creates or consolidates a dominant position than that which exploits it. Here we find the origin of a controversy which has been crucial for the future of European anti-trust policy.

(a) For many lawyers, Article 86 is not concerned with maintaining competitive market structure, because it permits the existence of dominant positions. It prohibits certain forms of direct misuse of power towards customers without going into the structural phenomena of the creation or growth of the dominant position. 'The second paragraph of Article 86 lists the various types of conduct by enterprises that are considered abuses...From this listing it can be inferred that practices of the type referred to in Article 86 are those having a direct effect on the market...The express reference to the prejudicial effects which the practices referred to would have for consumers, shows that the conduct concerned cannot be just an enterprise's internal structural conduct.'[18] This position is supported by R. Joliet, who says 'Article 86 is not concerned with the manner in which domination is acquired, maintained or increased whether by coercive or exclusionary unilateral practices or by mergers. Its goal is not to preserve competitive processes but to ensure that market domination is not actually exploited to the detriment of utilisers.'[19]

The example of price cutting given by Joliet[20] helps to clarify the position. The firm which reduces its price as a means of discouraging new entrants and follows a systematic policy of cutting prices to selected customers as a means of driving specific competitors out of the market can decide, once competitors are eliminated and dominance consolidated, to increase prices and secure monopolistic profits. According to this author, Article 86 can only be used against these predatory tactics once competition has actually been destroyed and unduly high prices fixed.

According to the unanimous view of legal writers and of the EEC Commission, a market dominant position is always beyond attack. But if Article 86 were to be applied to policies erecting barriers to entry and consolidating market dominant position, it is difficult to perceive why in such a case the market dominant position itself should not be dismantled, a consequence which is rejected by all.[21]

One implication of such an interpretation would be that the many forms of concentration, acquisition of interests or absorption observed in the Common Market would be beyond the purview of the rules on competition although these industrial operations could result in an irreversible change in European industrial structure and in growing domination by a small group of large firms.

(*b*) Economically, this approach to anti-trust policy can be criticised for taking a static view of the relationship between market structure, market conduct and market performance.

A dynamic approach on the other hand would take into account market conduct which affects market structure and, in time, changes the competitive situation.

Indeed, conduct which exploits a given monopoly position could be less dangerous for the consumer in the long run than predatory practices whose aim or effect is to modify the market structure by making the industrial environment unfavourable to actual or to potential competition. 'Horizontal and vertical mergers, pooling of patents, extensive advertising may be dangerous, not so much as means of exploiting the actual market power of the firm, but as means of increasing over time such power, through changes in the market structure.'[22] For example, it would be very short-sighted to prohibit a price policy which harms the consumer directly but at the same time to ignore the creation of monopoly positions which, by their nature, transform the conditions of supply and demand in such a way that the levels of prices, of quantities produced, and of various forms of expenditure will be harmful to the consumer's welfare.

It could be argued therefore that anti-trust policy should apply to all practices which are the result of monopoly power or which are designed to consolidate such power as long as they cause harm to consumers, directly or indirectly. Such a view is supported by several lawyers. Thus, according to Canellos and Silber, 'impropriety of exploitation' must be judged in the light of the general goals of the Community and the basic mechanisms relied upon to achieve those goals. Thus Article 86 may be used against mergers which involve the consolidation or extension of a dominant position and such transactions are forbidden as 'improper' if, by eliminating effective competition, they prevent competition from performing the role assigned to it in the Treaty.[23]

Analysing examples of abusive behaviour furnished by Article 86 itself, Cardon and Herbert[24] show that 'tying practices' could be defined from a long-run point of view where the consumer is only indirectly harmed by the change in competitive conditions, as well as from a short-run viewpoint where there is an immediate exploitation of the dominant position to the detriment of suppliers or purchasers. If one firm or a few firms are the sole suppliers of an essential good, they may indeed exclude other suppliers from selling connected goods since all prospective buyers of these other goods will come to be bound by tying contracts. This is a typical 'predatory and exclusionary' practice which tends to create and preserve a more concentrated market structure than would otherwise exist, and to raise barriers to the entry of new sellers into the market. Even if the actual prices and qualities of the goods concerned are fair, such practices are abusive because they tend to create and perpetuate an anti-competitive market structure.

This is the line of reasoning followed by the Commission. In the Continental Can case, it stated that since the concept of abuse is not defined more closely in Article 86, the Community's objectives set out in the Treaty of Rome must be considered before the examples of abuse given in Article 86 itself. An abuse is present where an enterprise conducts itself in a way that is 'objectively' wrong in relation to the goals of the Treaty: 'It is not, for example, a question of whether plaintiffs...as they claim...paid a fair price to TDV shareholders; what is important is whether plaintiffs through this acquisition virtually eliminated the actual, or at least potential, competition in these products between TDV and SLW prior to the acquisition.'

Thus the Commission considers that the market structure as such has to be protected: a change in the supply structure which virtually eliminates the alternative sources of supply to the consumer appears to be in itself an abuse. A similar decision was taken in the ZOJA case where an American firm (CSC) and its Italian subsidiary (ICI), holding a monopoly *de facto* for an intermediate product, stopped supplying a firm in the market for a final product derived from the intermediate product. 'This action was liable to lead to the elimination of one of the few producers on the market in question and thus severely impair competitive conditions in the Common Market.'[25] Although the Court annulled the Commission's decision in the Continental Can case – mainly because the relevant market was not adequately defined – it very clearly confirmed the soundness of its interpretation: Article 86 may be applied to mergers.

However, a basic ambiguity remains. According to the Court, it can, aside from any fault, be considered an abuse if one enterprise extends a dominant position to the point that the objectives of the Treaty are circumvented through a substantial alteration of the supply situation, so that the consumer's freedom of action on the market is seriously jeopardised. Hence, to be condemned, the extension must amount to a substantial alteration of the market structure. A quantitative criterion must be considered, which apparently becomes the main way of distinguishing between a dominant position and its abuse.

Even if the alteration of market structure is substantial, it could be argued, in line with Section 2 of the Sherman Act, that the abuse of a dominant position requires also that the consolidation of that dominant position be wilful rather than the consequence of a superior product, business acumen, or historic accident leading to internal growth.[26] O. E. Williamson has recently argued that industries containing a dominant firm in which a conduct offence was tenuously associated with dominance could be attacked expressly in terms of structural monopoly. 'The reach of antitrust enforcement could be extended to include industries in which dominance cannot be attributed even remotely to predatory or exclusionary business tactics. Industries in which dominance has manifestly resulted from chance event or default failures and which now enjoy apparent immunity would thus come within the ambit of section 2 enforcement without strain.'[27]

The Court, however, has stated that a company in a dominant position cannot improve it by any means whatever: 'the strengthening of the position held by the enterprise can be an abuse and prohibited under Article 86 of the Treaty regardless of the methods or means used to attain it', if the degree of dominance essentially affects competition.

Does this imply that a firm has the right to acquire a dominant position through internal growth and that any consolidation of that position once it exists, whether by internal growth or by acquisition or merger could be condemned? In its draft regulation on concentration, the Commission does not clarify this issue. The proposal states that 'this definition of concentration makes it possible to deal with all concentrations which are likely to prevent effective competition within the Common Market, whether of the horizontal, vertical or conglomerate type, and whether or not they involve undertakings in a dominant position'.[28]

But the comments make it clear that 'the proposed regulation only covers concentrations which bring previously independent undertakings under the same control. External growth...frequently takes place independently of the competitive capacity of the undertakings concerned. Internal growth, on the other hand, which does not fall under this regulation is as such not subject to any restriction in any antitrust legislation.'

There appears to be some inconsistency between this statement and that of the Court quoted above.

Market performance and the control of concentration

Once a broad interpretation of abuse is accepted, the possibility of allowing abuse of a dominant position because it brings about economic benefits for the public is important.

As is well known Article 85, para. 3 of the Rome Treaty formulates four tests according to which a restrictive agreement may be justified.

(1) The agreement must contribute to improvement of production or distribution, or to technological or economic progress.

(2) The public must share in the benefits of the improvement.

(3) The restriction must be indispensable for the achievement of these results.

(4) The restriction may not be such as to afford the enterprises involved the possibility of eliminating competition with respect to a substantial proportion of the commodity concerned.

This system has been criticised on the ground that such ill-defined and general grounds for exemptions entail judgements involving substantial administrative discretion. Using a trade-off between restriction of competition and increase of consumer welfare corresponds to a vague criterion that the Commission or the Court has no objective way of applying.[29]

Indeed, the EEC Commission has granted exemption in many cases, but without a real weighing up of competitive effects and public benefits. Article 86, unlike Article 85, makes no provision for such an exemption. It could be argued, however, that activities which promote technical or economic progress or improve production or distribution are not likely to be considered abusive.

Thus it would be through the interpretation of the concept of 'abusive' or 'improper' advantage that a public interest criterion could be developed in the application of Article 86 although so far there has been no guidance concerning possible public interest criteria to justify conduct which would otherwise be considered abusive. B. Yamey states that the British Monopolies Commission has judged each practice by a dominant firm on its merits in the particular circumstances of the firm and its industry. 'No doctrine has emerged to the effect that certain practices should be considered to be per se contrary to the public interest.'[30]

The draft regulation on concentration contains no further guidance on this matter. According to Article 1, para. 3, exemption from the general prohibition of 1(1) may be granted to mergers 'which are indispensable to the attainment of an objective which is given priority treatment in the common interest of the Community'. The general philosophy underlining this exemption rule could indicate some scepticism towards the competitive process as being capable of realising the best economic performance contrary to the attitude to competition discussed on p. 129 and could also express an intention of discriminatory implementation with regard to non-European firms.[31] The same distrust is to be found in the British laws on monopolies and mergers where a test of public interest is also included:

> The fundamental policy issue which is faced is whether competition is to be preserved as an end with a high priority, as a way of life worth preserving for its own sake, or rather, as a means merely to some ends, for example, progressiveness in industry, full employment, increased exports and price stability. The choice of the United States has been the first...The choice of the United Kingdom (as would surely be the choice of the European Economic Community) would undoubtedly be the second, holding competition to be a means to other desirable ends, or, at the most, an end with low priority which necessarily on occasions has to be sacrificed for other preferred objectives.[32]

However, the definition of these 'preferred' objectives is far from unambiguous.

(*a*) A first problem is the choice between macro-economic and micro-economic performance as an expression of the public interest.

Many commentators view the Community's competition policy as a part of its general economic policy intended to achieve such objectives as steady economic growth, full employment, and price stability. For example, it is stated in the *First Report on Competition Policy* (p. 6) that 'the Commission would like to underline the importance it attaches to competition policy as a means of fighting inflation, especially now, since inflation presents in many respects a structural obstacle to adaptation'.

Such a macro-economic approach, it may be argued, is probably better suited for defining an efficient anti-trust policy than the traditional partial micro-economic approach of Industrial Economics. According to Ferguson, the concept of workable competition emphasises the firm or the industry as the unit of study, largely ignoring the inter-industrial relations. But 'bringing each industry to a ceteris paribus or partial equilibrium second best does not guarantee, or even indicate, that the economic system itself attains a second best configuration'.[33] An exception is the case where the economy can be partitioned into independent subgroups: then an anti-trust policy that brings any one industry closer to its optimum is sufficient for an increase in total social welfare.

To avoid this piecemeal approach, it is suggested that a macro-economic approach to workable competition should be set out consisting of the specification of economic targets or objectives and statistical tests to determine the relationship between the targets and industrial structure. The economy – not just a particular firm or industry – is then said to be workably competitive if there is no feasible change in industrial structure that would make attainment of the targets more likely, given the probability limits imposed upon our knowledge by its origin in empirical research.[34]

Unhappily, these limits are very restrictive and we do not have testable, systematic and stable relationships between market structure, conduct or performance, and macro-economic targets. Even the administrated prices theory and its link with industrial concentration is still largely controversial.

(*b*) The usual focus of industrial economic analysis has been upon the relation between market structure and various indicators of industrial efficiency, mainly profitability. But although at this level we have more econometric results, there is disagreement about the implications of these results for social welfare.

First, the meaning of the available evidence is generally ambiguous. High monopolistic profits are not readily to be distinguished from the results of efficient management or of highly risky activities; low profits due to competitive pressure from poor performance produced by 'X-inefficiency'; overcapacity from prudent anticipation of demand; deliberately slow technical progress from wise decisions to reject unpromising products or improvements whose immediate adoption would be premature.

Second, the choice among various dimensions of public interest or consumer welfare requires a political compromise between conflicting and incommensurable values. It is, for example, the value system of the society which should determine whether, on balance, allocating a greater percentage of resources to activities such as advertising than would be the case under less 'imperfect' competition, contributes enough to consumer welfare to outweigh the losses resulting from the static inefficiencies of the reduced competition.[35]

A further example is given by recent studies on the performance of the largest European firms.[36] Contrary to a widespread belief in Europe no evidence of increasing profitability, faster growth or more intensive research efforts could be found to support the myth 'the bigger the better'. The main consequence of larger size is to reduce the variability of profit rates and hence the firm's exposure to risk.

The existing literature in Welfare Economics offers almost no assistance in answering the operational questions of policy raised by the risk-avoidance behaviour of large firms. And indeed the possible welfare effects of these forms of risk-avoidance are various. 'Some reduce the rate of economic progress or cause an outright waste of resources; some increase welfare through the pooling of risks; and some have primarily redistributive effects, the value of which depends on one's own views of the better and the best.'[37]

These illustrations confirm the fact that using a 'common interest of the Community' criterion requires that the Commission and the Court make a political choice. In trying to judge cases on the basis of their contribution to macro- or micro-performance, the European authorities make competition policy a part of their overall economic and industrial policy, so that the function assigned to competition becomes much less central than officially stated.

Our own point of view is that in so far as the intention is to preserve a role for competition policy in Europe, it would be better to delimit clearly the function of each public tool. The job of the anti-trust authorities would then be to examine mergers or agreements on the basis that, to escape the prohibition of the law, the consequent reduction of competition must be insignificant. The premise of this policy thus remains that competition is the best way to serve the public interest, and that the legality of market conduct depends on the extent of its anti-competitive effect. It must of course be possible to question such a premise, but at a different level of public policy.

Conclusions

Until 1971 European anti-trust practice focused on Article 85, while Article 86, in effect, remained an empty threat in spite of many learned comments to the contrary. With the Continental Can case and the Commission's draft regulation on concentration, however, a new situation is emerging. It is now possible to act against all the various forms of action which could restrict European competition, including conduct which modifies market structure by making the industrial environment less favourable to actual or to potential competition. However, several difficulties remain.

First, the determination of a dominant position should be more clearly based on a structural approach. Even then, the search for the relevant market, geographically and in product terms, is not an easy task given present-day developments in European industrial structure.

Second, although the link between the existence of a dominant position, whatever its origin, and abusive conduct is almost automatic, neither Article 86 nor the draft regulation implies that any dominant position is itself an abuse. Further, there is a persistent ambiguity concerning policy which might discriminate between the ways in which a dominant position is obtained or consolidated.

Third, the public interest criterion, as it may be deduced from the concept of abuse, and as stated in the draft regulation, is at present an empty box. But it could become the source of a dangerous discretionary and discriminatory power. For example, the grant of exemption could be linked with social, regional or industrial policies so that allowing an anti-competitive merger or agreement would depend on its being linked with a policy goal quite independent of competition policy.

Our belief is that this leads to a very inefficient confusion of functions. It would be much better to leave the application of European competition law to an independent institution in order to safeguard against political pressures and surreptitious compromises.[38] It is only with clearly specialised bodies that conflicts of interest between the promotion of competition and social, regional or industrial requirements can be solved by responsible political choices.

Notes

1 EEC Commission, *First Report on Competition Policy* (Brussels, April 1972), p. 11.
2 C. D. Edwards, *Control of Cartels and Monopolies* (Dobbs Ferry, N.Y.: Oceana, 1967), p. 283.
3 P. Canellos and H. Silber, 'Concentration in the Common Market'. *Common Market Law Review* 7, no. 2 (April 1970), p. 12.
4 EEC Commission (see note (1) above), p. 80.
5 Memorandum of the EEC Commission, 'Concentration of enterprises in the Common Market, Dec. 1965'. *CCH Common Market Reports* no. 26 (March 1966).
6 See D. Schwarz, 'Zum Stand der Wirtschaftskonzentration im Gemeinsamen Markt'. In *Der Bürger im Staat* 4 (1973), p. 10; A. M. Kumps, *Le conglomérat, nouvelle forme de concentration* (*La Renaissance du Livre*: Bruxelles, 1974), chapter 3.
7 For an explanation of this apparent contradiction see J. Vandamme, 'L'Arrêt de la Cour de Justice du 21 février 1973 et l'interprétation de l'Article 86 du Traité CEE'. *Cahiers de Droit Européen*, nos. 1–2 (1974), pp. 123–4.
8 Quoted in E. Singer, *Antitrust Economics* (Prentice-Hall: New Jersey, 1968), p. 266.
9 Doc. COM(73) 1210 final (Brussels, 18 July 1973).
10 See A. Jacquemin and L. Phlips, *Concentration, Size and Performance of European Firms*, Working Paper no. 7409 (Université de Louvain), p. 3.
11 N. Owen, 'Competition policy and the Common Market', unpublished mimeo p. 6.
12 EEC Commission's *Memorandum on Concentration* (see note (5) above).
13 Commission Decision of 2 June 1971, see *Official Journal* no. L134 (20 June 1971).
14 EEC Commission (see note (1) above), p. 75.
15 EEC Commission, *Third Report on Competition Policy* (Brussels, May 1974), pp. 60–1.
16 L. Telser, 'Abusive trade practices: an economic analysis', *Law and Contemporary Problems* 3 (Summer 1965), p. 504.
17 *Antitrust Developments in the European Common Market*, Report of the

Subcommittee on Antitrust and Monopoly of the United States Senate Committee on the Judiciary, 88th Congress, 2nd Session (1964), p. 19.

18 Argument put forward by the Plaintiffs in the Continental Can Case. *CCH Common Market Reports* **2** (1973), p. 8287.

19 R. Joliet, *Monopolisation and Abuse of Dominant Position* (Faculté de Droit de Liège, 1970), p. 293. See also E. Cerehxe, 'L'Article 86 du Traité de Rome'. *Cahiers de Droit Européen* **3** (1972); and L. Foscaneanu, 'L'Article 86 du Traité de Rome et la decision Continental Can, une interprétation contestable d'un texte mauvais'. *Jurisclasseur Périodique* **1** (1972), 2452.

20 R. Joliet, *Monopolisation and Abuse of Dominant Position* (see note (19) above), pp. 248–52.

21 *Ibid.*, p. 252.

22 A. Jacquemin, 'Market structure and the firm's market power'. *Journal of Industrial Economics* **20** (1972), no. 2, pp. 122–34.

23 P. Canellos and H. Silber (see note (3) above), pp. 163–4. See also P. Capteyn and P. Verloren van Themaat, *Inleiding tot het recht van de Europese Gemeenschappen* (Deventer: Brussels, 1970), p. 225.

24 M. Cardon and F. Herbert, *Evolution récente de la notion d'abus de position dominante*, Working Paper no. 719 (CRIDE, Université de Louvain). See also M. Waelbroeck in *Le Droit de la Communauté Européenne* **4**, *Concurrence* (editions de l'Université de Bruxelles, 1972), p. 70.

25 EEC Commission, *Second Report on Competition Policy* (Brussels, April 1973), p. 54.

26 Compare with *US v. Grinell Corp.* (384 US 563, 1966), pp. 570–71.

27 O. E. Williamson, 'Dominant firms and the monopoly problem: market failure considerations', *Harvard Law Review* **85**, no. 8 (1972), p. 1531.

28 Doc. COM(73) 1210 final (Brussels, 18 July 1973), p. 9.

29 See A. Jacquemin, 'The criterion of economic performance in the antitrust policies of the US and the EEC', *Common Market Law Review* **7**, no. 2 (1970), p. 219.

30 B. S. Yamey, *Some reflections on the British policy towards monopoly and restrictive business agreements*, Working Paper no. 731 (CRIDE, Université de Louvain).

31 See A. Jacquemin, 'Recent application of European rules on competition to foreign firms', *Anti-trust Bulletin* **19**, no. 1 (1974), pp. 169 and 177.

32 R. Goyder, 'Public control of mergers', *Modern Law Review* **28**, 1965, quoted by R. Joliet (see note (20) above).

33 C. F. Ferguson, *A Macroeconomic Theory of Workable Competition* (Duke University Press: North Carolina, 1964), p. 46.

34 *Ibid.*, p. 80.

35 See for example K. Cohen and R. Cyert, *Theory of the Firm* (Prentice-Hall: New Jersey, 1965), chapter 18; R. Bishop, 'Monopolistic competition and welfare economics'. In R. Kuenne (ed.), *Monopolistic Competition Theory: Studies in Impact* (Wiley: Chicago, 1967), p. 263.

36 See for example A. Jacquemin, 'Size structure and performance of the largest European firms', *Three Banks Review* **4** (1974), pp. 393–408; J. Adams, 'Firm size and research activity: France and the US'. *Quarterly Journal of Economics* **84** (1970), pp. 386–409.

37 R. Caves, 'Uncertainty, market structure and performance: Galbraith as conventional wisdom'. In J. Markham and G. Papanek (eds.), *Industrial Organisation and Economic Development* (Houghton Mifflin Co.: Boston, Mass., 1970), pp. 283–302.

38 See A. Jacquemin, 'Le Critère de l'intérêt public et le project de réforme de la politique canadienne de concurrence', *Canadian Journal of Economics* **4** (1971), pp. 395–401.

COMMENT

R. G. OPIE

At the beginning of his chapter Professor Jacquemin states that 'the function assigned to competition seems to be central'. In the UK nowadays, it also *seems* to be. The new legislation of 1973 introduces competition explicitly, even if only as a means to other things and not as an end in itself.

Two questions arise – why? and what does one mean by competition? The answer to the first question must be largely political, even party-political. In a reaction to the attempts by Mr Wilson's Governments of 1964–70 to plan the national economy, and to its later programmes of more detailed intervention in prices and incomes, in location decisions, in innovation and rationalisation decisions, Mr Heath and his Ministers in the early days and months of his Government expressed a much stronger commitment to free market forces. They turned words into deeds by abolishing a number of interventionist institutions, such as the National Board for Prices and Incomes and the Industrial Reorganisation Corporation, and wound up such policies as the regional employment premium.

Ministers' commitment to the primacy of market forces working in a competitive environment was further expressed in the Fair Trading Act of 1973 with its explicit references to competition in the list of elements of the 'Public Interest'. Indeed this commitment seemed at some stages to have gone so far as to amount to a recommendation of perfect competition – anything less was very imperfect. Since the Minister in charge of the Government's competition policy had also just carried out the ritual slaughter of the Consumers' Council (a body which seemed to many to have a potentially important role in improving the operation of market forces by the spread of market knowledge), it seemed possible to say the least that the Government of the day was not wholly clear in what it might mean by competition.

Happily, the same doubts are roused by the lengthy passage from the EEC Commission's First Report on Competition Policy quoted in Professor Jacquemin's first paragraph. Indeed the first sentence claims that competition 'guarantees the widest possible freedom of action to all'. One could beg to differ. Under perfect competition, the producer has hardly any freedom at all. Indeed quite a good examination question asks 'What *does* a perfect competitor compete about?' Again, a consumer faces an array of homogeneous goods – a freedom to choose that confers little. Indeed this passage – like another famous rule about 'the greatest good of the greatest number' – avoids the really interesting question of the balance of freedoms, how much freedom for how many? The essence of oligopoly after all is discretion, or arbitrary behaviour or, in other words, a 'freedom from market pressures'.

The dilemma surfaces again on page 132. 'Market domination' confers an ability to influence a market in a manner which is 'in principle foreseeable for the dominant enterprise'. I think I don't understand this section or its corollaries. In my view, oligopoly is a state of great uncertainty invaded by efforts to increase certainty – elements of both continue, just as they do in an environment of atomistic competition. Indeed, I deduce that the EEC has a not much clearer idea of 'competition' as an ideal than we do. One must be grateful, however, that 'the establishment of a dominant position is lawful'. That has after all been seen as the logical outcome of successfully ruthless competition ever since the days of Piero Sraffa.

On page 132 Professor Jacquemin turns to the problem 'of defining the relevant market'. Although this is an academically interesting and politically teasing point, it is not a decisive issue. It is made important only by the style of anti-monopoly policy, which seems to need a threshold to contain its investigations. My preference has long been for a policy which investigates the power of the large firm as such, as well as firms which happen to control a large share of a particular product market. Large firms tend as a general rule to be diversified, multi-product, multi-market conglomerates to varying degrees. I believe that such large firms with an overall corporate strategy are more important than simply as a sum of their parts. Under present (and past) British monopoly legislation, it is possible only to investigate the parts if a particular 'part' happens to supply more than some statistically critical share of a product market (not even an 'economic' market). This is a damaging limitation within the legislation.

Professor Jacquemin asks the question whether it is clear that 'a diversified firm...has a competitive advantage over a single product firm'. He agrees that it may, because capital markets are imperfect, and that a multi-product diversified or conglomerate firm may operate as a mini-capital market in itself, with knowledge and rationality superior to those of a more diversified and impersonal market.

Whether the answer to Professor Jacquemin's question is clear to economists or not, it is to businessmen and especially managers. Size is everything, or almost so. It is important to survival, to power, to security. And size requires diversity. Size (with a given *rate* of profitability) provides funds, and thus finances growth – and a firm diversifies as it runs out of growth opportunities in its own line of business. Hence, in the absence of further research, and as a generalisation, most of us would back Goliath against David every time – and so would Goliath's and David's colleagues.

Even so, society cannot allow Goliaths to run wild. Hence I welcomed the tone on page 133 – I would like to introduce into the legislation and the policy, the matter of size *per se* not solely as a trip-wire to detonate an investigation, but also as a consideration in the judgement on the large firm. This is at least in part the situation with mergers in the UK. It was also part of the aborted legislation for a Commission for Industry and Manpower in 1970 in the UK. If size is relevant to merger enquiries, it is at least as relevant in investigations of dominant firms. In my view, *large* firms are just as 'dominant' as firms with a large market share.

The very first sentence of Professor Jacquemin's section on 'Market conduct and abuse of a dominant position' raises the question of what would count as taking 'proper' advantage of a dominant position? Would it be proper to compete another oligopolist into bankruptcy? Would it be proper to use one's own funds to finance research and development, an outlet which cannot easily be financed on the capital market? Or is there in fact no proper behaviour for a large and oligopolistic firm? Professor Jacquemin suggests as much (p. 143) – 'the link between the existence of a substantially dominant position and abusive conduct is almost automatic'.

I find this view somewhat hard to accept. So too perhaps does Professor Jacquemin. He also writes about the ambiguity of judgements about the practices of large firms. In particular, I find it hard to accept the view that a dominant position tends to result in resource misallocation. Compared to what, pray? Compared perhaps to Samuelson, or Scitovsky, or the Review of Economic Studies, but compared also to any real-world alternative? And is such 'misallocation' both static and dynamic?

If we are looking for real-world judgements, how can one accept the view that 'it is more important to attack the conduct which creates or consolidates the dominant position than that which exploits it'. To do so would guarantee that even if we do root out the evil, we also lose the benefits of size, whatever they may be. So long as one accepts that size does confer some social (as well as private) benefits, policy must surely aim to root out only the disadvantages, viz the bad practices, in particular cases. *Ad hoc*-ery once more. Thus I would harden Professor Jacquemin's judgement and say not that 'it may sometimes be hard' but that 'it is always hard and often impossible' to determine 'if a specific practice exploits unduly the position...'

I find pp. 138–9 of Professor Jacquemin's paper on market structure and changes therein somewhat ironic. He states that in the view of the Commission 'the market structure as such has to be protected'. Indeed 'change in the supply structure which virtually eliminates the alternative source of supply for the consumer appears to be in itself an abuse'. Does he mean '*the* alternative' (i.e. the last step to complete monopoly – a relatively rare situation) or merely *an* alternative, or even an important alternative? If it is either of the two latter options, we should note that e.g. the vast majority of mergers in the UK in the last decade, in both number and value of assets taken over, have been horizontal mergers, i.e. mergers which reduce numbers of competing suppliers to those further downstream. I am highly sceptical of the so-called 'benefits of mergers', whether they be horizontal, vertical or oblique, but one should at least note that with horizontal mergers where the possible structural dangers are greatest, so too are the possible structural benefits. I emphasise 'possible', since so many mergers turn out to be gravely disappointing to both insiders and outsiders. But if the benefits of *horizontal* mergers are small, where else, pray, are they likely to be substantial?

It is in Professor Jacquemin's section on 'Market performance and the control of concentration' that the real dilemma is posed. We should not take up the position that dominant positions are necessarily bad, or necessarily good, nor even that good practices may outweigh the bad. Nor should we argue that, because something good is done by a large firm rather than by a small one, that fact alone makes the potential good an actual bad. We should rather try to eliminate the bad in order to enhance the good.

6

Policies towards market power and price discrimination in the EEC and the UK

M. HOWE

The competition policy rules contained in Articles 85 and 86 of the Treaty of Rome applied immediately the UK joined the European Economic Community. Article 85 deals with restrictive practices and agreements between firms, Article 86 with the abuse of dominant market positions. The competition policy rules of the Community apply to UK firms only when inter-EEC trade is affected. There is nothing to prevent the formulation of domestic policies by national governments and there is no intention to harmonise anti-trust policies. Indeed, at the time that British accession to the Community was being debated and negotiated a major codification and extension of the existing UK legislation was under way, and the new Act, the Fair Trading Act of 1973, had virtually no regard to EEC policy. However, Articles 85 and 86 reflect a different approach to the control of monopoly to that developed in the UK since the initiating legislation of 1948. These differences will be discussed and evaluated in this chapter in the context of the treatment of price discrimination which has always been regarded as a significant aspect of monopoly behaviour. The views expressed here are those of the author and should in no way be taken to express the views of the Monopolies and Mergers Commission, or any other official body.

The chapter is in four parts: the first part provides an abbreviated economic analysis of price discrimination; the second and third examine the approach to price discrimination adopted in the EEC and the UK respectively and entail some discussion of the general policies adopted in seeking to control the exploitation of market power; the conclusions to be drawn from this examination in the light of the economic analysis are contained in the final part.

The economics of price discrimination
Economists have generally been critical of discriminating market be-haviour, including the practice of price discrimination; that is, selling different units of output at different prices not related to difference in

costs. Since price discrimination can take a large number of different forms, can be analysed at several different stages of the process of production and distribution, and can have a variety of effects including that on the allocation of resources, a generally unanimous view is perhaps surprising. In fact the unanimity can probably be traced to the fact that price discrimination is a symptom of market imperfection. If competition is completely effective, price discrimination will not persist. Sellers will not be able to extract different net prices for different parts of their output. Net prices will tend to equalise under pressure from both the seller and the buyer sides of the market. If price discrimination is more pervasive the less effective is competition on either side of the market, and if competition is widely held (though not without qualification) to be more conducive to welfare than monopoly, a hostility to the practice among economists is not surprising. Indeed the practice of price discrimination is usually analysed in the context of the behaviour of the pure monopolist. The monopolist practising price discrimination is already established. Neither the creation nor the preservation of his monopoly position depends upon the practice of price discrimination and the implementation of that practice involves him in no additional costs. The buyers' side of the market is (usually implicitly) assumed to be perfectly competitive. How perfectly the monopolist can discriminate (in terms of Pigou's first, second and third degrees of price discrimination) then depends upon characteristics of his product and its buyers.

In all cases, however, the practice is essentially regarded as a means by which the monopolistic seller is able to increase his own short-run profits above the level attainable by a policy of uniform pricing in given demand conditions.

The practice therefore has clear enough effects on the distribution of income. Income will be redistributed from the buyers as a group to the discriminating seller who would in any case be expected to earn an above-normal rate of return on his investment in the long run without discriminatory pricing. With first degree price discrimination, indeed, the practice will enable the seller to expropriate the whole of consumers' surplus. In the usual case (where the possibility is not considered that economies of scale may be enjoyed as a result of the discrimination) income will also be redistributed within the buyers as a group, those buying at the relatively low prices benefiting at the expense of those buying at the relatively high prices. It is a commonplace to observe that attitudes to income distribution effects depend upon value judgements. So does the question of whether it is 'fair' that different buyers should pay prices which yield different net amounts to the seller when the costs of supply are taken into account. Economists have generally shied away from expressing a view on this aspect, perhaps content to rest their attack on any distributional consequences of price discrimination upon their general hostility to the monopoly power from which the practice is seen to spring.

The effects of monopolistic price discrimination upon the output of the sellers' industry and upon resource allocation are of more direct concern yet are less clear. In the extreme case of first degree price discrimination the output of the discriminating monopolist is identical to that of the perfectly competitive industry. In the case of second degree discrimination, output will be closer to the competitive level than where price is uniform but not necessarily identical with it. Second degree price discrimination is common. Into this category can be fitted the common situation where a seller produces a line of similar but differentiated products and charges prices which are not proportional to the marginal costs of supplying the different items, as well as discriminatory pricing of a standard product, for example according to the usage made of that product by different buyers as with certain office equipment. Finally, in the case of third degree discrimination where different prices are charged in separable markets but price is uniform within each market, output may be less than, equal to, or greater than the monopoly output depending upon the shape of the relevant demand functions. Third degree price discrimination is a widespread practice, differential prices in home and export markets, and on sales of components to original equipment manufacturers and in the replacement market being common examples. But the resource allocation effects are ambiguous.

A further ambiguity arises from the possibility that, with discrimination, a given output may be produced more cheaply. In the limit it may be unprofitable to produce any output if a uniform pricing policy is insisted upon. These possibilities may occur in industries subject to increasing returns to scale. Price discrimination aimed at expanding output may be considered acceptable in such circumstances. This case is normally discussed in the context of public utilities, however, and in such industries the behaviour of the discriminator will be subject to some sort of control or regulation. Hopefully, this may ensure a tolerable compromise between the benefits and any possible disadvantages of price discrimination. Increasing returns to scale are not, however, limited to public utilities. The possibility therefore arises that a private monopolist may be unable fully to exploit economies of scale or even to contemplate operating at all in a particular market unless he has the opportunity to practice price discrimination. The question in such a case is how to balance the gains that would not otherwise be forthcoming against the income distribution and 'fairness' issues raised by discriminatory pricing and (if the buyers are not final consumers) the possible effects of discrimination on the competitive process at the buyers' stage of the process of production and distribution.

This latter point is an aspect of price discrimination less often considered by economists. The usual focus is exclusively upon the monopoly seller. But if the effect of discrimination is to charge different net prices to different buyers, and if those buyers are in competition with each other, it is obvious that discrimination by the seller puts certain of its buyers at a competitive disadvantage. In contrast to the usual analysis, the discriminatory pricing of the seller may be dictated by the interests of certain of its buyers. Larger, more powerful buyers may be able to demand lower prices from their suppliers than are reflected in any lower costs of supplying them. The benefits enjoyed by the large buyer may not only take the form of lower prices. Quantity discounts are the rule in most industries. If such discounts correspond to cost savings to the supplier in dealing in large quantities, and clearly there usually will be some savings in administration and distribution if not in manufacture, the discount structure will not be discriminatory. Commonly, however, the discounts offered will reflect the bargaining power of the larger buyers and the relation of the discounts to cost savings is therefore rarely close. This is evidenced by the frequency with which quantity discounts are related to the annual purchases of the buyer, usually of all the products of the seller, rather than to order size or delivery consignment. Another similar and common situation is where certain retailer customers are granted wholesaler terms which do not correspond closely to any costs of the wholesaling function that they may incur but do reflect their size and bargaining power.

In the situations just described the seller may have little option but to acquiesce in the pressures and demands of certain buyers although he may see little positive benefit to himself from his concession either in the short or in the long run. His choice may be to grant a lower price or to risk losing an important slice of business altogether. Obviously the seller cannot be presented with such a choice where he enjoys a complete monopoly. This form of discrimination can therefore only arise when competition is imperfect on both sides of the market but when the sellers' side is not completely monopolised.

Although discrimination may be forced upon such a seller in that it reduces rather than increases his own short-run profits it may nevertheless offer him long-run benefits. Thus the discrimination may serve to increase entry barriers to his own market by cementing the more significant seller–buyer relationships. There is also the possibility that the seller may see some prospect of ultimate financial gain from his concessions to particular buyers. With given demand conditions this prospect requires that the favoured buyer(s) is able to use his price advantage to enhance his own market power, at the expense of those buying on worse terms. If the buyer is able to monopolise his own market the seller may expect to see some eventual advantage in the price at which he sells to that buyer. The consequences of the sellers' discriminatory pricing therefore would be disadvantageous not only to the competitors of the beneficiary of the discrimination but also to the final consumers who would ultimately have to pay higher prices. There may be further disadvantages if the surviving firm(s) is not the most efficient of the original competing group. In this context it is the relative size rather than the relative efficiency of certain buyers which enables them to extract favourable terms. More efficient firms may be forced out, creating a further loss in that the remaining firm(s) uses a greater quantum of resources to produce a given output than those that have left the industry.

These can only be long-run possibilities, however, and usually extreme at that. If the favoured buyers reduce their own prices, or use their advantage in other ways to promote their own sales, competition will be stimulated at the buyer stage in the short run, and while the discrimination may be unfair between buyers it has to be substantial and to affect a large proportion of the business of the firms concerned to threaten their long-run survival. Even if the larger buyers do obtain some advantage in their own market, if that advantage is to be turned into monopoly power they will need the protection of entry barriers. If the buyers' market is not monopolised then there is no scope for the discriminating seller to share monopoly gains. And, of course, the sellers' own market power will have been constrained by the pressures from the large buyer(s).

In fact it seems likely that the benefits hoped for by the seller in conceding discriminatory terms to large buyers will be less a share of monopoly gains ultimately extracted by those buyers than an expectation that the larger buyers may be more effective in expanding demand (at any set of prices) by promotional activities and so on, an expansion which will then benefit his own sales. Indeed it is not just large buyers who may be granted favourable prices or discounts for this reason. Firms do not see themselves as operating in given demand conditions; on the contrary they will be on the lookout for means of expanding demand. Favourable terms may therefore be granted to particular buyers who, by virtue of their management, technical facilities, locality or whatever, appear promising and expanding sources of business to the seller whatever their present size. Courting particular customers can be part of the competitive strategies of sellers.

Even assuming given demand conditions it must be recognised that seller competition in oligopolistic markets, which obviously abound in contemporary economies, may take the form of local or temporary price concessions, special discounts, allowances or other deals as a less overt and aggressive way of seeking additional business than uniform, publicised price changes with all the uncertainties these entail in conditions of oligopolistic interdependence. New entrants may find it particularly attractive to compete this way with less risk of disturbing established sellers. The outcome of this form of competition must be a discriminatory pattern of net prices. But the pattern would not be expected to be as systematic or as persistent as that which results from avowedly discriminatory policies of sellers. Changing market conditions and changes in the awareness of the situation on the part of other sellers and of buyers may lead to price/discount adjustments which change the pattern. Economists have always recognised that, in oligopoly, price shading and concealed concessions may be the order of the day. Yet discussions of price discrimination have rarely extended to this case but have concentrated upon the analysis of discrimination within complete monopoly. Discrimination may therefore have the advantage that in appropriate market conditions it can represent a loosening up of what might otherwise be a tightly co-ordinated oligopoly. It is difficult to be precise about the market structure in which price discrimination may be beneficial in this way, except to describe it as oligopolistic, but the benefits of such discrimination would take the form of a larger output than would result from more co-ordinated behaviour and, perhaps, greater pressure upon the oligopolists in respect of internal efficiency and innovation. In short, discrimination may promote more effective competition in some market structures than would exist without the practice.

A similar example can arise with respect to freight absorption. A practice of strict f.o.b. pricing is non-discriminatory (with respect to freight costs) but has the effect, certainly where freight costs are significant and producers scattered, of creating a network of 'natural monopolies' in locations around the various producers. Competition among such producers aimed to win business in each others' territories may take the form of freight absorption on particular transactions resulting in an unsystematic pattern of discriminatory net prices.

Mention of freight costs and pricing systems leads to the point that discrimination can be associated with the suppression of competition. A variety of collectively enforced collusive practices will have discriminatory effects. Outside the area of exclusive dealing, aggregated rebates and so on, the classic example is perhaps industry-wide, basing-point systems. Such systems are invariably designed to reinforce collusive behaviour among sellers and they result in discrimination between buyers according to their location in relation to the industry's basing point(s). The disadvantages of basing-point systems are primarily the disadvantages of collusion between the sellers. The discriminatory content, however, may distort the allocation of resources at the customer level, most spectacularly, perhaps, by distorting location decisions.

Finally, a seller may employ discriminatory tactics in order to create a monopoly. The distinction between oligopolistic competition resulting in unsystematic discrimination between buyers and systematic and persistent discrimination with predatory intent may be fine, but it is real.

Predatory price discrimination involves the seller making price reductions in particular localities or to particular groups of customers with the avowed intention of eliminating competitors, competitors to whom those localities or customers are important sources of business. The seller must enjoy sufficient market power to finance the loss of short-run profit yet must anticipate an extension of that power as a result of his discriminatory tactics such as to more than compensate for that loss. However, not only have many economists questioned the likelihood of such a combination of circumstances, they have also made the point that firms can usually find less risky and less costly ways of securing additional monopoly profits.[1]

This brief survey of some of the economics of price discrimination has served to demonstrate that the practice can indeed take many forms and have a variety of effects.[2]

The analysis above supports neither a policy of condoning price discrimination, nor one of invariably condemning it which would in any case be impracticable given the ubiquity of the practice. Apart from the prevalence of market imperfections it is virtually impossible for administrative reasons to establish price lists and discount structures which are at all times cost related. Discrimination which seems unambiguously harmful is predatory discrimination operated by one seller against another and discrimination which is the result of collusive action by a group of sellers. Discrimination may have advantages when it is the outcome of oligopolistic competition, the loosening of inter-seller discipline more than offsetting any disadvantages. Price discrimination aimed at maximising short-run profits has more ambiguous results when practised by a complete monopolist; the most beneficial case, from a resource allocation point of view (first degree discrimination), is relatively rare, but all cases may lead to a greater output than uniform pricing, and discrimination may be necessary in some circumstances if any output is to be produced at all. Finally, discrimination resulting from buyer pressure can stimulate competition although in the long term it could conceivably lead to an increase in market power at the buyer stage. Certainly the favoured (usually larger) buyers will enjoy an advantage over their competitors which is not justified in terms of cost savings. This, of course, applies to all price discrimination, whatever its motives or causes, where the sellers' customers are not the final consumers; and it provides the criterion by which economists identify the practice.

EEC policy towards price discrimination

The starting point of EEC competition policy is the proposition that a competitive decentralised economic organisation is more likely to contribute to the welfare of the community than is monopoly. It would be inaccurate to suggest that industrial policy within the Community has been exclusively dictated by this proposition. There have indeed been conflicts between competition policy and other forms of industrial policy in the EEC as elsewhere as well as disagreements over the efficacy (and meaning) of competition. Yet Articles 85 and 86 prohibit collusive practices of various sorts and the 'abuse' of dominant market positions as incompatible with the purpose of the Common Market. They appear to represent a stronger commitment to competition than that found in the British legislation, particularly outside the area of restrictive practices.

The Article relevant to the subject matter of this paper is largely Article 86. It is only very recently that the European Commission has directed itself to the interpretation and enforcement of this Article. The main impact of Article 86 both in the Community and on UK firms and the UK Government has been the successful extension by the European Commission of the provisions of that Article to the control of mergers following the Continental Can case. Otherwise the Article has so far been little used.

It is worth setting out Article 86 in full. It provides that any abuse by one or more enterprises of a dominant position within the Common Market or within a substantial part thereof shall be prohibited as incompatible with the Common Market, provided that trade between any member states is affected. The Article also provides examples, not intended to be exhaustive, of 'abuse' –

> (i) directly or indirectly imposing unfair purchase or selling prices or other unfair trading conditions;
>
> (ii) limiting production, markets or technical development to the prejudice of consumers;
>
> (iii) applying dissimilar conditions to equivalent transactions with other trading parties thereby placing them at a competitive disadvantage;
>
> (iv) making the conclusion of contracts subject to acceptances by other parties of supplementary obligations which, by their nature or according to commercial usage, have no connection with the subject of such contracts (i.e. 'full-line' forcing).

It is clear that price discrimination *per se* is not prohibited for it must be exercised by firms in dominant positions in order to be attacked (but see p. 162 below). In fact, leaving aside the age-old problem of defining the relevant market, the main issues surrounding interpretation of Article 86 have been the meaning to be attached to 'dominant position' and to a lesser extent 'abuse'.

No definition of a 'dominant position' is provided in the Treaty of Rome. However, in the landmark Continental Can case the Commission offered the following definition.

> Undertakings are in a dominant position when they have the power to behave independently which puts them in a position to act without taking into account their competitors, purchasers, or suppliers. That is the position when, because of their share of the market or of their share of the market combined with the availability of technical knowledge, raw materials or capital, they have the power to determine prices or to control production or distribution for a significant part of the products in question. This power does not necessarily have to derive from an absolute domination permitting the undertakings which hold it to eliminate all will on the part of their economic partners, but it is enough that they be strong enough as a whole to ensure to those undertakings an overall independence of behaviour, even if there are differences in intensity in their influence on the different partial markets.

The key phrase would appear to be 'the power to behave independently'. Obviously this must mean more than the decision-making discretion which all firms enjoy outside perfect competition. Discretion effectively constrained by the actions of competitors can hardly denote a dominant position. Likewise, the most important seller in a market does not necessarily occupy a dominant position. Dominance implies the absence of effective constraints on the conduct of the major seller. It has not proved possible to lay down a particular market share which would identify dominance. A fuller analysis of market structure, embracing all its dimensions, will normally be necessary to the consideration of whether any constraints offered by competitors are effective in limiting market power sufficiently for anti-trust intervention to be unwarranted. In extreme cases a simple analysis may suffice. Thus in the GEMA case, one of the few cases so far brought under Article 86, GEMA, a German authors' rights society, was the sole body operating in West Germany for the purpose of protecting authors' rights in musical works. But in less obvious cases it is even difficult to see how the absence of effective competition can be established by reference to market structure alone, however comprehensive the analysis.

If it is to be established that a firm enjoys a dominant market position such that its competitors can have no significant effect upon prices, production and distribution in the market, support may have to be drawn from an investigation of the price and production policies, and perhaps the profitability, of that firm. The emphasis upon effective competition suggests that in many cases the ultimate test of market dominance must be the way in which the market actually works rather than how it is structured. The neat progression from market structure to market conduct implied by the wording of Article 86 may often prove unattainable, some analysis of conduct and performance being necessary even to establish dominance. Thus the absence of price discrimination might be regarded as evidence that competition is effective: the neat progression from structure to conduct may become circular.

Before leaving the interpretation of 'dominant position', it is worth emphasising the point that Article 86 can apply to the abuse of dominant positions by more than one firm. Abuse of a dominant position by a number of firms which is the result of a restrictive agreement is also caught by Article 85, for the two Articles are not mutually exclusive. Moreover, Article 85 also applies to 'concerted practices' of firms as well as to formal and informal agreements and hence would appear to cover the parallel behaviour so often attributed to oligopolists. Presumably therefore, Article 86 applies if two or more firms, both occupying dominant positions, exploit those positions yet do not behave in parallel fashion. More arguably, it might also apply if two or more firms, taken together, occupy a dominant position but do not behave in a way which amounts to 'concerted practices' or tacit collusion. It can be questioned, however, whether in those circumstances the relevant firms could be said to 'have the power to behave independently'. Without collusion the independence of any one firm must be constrained to a major extent by the market power of the other(s) in the same market. The looser forms of oligopoly, with no one firm enjoying a dominant position, may therefore escape the net of Article 86.

This may well be important as far as price discrimination is concerned. If Article 86 cannot be extended to embrace oligopolists whose behaviour does not amount to 'concerted practice', discrimination which arises unsystematically as a result of the more covert forms of competition that may be adopted in such markets would seem to be beyond attack even though different buyers face 'dissimilar conditions' and though some will suffer a 'disadvantage'. On the other hand, if dominance is established any discriminatory behaviour runs the risk of being abusive since, whatever its form, whether in price, refusal to supply or anything else, and whatever the motive of the discriminator, it must put competitors of the beneficiary at a disadvantage. The scope of Article 86 is therefore wide ranging indeed given the pervasiveness of discrimination as defined in the Article. The question is, in what more precise circumstances will discrimination constitute an 'abuse'?

An interpretation of abusive behaviour follows from the interpretation of a dominant market position. According to the European Commission, abuse must be understood as an 'objective misconduct' in the light of the aims of the Treaty and the emphasis is clearly on observable behaviour. Behaviour will only constitute an abuse if it is behaviour that would not materialise if competition was effective and if the dominant position therefore did not exist. Predatory price discrimination, aimed at putting other sellers at a disadvantage and further increasing the seller's market power in the long run, would appear to constitute an abuse as 'imposing unfair selling prices' and hence is presumably prohibited if it affects trade between member states (as it is under US anti-trust law). Classic monopolistic price discrimination aimed at increasing the seller's short-run profits may also fall foul of the same provision if either the resultant profits or the discriminatory prices are regarded as unfair, not withstanding any resource allocation benefits (compared with uniform monopoly prices) of the practice. The discrimination illustrated in the Article as a possible abuse seems clearly intended to focus upon the effects of discrimination upon competition at the buyer stage of the process of production and distribution, the focus least often considered by economists.

It is not obvious whether the objection is solely to the unfairness of discrimination (the sort of objection which led to the Robinson–Patman Act being passed in the USA as the result of pressure from smaller retailers) or to the possibility that market power of the favoured buyers may be enhanced in the long run, or to both. What is obvious is that arguments can be expected over the meaning of 'dissimilar conditions' and 'equivalent transactions'. As in the Robinson–Patman Act, price discrimination is more likely to come under suspicion when prices vary between buyers than when prices are uniform yet the costs of supply vary, if only because prices are more observable than are costs. Consequently a defence to the charge of abuse will be that price differences *do* reflect cost differences although experience with the Robinson–Patman Act illustrates the practical difficulties. The American Act also allows discrimination which is the result of meeting a competitor's price, a defence which has also caused difficulties.[3] However, competition at the buyer stage may be discouraged rather than encouraged as price flexibility and experimentation is made more difficult.

The discrimination provisions of Article 86 were invoked as part of the European Commission's case against GEMA. GEMA was a German authors' rights society with a monopoly position in Germany. It had acquired the power to exercise in Germany the rights of other authors' rights societies established elsewhere in the Common Market. GEMA was held to have discriminated against the nationals of other member states who were denied full rights in the society.

A more interesting case of discrimination is to be found under Article 85 in the Commission's decision on Kodak's conditions of sale. Article 85 generally prohibits agreements between undertakings and concerted practices 'which have the object or effect of preventing, restraining or distorting competition within the Common Market' and it goes on to quote 'in particular' discrimination defined in the same terms as in Article 86. The intention would appear to be to attack collectively imposed discrimination under Article 85 and discrimination imposed by an individual seller with a dominant position under Article 86. The Kodak case has thrown this interpretation into some confusion. Kodak had introduced standard conditions of sale which, according to the European Commission constituted an 'agreement between under-takings', though vertical in nature, as they formed part of the contracts between each of Kodak's five European subsidiaries and their direct buyers. These conditions required payment for all transactions with Kodak in a given territory to be made to the Kodak subsidiary established in that territory. According to the Commission, this had the effect of preventing a buyer in one member state from directly importing from another member state in which Kodak's prices might be lower. This amounted to an ingenious way of separating markets for the practice of third degree price discrimination. However, the conditions of sale were attacked by the Commission under the general prohibition of Article 85 since they had the effect of restricting inter-state competition, without reference to the discrimination aspect. Negative clearance was granted to Kodak only when the offending conditions of sale were removed.

Whether this decision amounts to a general prohibition of dis-crimination practised by the individual seller when imposed by vertical agreements, a prohibition which was apparently explicitly rejected in the drafting of Article 85, has been a matter of debate with the majority holding that discrimination cannot be attacked without either an agree-ment between firms or a dominant market position.[4]

UK policy towards price discrimination

The 1973 Fair Trading Act defines a 'monopoly' situation according to formal criteria rather than by reference to the concept of market dominance. Under the simplest criterion a monopoly situation is said to exist in the supply of goods and services of any description (except for specific exclusions listed in schedule 7 of the Act) if at least one-quarter of all the goods of that description which are supplied in the UK, including imports, are supplied by one firm. If this criterion is satisfied then the conditions necessary for a full investigation by the Monopolies Commission are met. But there is no presumption in the legislation that a one-quarter share of the market in the hands of one firm is incompatible with effective competition. It is for this reason that the criterion should be regarded as formal rather than economic.

An important consequence is that the problem of market definition is less than with the market dominance approach. If the Commission is asked to undertake a particular enquiry its first task is to establish whether or not a monopoly situation prevails in the supply of the goods or services as described. If this is established and the Commission proceeds to a full investigation, it will then need to consider the appropriateness of the market definition implied by the description in its assessment of the working of the market.

The concept of market dominance, so characteristic of European anti-trust legislation, may have no place in British Law but the concept has influenced the choice of the one-quarter market-share criterion and the application of that criterion in the selection of cases for investigation by the Monopolies Commission. The 1973 Act reduced the critical market share from one-third to one-quarter. Although the basis for this reduction was the view, derived from the mounting empirical information on seller concentration and on the relationship between seller concentration and various dimensions of economic performance, primarily profitability, that significant market power can be exercised with less than one-third of the market, in the great majority of cases so far referred to the Commission the market share of the firms satisfying the criterion has been substantially above one-third. But UK policy also recognises that market power cannot be identified by reference to market share alone. An estimated market share of one-quarter is a necessary but not normally a sufficient condition for action to be initiated, and before a Monopolies Commission enquiry is set in motion other dimensions of market structure as well as available information on conduct and performance are likely to be considered. Certainly this is how the Office of Fair Trading (OFT) is beginning to formulate its approach to its task of making monopoly references under the 1973 Act.[5] In this important preliminary stage of the application of British monopoly policy the analysis of market power carried out by the OFT is of a basically similar kind (if less exhaustive) to that which the European Commission must conduct to establish market dominance.

There is an alternative criterion by which a monopoly situation can be established under the 1973 Act in terms virtually identical to the wording of Article 85. Under this criterion a monopoly situation will exist if two or more firms so conduct their affairs as to 'prevent, restrict or distort competition' except by virtue of agreements or arrangements which are covered by the restrictive practices legislation. Such a situation is described in the Act as 'complex monopoly'. This provision would allow the Commission to investigate the parallelism of action associated with tight oligopoly and price leadership as analysed in the Commission's general report on parallel pricing.[6] Clearly an analysis of market behaviour, rather than market structure alone, is essential if the OFT is to establish the likelihood of a monopoly situation under this alternative criterion. Relatively few references have been made with this criterion specifically in mind. Examples are bread and flour (under the similar provision of the earlier legislation), diazo copying materials and insulated electric wires and cables (under the 1973 Act), and a number of professional services, e.g. architects' and surveyors' fee scales. If an enquiry by the Commission should be initiated, the Commission's task in formally establishing that the conditions of the Act are met is clearly more difficult than with the simpler 'single firm' criterion.

The concept of 'abuse' of market dominance, the cornerstone of Article 86 of the Treaty of Rome, is also not to be found explicitly in the British legislation. Of course the legislation is founded upon the possibility that market power can be misused and as has been noted above, a reference is not likely to be made to the Commission without some grounds for suspicion of the behaviour or performance of the leading firms. Yet the authorities are at pains to emphasise that the initiation of a Monopolies Commission enquiry carries no implication of guilt. Instead under the earlier statutes, if the Monopolies Commission confirmed that a monopoly situation did indeed exist in the supply of the goods described in the reference, then it had to report whether those monopoly conditions or any 'things done...as a result of, or for the purpose of preserving those conditions operate or may be expected to operate against the public interest.' The Commission could be given a reference limited to the facts when it would not have to decide whether the conditions or the 'things done' operated against the public interest. There has only been one such reference. No attempt was made to indicate what the 'things done' might be. In the 1973 Act the phrase 'things done' has disappeared and the Commission is to consider 'steps (by way of uncompetitive practices or otherwise)...taken ...for the purpose of exploiting or maintaining the monopoly situation' and 'actions or omissions attributable to the monopoly situation'. This is largely a technical change. But it is of some interest that in a list of 'acts or omissions' which may be the subject of a limited enquiry by the Commission is 'any preference given to any person (whether by way of discrimination in respect of prices or in respect of priority of supply or otherwise)'. The 'public interest' is not defined though the Acts include some pointers. Those listed in the 1973 statute are something of a mixture of means and ends but include 'the desirability of maintaining and promoting effective competition between persons supplying goods and services in the UK'. This change may appear to reflect a more positive commitment to competition, but in fact no major change should be expected in the Commission's interpretation of the public interest. The Act merely spells out the sort of considerations that have influenced the Commission in recent years. The attitude to the practice of discrimination therefore remains neutral. In contrast to the prohibition of Article 86, it is for the Monopolies Commission to decide whether price discrimination, as operated in any particular case, has effects which are against the public interest. It may then make recommendations designed to eliminate these effects, including termination of the practice. If accepted by the Government, its recommendations may be implemented by negotiation or by statutory order. The reports of the Commission, covering a variety of industries, reveal that discriminatory practices are indeed widespread. There has been some variation in the Commission's reaction in its different reports, however. It is of interest how far this variation is consistent with the brief analysis of the economics of price discrimination in the first part of this chapter.

At the outset it should be emphasised that the Commission has offered few 'expressions of principles' on the practice and when it has these have invariably been guarded. The Commission is disinclined to establish any body of 'case law' on this (or any other) subject, insisting on judging each case on its merits. In this respect it operates quite differently from the European Commission which is charged with interpreting and enforcing legal rules. One of the few general statements of the Commission can be found in the chemical fertilisers report:

> It seems to us that in the absence of effective price
> competition a monopoly supplier can generally speaking
> best serve the public interest by ensuring that so far as may
> be practicable his price for any one product to any
> particular consumer or class of consumer reasonably
> reflects the true cost of supplying the product to that
> consumer. But we cannot regard this as a rule to be applied
> indiscriminately (*sic*).[7]

Without the qualification, this statement expresses the view that welfare is promoted by the resource allocation rules associated with competition and that the task of monopoly policy is, as far as is practicable, to bring about the competitive outcome including the eradication of discrimination. But the qualification is clear. And it is emphasised in other reports. Thus, in electrical equipment for motor vehicles, the Commission uncovered a whole host of discriminatory practices but insisted 'We do not think that price differentiation must necessarily be adverse to the public interest'.[8] The matter for consideration is in what circumstances the Commission has insisted that prices should be cost related and in what circumstances it has approved exceptions.

The great majority of the firms investigated by the Commission have enjoyed substantial shares of the market as defined by the goods described in the reference (sufficient one suspects to constitute a dominant position under the interpretation of Article 86 referred to earlier in this paper, assuming the UK is understood to constitute a 'substantial part' of the Common Market). In analysing the views of the Commission on the discriminatory practices of such firms it is convenient to begin with the effects on competition between the selling firms.

The Commission has generally been critical of price discrimination by dominant firms aimed at eliminating competition, containing the threat represented by any existing competition or preventing the emergence of new competition. It has not uncovered many clear-cut examples of predatory price discrimination. Localised price cutting by a fighting company of British Oxygen Company remains the outstanding historical case.[9] Hoffman–La Roche was criticised for low priced sales to hospitals intended to keep competition out of the market and the Commission recommended that the company should not differentiate between customers and classes of customers except to the extent to which this was 'justified by normal commerical considerations such as savings in cost arising from bulk supply'.[10] Courtaulds was charged with selective price cutting 'as a means of protecting the monopoly position against the impact of competition'.[11] Yet the Commission has not universally condemned this form of discrimination. Thus in one report it noted of Joseph Lucas that 'we have little doubt that for some years coils for initial equipment were supplied at a loss in order to discourage vehicle manufacturers from placing their orders with AC-Delco'[12] but did not criticise the company. It went on:

> It would in our view be unrealistic to suggest that price
> differentiation for the purpose of meeting competition at the
> point where that competition is having most effect must be
> improper...Although it may be difficult at times –
> particularly when one party is much more powerful than the
> other – to distinguish between price differentiation that
> intensifies competition and that which is intended to
> suppress competition we do not consider that Lucas can be
> said to have abused its position in this respect.[13]

Although this conclusion may have been surprising as Lucas had almost 80 per cent of the market and yet incurred losses, the general point made in this quotation goes to the heart of the Commission's problem. 'Meeting' and 'suppressing' competition are both dynamic responses to market conditions and may be characterised by similar cost–price relationships on particular transactions. It may be impossible to distinguish between them even by the most detailed analysis of market structure and behaviour.

A case in which the Commission had less difficulty in arriving at its verdict was starch and glucose in which the leading firm was Brown and Polson. Discriminatory pricing on a wide scale was observed which, according to the Commission, 'must in considerable measure reflect competition among the suppliers'.[14] Brown and Polson's market share was only 43.44 per cent, however, and this case represents a clear example where the Commission hoped that price discrimination would help to loosen the degree of oligopolistic co-ordination. In its general report on parallel pricing the Commission also recognised that discriminatory pricing might serve to undermine the discipline of highly structured oligopolies and would not necessarily operate against the public interest.

In the Brown and Polson case much of the discrimination took the form of discounts. The Commission's reports reveal the wide variety of discount structures encountered in industry. Because of the practical difficulties of relating all discounts to costs it is not surprising that discount structures are invariably technically discriminatory and have presented the Commission with some difficulties. In its report on electric lamps, the Commission offered one of its rare statements of principle.

> The prices to individual buyers should be related to the cost of supplying them and to the value of the business to the supplier. Since distribution costs vary with the quantities delivered the most appropriate method, and the one most conducive to efficient distribution, is a suitable scale of discounts related to the size or value of individual consignments. We would, however, see no objection in the circumstances of this industry to terms which also, if a manufacturer so wished, give some recognition to the size of the whole order (covering more than one consignment) or to the value of the total business which a buyer places with him. We would also see no objection to the provision of different scales of discounts for wholesalers, retailers and other buyers if the manufacturers considered it desirable to give wholesalers and retailers some extra

> reward in recognition of their part in selling and
> distributing. We can see no reason, however, for any
> differentiation in treatment between one class of user buyer
> and another which is not related to the cost or value of the
> business to the supplier.[15]

This is not unequivocal preference for cost-related discount structures, although the Commission did in fact recommend in this case that the quantity terms given by lamp component manufacturers should not be based 'otherwise than upon the quantities purchased'. Also in the case of Courtaulds the Commission did not consider special prices to large users were justified as large orders 'do not appear to produce sufficient economies to justify discounts'.[16] In other cases discounts, arbitrary in relation to costs, have not been criticised, however – glass is one case and wire ropes another. Loyalty discounts and discounts explicitly linked to exclusive dealing are more often than not criticised. Thus Metal Box (with a market share of 77 per cent in metal containers) had a complex discount structure which was accepted as broadly cost related. But an overriding discount, conditional on exclusive buying, and an incentive discount over and above the normal discount were criticised as prejudicial to the main competitors.[17] The main case in which a loyalty discount was not criticised was flat glass.[18] Ordinary quantity discount structures can have similar effects of binding particular customers more closely to existing sellers. This is particularly the case with discounts related to total turnover although these have not always been criticised by the Commission.

It is of some interest to consider next the use of price discrimination as a means of increasing a seller's short-run profits. Price discrimination observed in practice rarely matches the models of discriminating monopoly exactly, for discrimination is usually aimed as much at holding or extending a firm's market share as at exploiting its present share. An example which combines both aspects is 'two tier pricing' as between original equipment and replacement markets. This has been condemned in a number of cases, most notably electrical equipment for motor vehicles:

> We believe that the practice is pursued for the purpose of
> maintaining market dominance and that the position of
> dominance so achieved can be used to secure an excessive
> rate of profit overall. We regard the practice therefore as
> objectionable in principle and against the public interest in
> as much as it tends to perpetuate the dominance of
> individual component manufacturers in their particular
> fields, eliminating competition and providing opportunities
> for excessive profits.[19]

Side by side with this example of third degree discrimination can be set a number of cases of price discrimination between different buyers or classes of buyers. British Oxygen with 96 per cent of the oxygen market at the time of the enquiry, was an early example. Having found its pricing policy to be against the public interest, the Commission declared:

> In our view the underlying principles should be that there should be no discrimination either between individual consumers or between classes of consumers in particular circumstances, that the scale of charges should be based on relevant costs, and that they should be made known to all consumers.[20]

The Commission's criticisms were undoubtedly stimulated by the high level of profits reported in these cases. It did not give particular attention to the output (resource allocation) aspect of discrimination except to note in the electrical equipment case that the discrimination practised may have been in the companies' *private* interests; for example, in order to exploit scale economies.[21]

Turning now to the effects of sellers' price discrimination on competition between the buying firms, the Commission has had little to say on this aspect. Most of its comments have concerned the issue of fairness between buyers, the issue that seems to underlie the reference to discrimination in Article 86. Thus in criticising Courtaulds' discrimination in favour of its own subsidiaries: 'a preference given to one company implies discrimination against others, and the special aspect of Courtaulds' position is that companies which are, or feel they are put to a disadvantage by Courtaulds' pricing or supply preferences have no alternative supplier to turn to'[22] although in other cases, e.g. electrical equipment for motor vehicles, it has felt that, despite discrimination, buyers were large enough to look after their own interests. There are those who feel that the disadvantage of the smaller buyers in the face of discrimination in favour of larger firms has been neglected in UK anti-trust. The Bolton Committee on Small Firms took this view, particularly in the context of retail trade. Having argued that scale economies to large retailers are 'comparatively slight', it went on: 'We do not believe that these true cost savings wholly account for the very large price differentials achieved by some multiples. In these cases the distributors are using their great buying power to exact concessionary prices.'[23] So long as competition between the multiples continued there need be no detriment to the consumer but, in the long run, it argued, 'the benefit to the public is likely to be transitory and may be dearly bought in terms of a long term reduction of competition in the industry'.

The Committee considered the desirability of legislation on the lines of the US Robinson–Patman Act but recognised the force of the critical comment on the operation of that Act at least as far as the protection of competition and consumer interests is concerned. Instead, it recommended that the Monopolies Commission be asked to investigate the general problem of the market power exercised by large firms through their buying policies. So far this recommendation has not been acted upon. Complaints by aggrieved buyers will have to be considered in any particular enquiry of the Commission (as in the cellulosic fibres case for example). But, until the last year or so, the Commission has had relatively few enquiries involving consumer goods handled by the retail trade and hence little opportunity to comment upon the development referred to by the Bolton Committee.

Another aspect which has received little adverse comment by the Commission over the years is discrimination in the matter of freight charges. There was no criticism of systems of uniform delivered prices, for example, in the industrial and medical gases, chemical fertilisers, flat glass, metal containers or wire ropes cases, although other discriminatory behaviour was criticised in at least some of these reports and there was a critical minority report in the first two cases, and although uniform and non-uniform delivered price systems existed side by side in the metal container industry. The only report which has so far found uniform delivered prices to be against the public interest is plasterboard.[24] British Plasterboard were the sole UK producer and a significant reason for the Commission's decision in this case was the view that entry could be inhibited by the practice, given the importance of transport costs and the location of the company's plants in relation to sources of raw material. It recommended British Plasterboard should adopt a system of differential delivered prices, prices varying according to transport costs to the 419 haulage zones used by the company in its internal costing. In its way this is one of the most dramatic Commission recommendations on the subject of discrimination; in it the Commission recognises that there can be discrimination without what it tends to call 'price differentiation'; it accepts that its recommendation could have regional effects but considers that these are best dealt with separately from the effects of competition; and it recommends a quite precise alternative system which it believes practicable.

This review of the treatment of discrimination in a number of the Commission's reports shows that the major concern has been with the effects of discriminatory behaviour on actual and potential competition at the seller stage. From time to time it has made observations on the practice which imply a preference for the static rules of resource allocation, but its application of such rules has been heavily qualified.[25] Its reports frequently place discrimination in a dynamic context, objecting to the practice if it seems designed to reduce competition and accepting it if competition would otherwise be less effective. It cannot be claimed, perhaps, that on any particular aspect of the practice the Commission has always been consistent. There are a number of reasons why apparent inconsistency can occur. These no doubt include the varying impact of complaints from aggrieved parties in particular cases; difficulties in some cases in obtaining the necessary cost information to establish the extent and magnitude of discrimination; the extent of other practices by the monopolist which the Commission is inclined to criticise and which may overwhelm the effects of price discrimination; and differences in the Commission's judgement of the effect of the practice on the public interest in different cases, particularly over such a long period as from 1948. The Commission must also give consideration to the practicality of its recommendations. Thus the discrimination inherent in discounts with exclusivity provisions can more readily be set aside than can discriminatory quantity discounts; uniform delivered pricing can more easily be replaced by a system relating prices more closely to freight costs when a firm produces relatively few products than when it produces thousands; a rigid non-discriminatory price structure can more fairly be imposed on a 100 per cent monopolist than on a firm with competitors who could not be similarly treated. UK monopoly policy, after all, is concerned in the last analysis with intervention, and the design of sensible recommendations for dealing with any misuse of monopoly power is as important as sensible analysis of such misuse. And because UK policy is administrative rather than legal in character some degree of apparent inconsistency may be the inevitable price of the policy's greater flexibility.

Conclusions

So far Article 86 has had little direct effect on UK monopoly policy (outside the field of merger control) in some contrast to Article 85. Consideration has had to be given to possible changes in the measurement of market shares under the UK legislation as progress is made towards a unified EEC market and an increasing degree of consultation is taking place between the UK and EEC agencies on matters of interpretation and enforcement of the Treaty of Rome competition policy rules. The visible effects so far are few, but this is unlikely to prove a permanent state of affairs. If more vigorous action is taken by the European Commission on abuse of dominant positions, UK firms could fall foul of the Treaty. Thus, if the UK is regarded as a substantial part of the Common Market and if a UK firm's discriminatory tactics did affect inter-EEC trade, e.g. by making imports from other states more difficult, then Article 86 would apply. Indeed, a firm could find itself subject to investigation under both the EEC and the

UK policies. Under the EEC arrangements it could expect to be embroiled in argument over the definition of the relevant market, the analysis of market dominance and the meaning of 'dissimilar conditions' and 'equivalent transactions'. But if dominance and discrimination were established it would have to expect prohibition of its practice with no reference to the 'public interest' or to any possible benefits of its discrimination. Under the UK arrangements it could expect a more formal approach to the identification of monopoly but more flexibility (and uncertainty) in identification of the practice of discrimination and the interpretation of its effects in the light of the public interest as conceived by the Monopolies Commission. Unlike the European Commission the Monopolies Commission would not be bound to initiate action to stop the practice by the making of an appropriate recommendation. However, were parallel proceedings to be instituted and if a conflict of laws did occur then the EEC law would prevail.

Although there are clear differences between the EEC and the UK approaches to the practice of price discrimination they are similar in one respect. Price discrimination concerns the behaviour of firms in markets where competition is less than perfectly effective. As they have evolved so far, both policics have been directed at that behaviour rather than at the conditions which have rendered competition to some degree or other ineffective. Article 86 can be activated only when a firm occupies a dominant market position and discriminatory behaviour by such a firm is prohibited. It is only under the new controls on mergers that market structure itself can be controlled. The Monopolies Commission has had to investigate markets with a wide variety of structures though usually with a single dominant firm. It has discretion about whether to criticise discrimination as being against the public interest but when it has done so its recommendations have been aimed at the behaviour of the firms operating the practice. Although, in contrast to the European Commission, the Monopolies Commission can make recommendations bearing directly on the structure of the market investigated, it has rarely done so. Market structure is not easily changed and if the change is from a higher to a lesser degree of monopoly or oligopoly it cannot be certain that behaviour and performance will also change, or change for the better. This is not to argue on any general grounds that a more vigorous action on market structure by the UK anti-trust agencies as a whole might not be justified in present circumstances; nor that such action might not prove an effective way of limiting abusive market behaviour, for the deterrent power of anti-trust should not be underestimated. But in the context of price discrimination the Monopolies Commission's approach can be justified. Price discrimination is so widespread as to its forms and the types of market in which it can be operated, and its effects on the public interest are so various, that the discretionary approach has much to commend it. Moreover, such an approach is supported by the economic analysis of price discrimination which does not justify either universal condemnation or universal approval of the practice.

Notes

1 For a recent discussion see B. S. Yamey, 'Predatory price cutting, notes and comments', *Journal of Law and Economics* 15 (1972), pp. 129–42.
2 The most useful review of the many forms price discrimination can take in practice is still F. Machlup, 'Characteristics and types of price discrimination'. In NBER, *Business Concentration and Price Policy* (Princeton University Press: Princeton, 1955).
3 On the Robinson–Patman Act see A. D. Neale, *The Anti-trust Laws of the USA* (Cambridge University Press: London, 1970), chapter 9.
4 See G. Canenbley, 'Price discrimination and EEC Cartel Law: a review of the Kodak Decision of the Commission of the European Communities', *Anti-trust Bulletin* 17 (1972), pp. 269–81; F. S. Schemerman, 'Reflections on the Kodak Decision and price discrimination under Article 85 of the Rome Treaty', *Journal of World Trade Law* 5 (1971), pp. 533–44.
5 See 'Economic information system for monopoly references', *Trade and Industry* 14 (1974), p. 158.
6 Monopolies Commission, *Parallel Pricing* (Cmnd 5330, July 1973).
7 Monopolies Commission, *Report on the Supply of Chemical Fertilisers* (HC 267, 1959), para. 669.
8 Monopolies Commission, *Report on the Supply of Electrical Equipment for Mechanically Propelled Land Vehicles* (HC 21, 1963), para. 996.
9 Monopolies Commission, *Report on the Supply of Certain Industrial and Medical Gases* (HC 13, 1956).
10 Monopolies Commission, *A Report on the Supply of Chlordiazepoxide and Diazepam* (HC 197, 1973), para. 238.
11 Monopolies Commission, *A Report on the Supply of Man-made Cellulosic Fibres* (HC 130, 1968), para. 193.
12 Monopolies Commission (see note (8) above), para. 1000.
13 *Ibid.*, para. 1060.
14 Monopolies Commission, *A Report on the Supply of Starch, Glucose and Modified Starches* (HC 615, 1971), para. 167.
15 Monopolies Commission, *Second Report on the Supply of Electric Lamps* (HC 4, 1968), para. 81.
16 Monopolies Commission, (see note (11) above), para. 185.
17 Monopolies Commission, *A Report on the Supply of Metal Containers* (HC 6, 1970), paras. 311 and 320.
18 Monopolies Commission, *A Report on the Supply of Flat Glass* (HC 83, 1968), para. 147.
19 Monopolies Commission (see note (8) above), para. 996.
20 Monopolies Commission, *Industrial and Medical Gases* (HC 13, 1956), para. 275.
21 Monopolies Commission (see note (8) above), para. 993.
22 Monopolies Commission (see note (11) above), para. 193.
23 Bolton Committee of Inquiry on Small Firms, *Small Firms* (Cmnd 4811, 1973), paras. 16 and 20.

24 Monopolies Commission, *A Report on the Supply of Plasterboard* (HC 1, 1974), para. 153.

25 More so than conceded by a recent critic. See A. Knight, *Private Enterprise and Public Intervention: Courtaulds Experience* (Allen & Unwin: London, 1974), chapter 6.

COMMENT

J. HARDIE

It is reassuring to have from one of those responsible for the enforcement of anti-trust policy a paper on price discrimination which accepts
the practice as a fact of life, and often a desirable fact at that. It is easy
for economists with a simple grounding in welfare economics to take
any variations in price/cost ratios as evidence of a discrepancy between
marginal cost and price: and hence *prima facie* culpable. Even those
who have gone to the trouble of reading Pigou and Joan Robinson on
the subject can find it difficult to relate their conclusions to real
commercial situations. Dr Howe's chapter is a substantial step towards
bringing theory and practice together.

I want to start with two, short, unconnected points.

First, the practical difficulties involved in calculating the margins
earned on different products, or on the same product sold in different
markets, are substantial. In almost all cases of price discrimination, the
products are produced in conditions of joint costs – of manufacturing,
marketing, research and development, and everything else. It is the
conventional wisdom that product profitability can only be computed
by the use of arbitrary allocations of cost between the jointly produced
products. Such arbitrary allocations are the responsibility of account-
ants. The results are treated by economists with a mixture of despair
and respect. That is, they are respected as emanating from Peats or
Cooper Bros., and hence being in accordance with best accountancy
practice. The despair arises from the knowledge that the methodological
basis of the calculations is unexplored and hence untrustworthy. Of
course, some figures of some kind have to be used. But if you are
shooting a man, you like to know not only that the ballistics expert has
done his best: but also that his best is pretty good. This condition does
not seem to me to be fulfilled at present. More generally the most
obvious area where progress might practically be made in anti-trust
enforcement is in clearing up the relationship between accountancy
evidence and the evidence which economists need to identify particular
industrial situations or behaviour. The computation of profitability on

capital employed for the business as a whole is another area of monstrous conceptual and practical difficulty.

Second, there is the question of subsidisation. I am not talking here about the negative taxation used by governments to make, for example, bread cheaper for all or part of the population. But the same term is misleadingly used to describe the situation where a company, for straightforward commercial reasons, earns more margin on a product in one market than in another. This is often called cross-subsidisation. I think that it follows from chapter 6 that this means nothing more (in the case of similar products) than that price discrimination is taking place. If this is so, it would perhaps be better to drop the term 'cross-subsidisation'. In the case of home rates versus export, for example, it will often be true that net margins are higher at home than abroad. This does raise questions of equity of the kind which the paper mentions – the home buyers are paying more than the overseas buyers. But this is no more nor less than a difficulty raised by price discrimination in general.

I would now like to turn to the question of the relationship between market dominance and price discrimination. If you accept the analysis of Martin Howe's paper, it appears very unlikely that the existence or not of price discrimination can or should count for very much in the assessment of monopoly (or cartel) seller situations.

In the case of oligopoly without agreement (that is, commercial rivalry between a number of comparatively well-matched suppliers) the freight-absorption paradigm makes the point very clearly that the possibility of price discrimination will much increase the interpenetration of markets and crossing of product boundaries that are an important characteristic of competitive markets. There will always be local quasi-monopolies, both in the strict geographical sense, and in relation to particular groups of customers. Companies will always for one reason or another be more or less strong in various segments of the overall product market. If a company which is strong in one area is to be challenged there, its rivals will be much more eager to do so if they can limit the loss of net margin to the point where it is necessary to compete successfully, without losing profit on the intra-marginal business which they already have in their own area of strength.

This is a benefit of price discrimination in terms of what Martin Howe calls loosening up oligopoly. What of the costs? The main one may be that mentioned in Article 86(1), that competition at the level of the customers will be distorted if some buyers get their inputs more cheaply than others. But this has little to do with the dominance of the seller and for it to amount to much two conditions have to be fulfilled. First, the price discrimination must involve price differentiation. For example, in the freight absorption case the effect of price discrimination is actually to standardise the price at which customers buy – which presumably helps competition between them. Second, the input must be significant, or rather the savings on it significant as a proportion of total cost. This is not usually the case.

The supermarket example does of course represent a possible example of discrimination harmful at the level of the customers' industry. The point here, however, is not that a particular supplier offers discriminatory terms, but that most suppliers are made to. The danger is monopsony – or at least power on that side of the market. It can only be tackled by wholesale reference of suppliers to the Monopolies Commission, or by a Robinson–Patman Act. Piecemeal condemnation of the odd cheap deal agreed to by one particular supplier, dominant or not, will not achieve much.

Why should the fact that the discrimination is practised by a dominant firm or a cartel rather than by rival oligopolists make any difference?

First, the definition of monopoly might seem to exclude *ab initio* the argument that price-discrimination is used to invade other markets, and hence increase competition there. But the fact – which will be a fact in every case – that the demand curve is downward sloping shows that a lowering of price in certain markets or to certain customers will gain business: and that business must be at the expense of other products which are competing for a place among the customer's purchases. The fact that these products are not so closely related to the monopolist's as to include their producers in the definition of the industry which the monopolist dominates, does not on the face of it matter. So long as competition is deemed to be increased when a product penetrates to new customers, then competition is increased by a dominant firm's price discrimination as much as by an oligopolist's.

Then it may be that the dominant firm achieves very high profits via price discrimination. But the key question then is whether or by what criteria the profits are excessive. This is nothing to do with price discrimination. If the profits are too high, it does not follow that they should be lowered by eliminating price discrimination. An equiproportional cut in all prices will be preferable if the price discrimination has good effects on output and market penetration. The questions of the level of prices on the one hand and the variety of price/cost ratios on the other are quite distinct.

Third, the price discrimination may be predatory – i.e. designed to use superior strength to eliminate rivals from the market, and create or reinforce a dominant position. The paper mentions the difficulties of distinguishing predatoriness from the normal commercial behaviour of a company meeting competition or entering a new market. The main practical difficulty may be as much a matter of evidence as anything else. That is, the crucial question will be with what intention certain behaviour was undertaken. Even though, as usually happens, the company is quite open with the Commission, there will be many difficulties. The motives for accepting a low return will often have been mixed. Different members of the board or the management team will have had different motives. Anyway, everyone will have forgotten why they did it. The fact, if it is so, that low profits or losses resulted does not prove much as to intention: the gap between intention and results will always be wide, and no ex-post linkage is justifiable.

I conclude therefore that predatoriness can only rarely be proved with the certainty required for justice: and that the other defects of price discrimination may well be substantial, but they have not got much to do with dominance.

7
Competition laws which apply to member states

P. MATHIJSEN

Before examining in some detail the competition rules of the European Economic Community (EEC) applying to member states, it seems necessary to make a few remarks of a more general nature. The first of these remarks concerns the role assigned to the competition rules within the EEC and the second is intended to define which acts or measures are regulated by the EEC competition rules as opposed to those which, although they affect competition, fall within the province of other EEC Treaty provisions.

Attention should be drawn in the first place to the implications of Article 3(f) on which all the other Treaty provisions concerning competition are based. EEC Article 3 provides that 'for the purposes set out in Article 2, the activities of the Community shall include...the institution of a system ensuring that competition in the common market is not distorted'. This provision presupposes the existence of an economic system, in which both public and private institutions exercise economic control. Indeed, only in such a situation can competition exist not just between private undertakings but also between private and public institutions and even among the latter. In a state-controlled economy on the contrary there seems to be no role for competition. This might seem obvious to most people but it is certainly not accepted by all and therefore needs to be reasserted. It may also be said that the market economy system on which the EEC Treaty is based is that which prevailed within the member states both when the Communities were established and when they were enlarged. This economic system naturally follows from the liberal democratic political system to which Western European countries are so deeply attached, since democracy implies a separation of powers and a distribution of those powers over as many agents as is compatible with an efficient economic system.

The economic system envisaged by the European Treaties thus requires competition to be undistorted, which does not mean that it demands 'perfect' competition (*laissez faire*). To define the requirements of the Treaty rules, one generally refers to 'effective' competition i.e. economic circumstances under which producers and users enjoy a certain amount of liberty in their choice of what, where and how to produce or to buy.

Furthermore, such liberty is only possible when the goods that are produced or purchased can be freely exported and imported within the whole Community. It is one of the main objectives of the Common Market to establish and maintain precisely this free movement of goods, which is both a consequence of and a prerequisite for competition in the EEC. It follows that any act or conduct which interferes or threatens to interfere with this free movement violates the rules on competition and it can therefore also be said that the criterion for determining whether or not a given example of market behaviour (in the broadest sense) is prohibited under these rules is to be found in the answer to the question 'does this behaviour endanger the fulfilment of the objectives of the Common Market?'[1] In other words, does it put an obstacle in the way of free trade? If the answer is 'yes' then the activity under investigation violates the EEC Treaty. As will be remembered, many existing obstacles to free trade were eliminated as a result of the establishment of the customs union: customs duties on imports and exports, quantitative restrictions and measures having equivalent effect to the above have been abolished; others such as the so-called non-tariff trade barriers are in the lengthy process of being eliminated. And while total freedom of movement of goods will only be possible within an economic and monetary union, one of the objectives of the EEC competition rules is to prevent the establishment of new obstacles to free trade between member states.

It is further necessary to realise that the application of the competition rules is not limited to private undertakings and their market behaviour. These rules also apply to the member states in so far as their direct or indirect intervention in economic activity creates or may create specific distortions. Although national competition rules normally do not apply to the state acting in its capacity as public authority, the member states, since the integration of the nine national markets into a single common market, have been in a position to influence inter-state trade and competition very strongly. Whether they act directly, for instance as operators of public services or of state monopolies, or indirectly either through state-controlled enterprises or by improving the competitive position of private undertakings with state aids, the member states must abide by the rules of the game. Especially nowadays when state intervention shows a strong tendency to expand, it would be unthinkable to create and operate a customs union let alone an economic and monetary union if the member states were not submitted to certain rules in regard to those activities which might interfere with the normal functioning of the Common Market.

A distinction must now be made between those state activities which are regulated by the EEC competition rules and those which although 'distorting the conditions of competition in the Common Market' (EEC Article 101) must be eliminated through harmonisation of laws. The former constitute 'specific' distortions while the latter are to be considered as 'general' distortions; specific distortions result from acts which affect – favourably or unfavourably – persons or groups of persons; while general distortions result from differences between the provisions laid down by law, regulation or administrative action in member states. Consequently it is also correct to say that specific distortions which are prohibited by the EEC competition rules create discrimination while general distortions do not. For instance, in the case Wilhelm versus Bundeskartellamt the Court held that 'Article 7 of the EEC Treaty prohibits the Member States from applying their anti-cartel laws differently according to the nationality of the interested parties, but does not concern the difference in treatment resulting from differences existing between the lègislation of the Member States, as long as these provisions affect all the persons within their province on the basis of objective criteria and without regard to their nationality'.[2] This is also the reason why in the case of specific distortions the activities in question are 'prohibited' altogether unless exemption is granted by the Commission and in the second case it is provided only that the Council can issue directives to eliminate general distortions if necessary. In practice this means that, of all the Treaty provisions concerning distortions of competition, i.e. Article 7 (discrimination on the basis of nationality), Article 37 (state monopolies: discrimination between nationals of member states regarding conditions under which goods are procured and marketed), Article 85 (agreements, decisions and concerted practices which may affect trade and have the objective or result of distorting competition), Article 86 (abuses of dominant positions affecting trade between member states), Article 90 (public undertakings or undertakings to which member states grant special or exclusive rights), Article 92 (aids granted by a member state which distort competition and affect inter-state trade), Article 95 *et seq.* (discriminatory taxation of products of other member states), and Article 100 *et seq.* (elimination of those differences between national provisions which distort competition), only Articles 7, 37, 85, 86, 90 and 92 constitute 'competition rules' in the strict sense. Of this group Articles 7, 37, 90 and 92 *et seq.* concern member states and will now be examined.

EEC Article 7: discrimination on grounds of nationality

Article 7 prohibits discrimination on grounds of nationality by natural and legal persons as well as by member states. Discrimination consists of 'either treating similar situations differently, or different situations in the same way'.[3] Since, as pointed out above, all cases of specific distortion constitute discrimination of some kind (which does not mean that all cases of discrimination violate the competition rules), this provision enters our examination only in so far as the prohibited discrimination may affect competition within the Common Market, i.e. affect trade between member states. For the definition of this criterion one must refer to the judgement of the Court of Justice in the Consten and Grundig versus Commission case where the Court held that competition within the Common Market is affected when 'the implementation of the objectives of the Common Market is jeopardised'.[4]

In most cases, however, discrimination by member states which affects inter-state trade will have effects equivalent to quantitative restrictions and are consequently prohibited under EEC Article 30 *et seq*. This is the case for instance when preference is given to national products over imports in public purchases. Article 7 will therefore be used as a competition rule only in those cases where discrimination on grounds of nationality which affects inter-state trade is not prohibited by other Treaty provisions.

EEC Article 37: state monopolies

Article 37 concerns monopolistic rights of the member states in the buying or selling of goods. Services do not come within the scope of Article 37 as the Court of Justice decided in the Sacchi case.[5]

These monopolistic powers may be either exercised by the member states themselves or delegated to others. Since the purpose of state monopolies is to control the import, export and sale of goods their (potential) effect on trade between member states doesn't need to be demonstrated. The EEC Treaty does not require member states to abolish their state monopolies but, as with other exclusive rights (e.g. property rights), although their existence is not questioned the use that can be made of those rights is strictly limited and member states must progressively adjust their commercial monopolies so as to ensure they give rise to no discrimination regarding the conditions under which goods are procured from other countries and marketed within the member state. In other words, and this follows from the place of Article 37 in the Treaty (Part two, Title I, Chapter 2) – existing mono-polistic rights may not be used to prevent the free movement of goods. This 'freedom' must be strictly interpreted; according to the Court of

Justice nothing may stand in the way of inter-state trade: even an automatically granted import licence is considered to violate this rule.[6]

For this reason member states have found it simpler to abolish certain monopolies altogether rather than work out what adjustments are needed; Italy has abolished or is in the process of abolishing the following state monopolies: bananas, cigarette lighters, flints, salt, cigarette-paper and manufactured tobacco; France has abolished state monopolies in matches, powder and explosives, basic slag, potash and tobacco.

It should be noted, however, that the Treaty does not require the adjustment of monopolies in production; indeed, within a real common market where goods can be freely imported and exported everywhere regional specialisation in production cannot severely affect trade. Furthermore, mention should also be made of the fact that the exercise of monopolistic power in regard to direct imports from third countries remains unimpaired; for 'products coming from third countries which are in free circulation in Member States' (EEC Article 9(2)), the Commission has considered that monopolistic rights in relations with third countries constitute 'measures of commercial policy taken in accordance with this Treaty' (EEC Article 115); consequently, deflection of trade resulting from the implementation of Article 9(2) can be corrected by protective measures such as quantitative restrictions by the member state concerned, with the Commission's permission.

However, the subject of state monopolies has lost much of its practical importance since most of them have now been adjusted, if not altogether abolished.

EEC Article 90: public enterprises

Article 90(1) imposes an obligation on member states in respect of 'public undertakings and undertakings to which Member States grant special or exclusive rights'; this wording implies that the member states are in a position to dictate the market behaviour of these undertakings. In other words the Treaty assumes that member states 'control' their public enterprises and those to which they grant special or exclusive rights. It seems, therefore, useless to try and define what exactly is meant by 'public enterprises'. Although it appears safe to say that wholly state-owned undertakings are to be considered as 'public enterprises' and that this also applies when the state owns 51 per cent of the shares, there is no reason why state control may not be exercised with a lesser share of ownership.

Where member states have used these powers to 'instruct' the undertakings referred to in Article 90(1) to behave in a way which violates the rules of the Treaty, this Article now obliges these member states to stop using their powers in such a way and to refrain from doing so in the future. The maintenance of such 'instructions' by the member states would indeed be a 'measure contrary to the rules contained in the Treaty'. But Article 90(1) goes a step further in so far as it also obliges the member states to instruct those enterprises they control to abstain from all violations of the Treaty rules. Not giving such instructions is indeed equivalent to granting the undertakings referred to in Article 90(1) freedom to violate the Treaty and will thus constitute a 'measure contrary to the rules contained in the Treaty'.

Concretely speaking this means that if undertakings referred to in Article 90(1) violate certain Treaty obligations the member states can be held responsible, indeed Article 90(3) provides that the Commission may issue directives or decisions addressed to member states to ensure the implementation of Article 90. It also provides that member states may not 'instruct' undertakings they control to do certain things which would have been contrary to Treaty rules if done by the state itself; indeed, many rules apply only to member states and therefore cannot be violated by undertakings. Consequently it would be erroneous to speak of a Community policy towards public enterprises: there can be no such policy since the Treaty does not provide for one.

Article 90(2) provides for exceptions to the application of the Treaty rules in favour of 'undertakings entrusted with the operation of services of general economic interest'. This provision can be viewed as an 'escape clause' for certain undertakings. For instance, a post-office which prevents others from distributing mail will not be considered by the Commission to be abusing its dominant position. It is therefore up to the Commission to establish, on a case-by-case basis, whether or not the services rendered by an undertaking claiming to be exempted from certain Treaty obligations under Article 90(2) are 'of general economic interest'.

In its decision in the GEMA case[7] the Commission found that GEMA was not, despite its claim to the contrary, entrusted with the operation of services of general economic interest since neither the German law concerning copyrights nor the authorisation granted GEMA under Article 1 of this law contained anything to that effect.

In its judgement in the case of Luxembourg Public Prosecutor versus Muller *et al.*, the Court of Justice held that 'an undertaking which controls the most important waterway outlet of the State concerned, enjoys certain privileges in the conduct of its business and has close links with the public authority, can indeed come under EEC Article 90(2)'.[8]

More recently, in the Sacchi case[9] the Italian and German governments claimed that their national television systems were entrusted with the operation of services of general economic interest; the Court of Justice held that Article 90(1) allows member states to grant special or exclusive rights to certain undertakings, and to prevent other companies from competing with them, but that in fulfilling their tasks these public enterprises remain bound by the prohibition of discrimination. The fact that an enterprise entrusted with the operation of a service of general economic interest enjoys a monopoly position is not incompatible with Article 86 (which only prohibits the abuse of such a position).

It is interesting to note that if Article 90(2) grants exemption to undertakings this provision in fact applies to the member states and not to the undertakings themselves except where EEC Articles 77, 85 and 86 are concerned, since these are the only Treaty provisions which give the Commission direct rights with regard to undertakings. If, for instance, an undertaking entrusted with the operation of services of general economic interest were to refuse to purchase machinery because it was produced in another member state, the Commission would address itself not to the undertaking since in this field it has no powers to do so but to the member state concerned and would require it, possibly with a decision based on Article 90(3), to make the undertaking in question abandon this practice. The member state is in a position to do this since it 'controls' the undertaking through the granting of exclusive rights; any failure on the part of the state to do as instructed would be considered a violation of Article 90. If an undertaking referred to in Article 90(1), i.e. a public enterprise or firm to which a member state has granted special or exclusive rights, exercises preference in favour of national products then again the Commission's decision will be directed to the member state and not the enterprise itself. It has been argued that if the culprit is a so-called 'public enterprise', i.e. an undertaking which is directly controlled by a member state through its financial participation in the undertaking, then such a preference is in fact being applied by a state – through a public enterprise – and amounts to a measure having effects equivalent to those of a quantitative restriction which is prohibited by Article 30. This view tends to complicate the implementation of Article 90 since it makes a distinction between directly state-controlled and indirectly state-controlled undertakings; such a distinction does not seem to be justified.

Finally, in regard to Article 90(3) it must be mentioned that until now no such directive or decisions have been addressed to the member states.

It has often been stated that under the EEC Treaty provisions no distinction is made between so-called public and private undertakings because EEC Article 222 provides that 'this Treaty shall in no way prejudice the rules in Member States governing the system of property ownership'. It has been deduced from this provision that the EEC Treaty is not concerned with the nationalisation of private undertakings.

In principle this may be true, but it follows from the argument above that the Treaty imposes certain obligations on member states 'in the case of public undertakings and undertakings to which Member States grant special or exclusive rights' which it does not impose in the case of private undertakings. As stated above, the latter are covered mainly by EEC Articles 7, 85 and 86, but in Article 90(1) which deals with 'public enterprises' the Treaty refers to 'the rules contained in this Treaty'. As far as these undertakings are concerned the Commission must consider that certain kinds of behaviour which would not be objectionable on the part of private undertakings constitute violations of the Treaty by the member state which controls them. Being a 'public' undertaking, or an undertaking with special rights, the enterprises referred to in Article 90(1) must be considered to share some of the privileges and also some of the responsibilities of the member states themselves.

EEC Articles 92 to 94: state aids

It will be remembered that the 'system ensuring that competition in the Common Market is not distorted' was instituted 'for the purposes set out in Article 2' (EEC Article 3); at this point it might be useful to remind the reader of the fact that Article 2 sets out the fundamental objectives of the Community (harmonious development of economic activities throughout the Community, continuous and balanced expansion, increase in stability and accelerated raising of the standard of living) and also the main instruments or means through which these objectives are to be attained: establishment of a common market and progressive approximation of the economic policies of the member states. It is mainly the former of these means which is important in relation to state aids. And indeed, if the Common Market is the means to achieve the Treaty objectives, the establishment and proper functioning of the Market are of paramount importance.

From the point of view of undertakings, the Common Market appears as a geographical area where all enterprises operate under more or less similar economic conditions on the basis of their own capabilities and at their own risk. Industries in the various member states which operated behind protective barriers of all kinds until a few years ago are ready to accept the abolition of these barriers and meet competitors on their own ground on condition that such a challenge takes place under fair conditions; in other words that all sides abide by the 'rules of the game'. It follows that any state intervention in favour of one or more undertakings upsets the whole pattern. And this is why EEC Article 92(1) provides that 'any aid granted by a Member State or through State resources in any form whatsoever' is 'incompatible with the Common Market'. It goes without saying that assistance which has no effect beyond the borders of a given country does not affect the Common Market or the free movement of goods, i.e. 'trade between Member States'. Aids which do not affect such trade, and so do not affect competition between undertakings situated in different member states, are not considered incompatible. However, the draftsmen of the Treaty showed their realism in providing for exceptions to the general rule of incompatiblity of state aids with the Common Market since there are many cases where the full implementation of this rule would cause social distress or would prevent such distress from being relieved with the required urgency. As pointed out above, Article 2 gives as an objective of the Community 'an accelerated raising of standards of living' as well as 'the harmonious development of economic activities throughout the Community'. As the Court of Justice pointed out in the judgement in the Europemballage and Continental Can versus Commission case: the Treaty allows 'restraints on competition... under certain conditions because of the need to harmonise the various objectives of the Treaty'.[10]

The next question therefore concerns those restraints on competition in the form of state aids which are exceptions to the principle of incompatibility. In the first place it is of interest to point out that the Commission has for all practical purposes the exclusive right, subject to the legal control of the Court of Justice, to administer these exceptions. To this end member states are obliged to inform the Commission of any 'plans to grant or alter aid' (EEC Article 93(3)) in sufficient time to enable the Commission to submit its comments (two months according to the Court of Justice). If the Commission considers such aid to be incompatible (i.e. not coming within one of the exceptions), it will initiate a formal procedure thereby preventing the member state in question from putting the proposed measures into effect. This formal aspect is interesting in so far as it shows that the Commission has been entrusted with wide ranging powers in this field. Now what about the exceptions? The most important ones are regional development aids and industrial development aids which the Commission may consider 'to be compatible with the Common Market'. This means that although they affect competition and trade between the member states, i.e. do endanger the achievement of certain Treaty objectives, they can be accepted in order to facilitate the realisation of other objectives: delicate balancing of the priority of different objectives is needed, a judgement necessarily based not only on economic considerations but also taking into account social and political necessities. It will be clear that this presupposes wide discretionary powers for the Commission. On the other hand some legal certainty is required for the member states in their planning of regional and industrial development. This is one of the reasons why the Commission has, in close co-operation with the member states, established what is known as 'the principles concerning the general arrangements for regional aid', elaborated within the framework of the application of Articles 92 to 94 of the EEC Treaty.[11]

Unfortunately, the only point which is well known about these principles is the limitation of the amount of aid a member state may grant to an investor in the 'central regions' (that is, those parts of the Common Market which are industrially developed but face structural problems in adapting to current economic conditions) to 20 per cent of the total net value of the investment. There are other points which from the point of view of competition are much more important. One of these is 'regional specificity': the EEC Treaty admits restrictions on competition in order to facilitate the development of certain regions: consequently it must be established (1) that the region is in need of assistance compared to the other regions in the same country and in the Community as a whole and (2) that the proposed aids do really constitute an incentive to regional development. It is of course the Commission who, on the basis of information received from the interested member state, must establish these facts. In other words the Commission gets more and more involved with the economic policies of the member states and it is well known that these policies are not dictated only by social and economic considerations. But generally speaking it is possible, on the basis of statistics, to establish the general trend of the economic situation in a given region based on the level of investment, number of jobs created or lost, composition of the working population, emigration or immigration, rate of unemployment, average income, etc. The regional picture thus obtained can be compared to the general situation of the member state in question and of the Community as a whole. The latter of course is important since member states have a natural tendency to look only at their own problems.

Once it is established that the region a government intends to develop really constitutes a problem, the second question is whether or not the proposed aid system will contribute to the solution of that problem. Indeed, according to EEC Article 92(3)(c) only those aids which 'facilitate the development of certain...economic areas' can be considered by the Commission to be compatible with the Common Market. Any aids, the purpose of which is not to 'develop' an area (e.g. the saving of 'lame ducks'), can therefore not be accepted. Apart from the general question of whether or not assistance granted to undertakings can solve regional development problems, the form and the amount of aid granted should be such that competition and inter-state trade are distorted as little as possible.

As regards the more general question of the usefulness of aid to industry as an incentive to regional development a first distinction should be made between aid which aims at encouraging potential investors to invest in a given region and thereby creating employment (investment aids) and aid which is granted to existing industries in order to alleviate their production costs such as labour, raw materials and transport costs, etc. (production aids). Even in the case of investment aids the question can be asked whether in the long run, instead of giving financial aid directly to some undertakings (thereby putting them in a favourable competitive position) it would not be much better to improve the general economic, social and cultural infrastructure of the area in question: better roads and faster rail, better trained workers, better telecommunications, better schools and universities, better facilities for entertainment, better hospitals, etc. Is it an imprudent question to ask whether the millions which have been pumped into declining industries which have continued to decline would not have been better used from a social and economic point of view had they been invested in projects of general interest? Under the present system not only did most of the money go to a few firms with little or no results for the region as such, but the competitors of these firms in the rest of the Community were put at a disadvantage either by the fact that an undertaking which normally (i.e. under market conditions) would not have been created starts producing and selling, or because, with the help of the aid, the undertaking in question is in a position to sell at lower prices than would normally have been the case.

Whatever the answer to this general question may be it is generally accepted that investment aids can be a useful instrument of regional development if judiciously applied, i.e. where needed, when needed and only to those who need such aid. Alas, at the present time few governments have the courage to make such choices and are satisfied with incentives distributed at large, thereby paying a bonus to those firms which don't need them and not helping sufficiently when action is really required. That such policies can be extremely harmful for the functioning of the Common Market needs no further demonstration.

If investment aids are capable of jeopardising the attainment of the Treaty objectives, what is to be said of production aids? As previously stated, these are aids which directly reduce certain production costs, for instance the cost of labour. Do such aids really constitute an incentive to regional 'development' or do they simply aim to keep enterprises going which would otherwise be in difficulty? Furthermore, if such aid is granted 'across the board' to needy and non-needy enterprises alike what justification is there for this bonus to the efficient ones and for the others this disincentive to become more efficient? Such production aids have been justified as 'regional devaluation'. Technically speaking they can be compared to such a measure but only very partially, since a real devaluation makes imports more costly which is not the case here, and is normally accompanied by a series of measures such as credit restrictions intended as a brake on internal consumption; none of this, of course, happens when production aids are granted universally. The worst effect on competition that such production aids have is that, by allowing undertakings either to remain in business or to lower their prices, they have a direct effect on the competitive position of the beneficiaries and hence on trade between the member states while on the other hand the region itself does not necessarily profit by these aids to industry.

However, here also, it is recognised that such aids can under certain circumstances be a useful instrument for regional development.

Conclusion

State intervention in the economy can have direct and very harmful consequences for trade and competition between member states and consequently for the proper functioning of the Common Market. The Commission's task in administering the EEC competition rules applying to member states consists mainly of establishing priorities among the various objectives of the EEC Treaty and finding the right balance between the harmful consequences of the measures proposed or initiated by member states and the economic and social needs of so-called development areas in the Community. This requires insight not only into the particular economic and social problems of each member state but also into national and Community-wide political questions.

Notes

1 See judgement of the Court of Justice of 13 July 1966 in joined cases 56 and 58/64, Consten Grundig v. Commission. *Recueil de la jurisprudence de la cour* (hereinafter referred to as *Recueil*) XII (1966), p. 429.

2 Judgement of the Court of Justice of 13 February 1969 in case 14/68, Wilhelm versus Bundeskartellamt. *Recueil* XIV (1968), p. 1.

3 Judgement of the Court of Justice of 17 July 1963 in case 13/63, Italy v. Commission. *European Commission Report* (1963), p. 177.

4 See note (1) above.

5 Judgement of the Court of Justice of 30 April 1974 in case 155/73, Sacchi. *European Commission Report* (1974), p. 409.

6 See judgement of the Court of Justice of 15 December 1971 on joined cases 51 to 54/71, International Fruit Company v. Produktschap voor Groenten en Fruit. *European Commission Report* (1974), p. 409.

7 See *Official Journal* no. L134 (20 June 1971), p. 27.

8 Judgement of the Court of Justice of 14 July 1971 in case 10/71, Luxembourg Public Prosecutor v. Muller *et al. Recueil* XVII (1971), p. 730.

9 See note (5) above.

10 Judgement of the Court of Justice of 21 February 1973 in case 6/72, Continental Can Company Inc., Europemballage Corporation v. EEC Commission. *European Commission Report* (1973), p. 215.

11 See Act of Accession, Article 154; *Official Journal* no. L111 (4 November 1971), p. 1; EEC Commission, *First Report on Competition Policy* (Brussels, April 1972), part II, chapter 1.

8
A review of the main economic issues

K. D. GEORGE AND C. L. JOLL

In this chapter we draw together some of the issues that arise from the papers contained in this book, and attempt to answer some of the questions that recurred in discussion at the conference, for example:

Are the approaches of the UK and the EEC to the maintenance of competition really different? Or do differences in language and procedure mask essentially similar attitudes?

Should competition policy be concerned with the preservation of competitive market structure or with the regulation of non-competitive market conduct?

What are the prospects for harmonisation of competition policy between the EEC and its member countries, who at present have widely varying attitudes to this problem?

What should be done to make competition policy more effective, both in the UK and the EEC? The conference produced many suggestions, some of which we discuss here. These include the following considerations:

Should the EEC have a separate independent agency for the enforcement of competition policy to reduce the political influence on what are essentially economic questions? The present EEC system was criticised for its secrecy. Also, its effectiveness is severely hampered by lack of resources.

If the aim of policy is to preserve a competitive industrial structure then ought we not to have a system of 'guidelines' like that in the USA, forbidding mergers which would increase concentration by a certain amount and also to be looking more seriously at 'unmerging' or breaking up existing large firms?

Where the UK and EEC approaches do seem to differ substantially, e.g. in attitude to mergers, what lessons can either system learn from the other? For example, does the available evidence on the effect of mergers support the UK method of merger control which is to allow a performance based 'trade-off'?

Where does competition policy go from here? Recent developments suggest that policy is still evolving because we don't yet have an effective way of dealing with all forms of threat to competition. Is policy changing as fast as firms' behaviour, or must policy inevitably lag behind?

How important is competition in competition policy?

It is universally agreed by commentators in this area that competition as such has a higher priority among the aims of the EEC than of the UK. Thus 'the institution of a system ensuring that competition in the Common Market is not distorted' is given in Article 3 of the Treaty of Rome as one of the ways of achieving the fundamental purposes of the EEC, which are themselves laid down in Article 2 of the Treaty and were given in chapter 1 (p. 1). Both Professor Jacquemin and Professor Barna quote a passage from the EEC Commission's *First Report on Competition Policy* which may be said to express the philosophy on which EEC competition policy is based. This states that competition is regarded as desirable because it will guarantee freedom of action and choice, ensure efficiency and the optimal allocation of resources and so on. Thus the EEC's position may be regarded as intermediate between that of the USA, which provides a frame of reference for the discussion of competition policy where competition, for cultural and political as well as economic reasons, is regarded as a 'way of life' or an 'end in itself', and that of the UK. In the UK, competition is certainly seen as a means to an end, where the end is variously described in terms of efficiency in production and distribution, development of technical improvements, distribution of industry and employment etc. (see pp. 21–2). However, competition is not seen as invariably the best or only way of achieving these primarily economic aims and UK policy has contained very little presumption in favour of competition. The 1973 Fair Trading Act was the first piece of UK legislation to contain specific mention of competition as desirable on its own account rather than as one of a number of alternative means of achieving the aims of policy, all to be considered on an equal basis. Thus, although the pointers to the public interest contained in this Act include 'the desirability of maintaining and promoting effective competition between persons supplying goods and services in the UK' taken as a whole they are, as Dr Howe points out, 'something of a mixture of means and ends'.

If we accept that the philosophy of the EEC's policy is more strongly in favour of competition than that of the UK, then how does this difference show through in legislation on competition policy and in the way in which this legislation is enforced in practice? It is possible to point out ways in which the different provisions of legislation on monopolies, mergers and restrictive practices in the UK and the EEC reflect a greater commitment to competition in the latter. In the field of restrictive practices, UK and EEC policies are broadly similar in that a wide range of restrictive practices are prohibited but agreements may be permitted on certain conditions. It is in the specification of these conditions that the difference between the UK and EEC attitudes manifests itself. Thus in the UK, as described in chapter 1, an agreement may be upheld by the Restrictive Practices Court if it has beneficial consequences which outweigh the detriment to competition, and also agreements which are considered by the Government to be 'on balance in the public interest' or to be anti-inflationary can be licensed by the Government without the anti-competitive effects of the agreement being weighed up by the Court. In these cases there is plainly no presumption in favour of competition operating. In the EEC, however, a restrictive agreement must simultaneously fulfil four conditions in order to be exempt, and one of these conditions is that competition must not be eliminated from a substantial proportion of the product in question. Thus an agreement with a 'substantially' anti-competitive effect cannot be licensed in the EEC under any circumstances whatever or, to put it in UK terms, could never be considered 'in the public interest'.

UK legislation on monopolies and mergers expresses a less favourable attitude towards competition than that on restrictive practices, which are after all initially presumed to be against the public interest. Towards monopoly situations and mergers, however, the UK approach is basically to assess the effects of each situation separately and pronounce on whether these are against the public interest. The 'cons' to be assessed will consist of adverse effects on competition, but UK policy has given little guidance to the Monopolies Commission, which is responsible for this exercise, as to how these effects should be weighed in the balance against the beneficial consequences claimed for the monopoly situation or merger. EEC monopoly policy, that is Article 86, prohibits the abuse of dominant position and there is no provision for exemption. Much depends on the interpretation of this Article, but it could be taken as prohibiting any conduct which would not have occurred in a competitive situation, e.g. price fixing or restrictions on output. This would undoubtedly express a stronger determination to regulate the behaviour of large firms and make them behave 'as if' they were in a competitive situation, than can be deduced from the UK legislation which prohibits nothing and assesses anew in each case the effects of monopolistic practices to see whether the practice can be said to operate against the public interest in these circumstances.

The EEC legislation on merger control, if it follows the lines of the

8-2

draft proposal currently under consideration, will differ from UK policy in that the chief test of whether a merger shall be allowed to proceed is its effect on competition. Dr Markert describes the system as operating on a 'competition criterion with a limited public interest trade-off'. Thus mergers which result in 'the power to hinder effective competition' are to be prohibited and will not be exempt if the merger promises efficiency gains or to improve the performance of the firms or industry concerned. The EEC system does not operate a trade-off of adverse effects on competition versus beneficial effects on performance as does the UK merger control: where a merger is allowed in the EEC it must be because it is 'indispensable to the attainment of an objective which is given priority treatment in the common interest of the Community'. In other words the anti-competitive effects of the merger are accepted, not because it will promote industrial efficiency (since in the EEC competition is itself seen almost without qualification as the best way of achieving this efficiency) but because the merger works towards another goal of EEC policy which is considered a 'higher' goal than competition.

We can say, therefore, that EEC legislation does, on the face of it show a greater commitment to competition and a tougher line on monopolies mergers and restrictive practices as offences against competition than UK legislation. However, it must be stressed that both systems leave a substantial amount of scope for discretion in interpreting the legislation. And so we have to ask whether EEC policy has been more pro-competition than UK policy in application as well as in theory Have agreements, practices and mergers that would be condemned in the EEC been allowed to continue in the UK, or vice versa? This is a very difficult question to answer and so far, in spite of overlapping jurisdiction since the UK joined the EEC in 1973, there have been no cases tried under both sets of laws, which would illuminate this question. Many participants at the conference felt that the difference in attitude between UK and EEC competition policy is more pronounced in theory than in practice. Thus Professor Heath, in his comments on Professor de Jong's paper, says 'in the evaluation of competition policies within the EEC, the trend would appear to be towards attitudes adopted in the UK, in which situations are looked at in some detail in relation to their specific economic effects'.

In relation to merger policy Professor Barna says 'in spite of differences in philosophy between the EEC and the UK, I believe that in the practical application of mergers legislation these differences are more apparent than real'. This of course must be speculative since merger control hasn't started working in the EEC yet. There seems little doubt that the intention behind the proposed regulation was to be tougher on mergers than we are in the EEC, but whether this will b carried out will depend largely on the interpretation of the 'public interest exemption clause' which is couched in general terms. Participants at the conference from the EEC expressed the hope that the use of this clause will be restricted by the force of public opinion, so that their system won't become too like the UK one, which has allowed almost all mergers to proceed.

It is difficult to reach a conclusion as to how severe EEC monopoly policy is in practice, as it has been used so very seldom and until 1971, as Professor Jacquemin says, Article 86 remained 'an empty threat'. Is the EEC policy which prohibits non-competitive conduct and has hardly been enforced at all more or less severe than the UK system which has resulted in intervention in certain industries with the aim of modifying those aspects of large firms' behaviour which have been found to be against the public interest? It seems as though EEC policy is potentially more severe, but has in practice been less useful. Were more cases to be tried under Article 86 we should have a clearer idea of what behaviour constitutes an 'abuse' of dominant position and how this compared with the British concept of a practice being against the public interest. As it is, we don't know whether non-competitive conduct may be defended on the grounds of beneficial effects on performance, e.g. that it contributes to technical progress, and is thus considered non-abusive, or whether such conduct is abusive *per se*. Thus the fact that there is no provision for exemption in Article 86 cannot be taken to imply such per-se illegality. As Professor Jacquemin points out 'the European Authorities make competition policy a part of their general economic and industrial policy, so that the function assigned to competition becomes much less central than it is officially stated'.

There is no shortage of restrictive practices cases from which to draw conclusions on the relative toughness of the UK and EEC systems. By 1972, 37 000 agreements, of which 2873 were outstanding, had been notified to the EEC Commission, which had made only 57 formal decisions under Article 85, including 13 cases in which exemption was refused. In June 1972 the UK register contained particulars of 2875 agreements of which 2620 had expired or been terminated, although only about 60 had been tried before the Court, and 11 upheld. These figures immediately bring home two points: first, the vastly greater magnitude of the task facing the EEC Commission in administering competition policy; second, in both cases the number of agreements abandoned or expired far exceeds the number of cases heard by the relevant authority in which a decision to terminate an agreement was reached. This indicates that an adverse decision may lead to similar agreements being modified or abandoned.

Such figures will not reveal the whole effect of restrictive practices legislation on competition. They will underestimate the effect of legislation to the extent that it has a deterrent effect so that agreements which would otherwise have been concluded are not made or are voluntarily cancelled before registration. On the other hand the number of agreements terminated will exaggerate the effect of legislation if firms substitute non-registrable or non-prohibited forms of agreement for their original ones. The sheer number of agreements which have been registered in the EEC has meant that a very large proportion have had to be dealt with 'informally' so that limited resources can be concentrated on those types of restrictions considered most inimical to the aims of the Common Market. Some 34000 notified agreements have been dealt with in this way. In addition the Commission has received from the Council of Ministers authority to grant block exemptions for certain types of agreement and has actually made two such block exemptions for a limited time period. In addition to all this, various estimates suggest that over 50 per cent of agreements prohibited by Article 85 have not been notified to the Commission. Although notification is the only way of gaining exemption and may also lead to immunity from retrospective fines, these considerations have proved an insufficiently strong inducement to notify. Firms are likely to be most reluctant to notify those agreements least likely to be exempted and will prefer to take a chance that the overworked authorities won't get around to investigating their particular industry. Thus the practical problems involved in administering restrictive practices policy on a grand scale have made it imperative for the Commission to allow many types of restrictive activity to continue at least for the time being, and it would be foolish to suppose that Article 85 has succeeded in eliminating such practices from the EEC.

However, Professor de Jong is broadly content with the way in which restrictive practices policy has been applied in the EEC, and that the Commission has in the main been consistent in its interpretation of Article 85. The presumption of Article 85 in favour of competition has not, he says, been eroded by liberal granting of exemptions and the Commission has not hesitated to impose heavy fines to force firms to view the EEC's competition policy with respect. Professor de Jong's view may well err on the side of optimism in view of such considerations as the possible large number of agreements which have not been notified and also the uneven application of the policy, particularly in relation to the problem of enforcing cartel policy in a country like France where indicative planning is important. However, few economists would deny that there has been greater success in enforcing competition policy in the field of restrictive agreements than in the field of monopoly and mergers. It is in the latter that the greatest problems are found and a consideration of these will occupy the remainder of this chapter.

The control of monopoly: structure, conduct or performance?

'The anti-trust policies pursued by industrial countries vary mainly in the emphasis laid on the roles of structure, conduct and performance as criteria for determining the existence of monopoly power or for enforcing remedial measures' (A. Jacquemin). It is our intention here to examine the implications of this statement as applied to the UK and EEC; to see whether we should be most impressed by the similarities or differences in the existing approaches to policy; and to examine the need for reform.

Definition of monopoly

In the UK a monopoly situation is defined in the 1948 and 1973 Acts on purely structural grounds: such a situation is now said to exist where one firm supplies one-quarter of the total UK supply of any good. However, there is an alternative criterion to cover situations of oligopoly or 'complex monopoly', in this case a monopoly situation exists if 'two or more firms so conduct their affairs as to prevent, restrict or distort competition' and a structural analysis will be insufficient to determine whether this criterion is met.

The condition for a large firm to be covered by the EEC's anti-monopoly provisions is that it has a 'dominant position'. This is not defined in Article 86 but interpretation to date of this concept by the EEC Commission and the European Court suggests on the whole that it is not a purely structural concept (but see p. 201 below). No superiority in market share is necessarily identified with market dominance, defined by the Court as 'the power to behave independently, without taking into account their competitors purchasers or suppliers'. Since such a 'power' must necessarily be unobservable, this interpretation means that the existence of a dominant position can only be proved by the exercise of this power, i.e. by the appearance of non-competitive market conduct. Thus the insistence on a conduct test for the existence of dominance means that the EEC's criteria for identifying monopoly power will coincide with that for enforcing remedial measures. There will be no way of identifying a dominant position which is not being abused, yet the possibility of such a 'good' monopoly is inherent in the policy of both the UK and the EEC, which condemn not the existence of monopoly power but its undesirable consequences.

UK policy avoids this confusion by defining unitary monopoly positions at least in clearly structural terms. A structural criterion for the existence of a monopoly situation is certainly easier to use than the required conduct test for market dominance in the EEC. Difficulties of interpretation of Article 86 in this respect may well account in part for the relative lack of anti-monopoly activity in the EEC. It is to be feared that the same kind of problems may arise with the 'criterion for enforcing remedial measures' put forward in the Commission's draft merger control proposal, and that the Commission's failure to apply structural criteria may result in many mergers going ahead because it is not possible to prove conclusively, *ex ante*, that they will result in the power to hinder effective competition. Dr Markert notes that the West German merger control system started off in 1973 with a similar conduct criterion for the prevention of mergers, but this has subsequently been supplemented by structural tests to make the system more practicable.

Even with the use of the structural criterion for defining a monopoly position there remains of course the problem of how to define the appropriate market – this involves the two thorny problems of how narrowly or widely to define a market in terms of products and in terms of geographical extension. It should also be pointed out that in practice the distinction between the UK and EEC in the definition of a monopoly position is not so sharp as it may appear in theory. In the UK a market share of over 25 per cent is a necessary but not usually a sufficient condition for being referred to the Monopolies Commission, and in the preliminary investigations on monopoly situations undertaken by the Office of Fair Trading the EEC concept of a dominant position is not absent. Most firms referred to the Commission for investigation are certainly likely to command a substantial market share of the relevant products. However, the tone of the Conference was that there is a great deal to be said on practical grounds for competition policy criteria to be set in structural terms. Monitoring the structure of industry is part of the job of the Office of Fair Trading in the UK and of the Directorate General of Competition in the EEC and the information which they seek should be readily available and easier to collect than that on the behaviour of individual firms which is needed if this is to constitute either proof of the existence of a dominant position or the signal for remedial action, as in the EEC.

Criteria for enforcing remedial measures

The existence of a monopoly situation is in no way condemned in either the UK or the EEC. In the former the criterion for enforcing remedial measures is basically a test of performance: has the firm made excessive profits, has it been slow in meeting demand or in making technical innovations and so on. The criterion for action in the EEC would appear to be much stricter since, as we have seen, Article 86 may be interpreted as saying that any behaviour which could not occur in a competitive market is abusive and prohibited. UK policy obviously says less than this – non-competitive conduct will only be condemned if it affects the performance of the firm in a way considered to be against the public interest.

For both behaviour and performance, however, there are major problems of interpretation which are clearly pinpointed in both the papers presented on the monopoly issue. The problems arise because the authorities have to examine competition in a dynamic setting to which the static analysis of resource allocation is at best only of partial relevance. Thus as pointed out by Dr Howe it is not at all easy in a dynamic situation to distinguish between price discrimination designed to enhance and that designed to suppress competition. Similarly, it is not at all an easy task in a world of change and uncertainty to weigh up the pros and cons of information agreements and investment planning. Again, on the performance side the interpretation of evidence is not straightforward. A high level of profit may be due to monopolistic practices or to efficient management, or to the successful handling of high risk innovative activity. Thus without detailed analysis in each case it is not clear what kind of action is needed to improve the firm's performance.

As far as the practical application of monopoly policy is concerned it can be reported that since 1948 the UK Monopolies Commission has undertaken some 40 enquiries. It is pretty well impossible to say what effect there has been on the firms which have been investigated let alone on the large sectors of industry which haven't been examined at all. The deterrent effect of legislation depends on the probability of being referred to the Monopolies Commission on the one hand, and on the severity of the remedies imposed by the Government following such an investigation. The UK record can be blamed for being deficient in both these respects. Again, although it is possible for the Government to break up monopoly firms found to operate against the public interest, if firms examine the record rather than the potential powers they are unlikely to be worried by this possibility. There is no doubt that firms do very much dislike being referred to the Monopolies Commission, but this is more likely to be due to the amount of time taken up by an investigation and the adverse publicity involved than to the possible effect of the Commission's conclusions on the future operation of the firm.

In the EEC there is very little evidence indeed on which to judge the effectiveness of policy. Since use of Article 86 was first made in 1971 the EEC Commission has made only four decisions prohibiting abuses, one of which was reversed by the European Court, and in one case the abusive practice was voluntarily abandoned before the Court reached its decision. In view of the small number of cases undertaken the deterrent effect of the legislation seems likely to be extremely limited and there is still insufficient case law on the interpretation of the key concepts of Article 86 for many firms to know whether their practices would be considered abusive or not.

Remedies – the case for a structural approach

Both UK and EEC policy have so far intervened at the conduct stage and prohibited certain anti-competitive practices of those firms which have been investigated. Such a policy may be viewed as merely tinkering with the situation and unlikely to achieve any lasting improvement. If it is uncompetitive market structure which causes, or at least permits, the conduct which is condemned then in order to eliminate the conduct the structure of the market must be changed. If this is not done then firms will have to be constantly watched to make sure anti-competitive behaviour does not re-emerge and the resources simply are not available for this sort of monitoring. Also, the attack on certain business practices may lead to other forms of behaviour which make the structure of the market less competitive and so store up trouble for the future. This is particularly likely where the monopolistic practices condemned by policy are those which exploit present market power at the expense of consumers, while those which are aimed at increasing market power by the elimination of other firms are largely ignored. Thus by deciding to intervene in the dynamic process at the conduct stage and regulate firms' behaviour, market structure may be permitted, and indeed even induced, to change. Thus without a policy of controlling industrial structure there will be nothing to stop firms growing until they have attained such a position of dominance that the only remedy available, regulation of behaviour, is totally insufficient to make firms behave in the public interest and consumers have no viable alternative source of supply. Indeed, there was a strong feeling at the Conference that it is impossible to control effectively the behaviour of dominant firms.

There are in fact indications that the competition policy authorities are not entirely happy with the diagnosis of the monopoly problem expressed in past legislation and with the solution of conduct regulation. In the UK structural as opposed to conduct remedies for monopoly problems have been available since the Monopolies and Mergers Act was passed in 1965, empowering the responsible Department to 'provide for the division of any trade or business by the sale of any part of the undertaking or assets'. This radical increase in the powers of the Government to deal with monopolies implies a change of UK attitude towards the belief that recommending the discontinuing of certain practices might not be sufficient to make large firms behave henceforth in the public interest. Also, of course, the possibility of dissolution provides a corollary to the merger control system which was introduced at the same time: if a merger is judged likely to operate against the public interest the concentration of market power can be prevented, and if an existing concentration is found against the public interest it can be broken up. However, there is an asymmetry in practice: legal, financial and political problems militate against enforcing dissolution, and where the Monopolies Commission has recommended a measure of it the recommendation has not been accepted by the Government.

In the EEC there is no provision for the dissolution of existing concentrations. However, in a recent, and controversial, use of Article 86 it seems that this Article may be used to prevent the extension of a dominant position where this endangers effective competition. The EEC Commission's controversial use of Article 86 to preserve market structure arose in the Continental Can merger case of 1971. Although the merger was not prevented the statements of the European Court amount to a substantial reinterpretation of the scope of this Article. They state that it can be an abuse for an enterprise to extend its dominant position to the point that consumer's freedom of action on the market is seriously jeopardised. Thus it seems that Article 86 may be used to preserve market structures which are necessary for effective competition and that Article 86 may be used not only to prevent acquisitions by a firm in a dominant position but also to prevent that firm extending its dominance in a market as a result of a high rate of internal growth. However, Article 86 has never been used in this way and it seems doubtful whether it ever will be. As Professor de Jong says, 'High sounding principles do not normally convince the economist. He is interested in the way those principles are applied and if necessary enforced.'

In practice then there has been no resort to structural remedies to the monopoly problem in either the UK or EEC, but there was considerable agreement at the Conference that the way to give competition policy more bite is to concentrate more on market structure, and that the time has come to make this change. This point was made forcefully in discussion by Mr Sutherland and Professor Barna, both of whom advocated a measure of dissolution or unmerging as a means of dealing with monopoly situations, a recommendation which has to be coupled with recognition of the need to empower the Monopolies Commission to investigate companies as well as individual markets. What is the case for a move in this direction?

First, there are the difficulties already noted in relying on a conduct approach – the problems of interpreting the evidence, of enforcing a change in business conduct, the need for monitoring the behaviour of dominant firms and all that this entails in terms of the resources needed by the enforcement agency if it is to do a worthwhile job. It is probably fair to say also that the extent to which the enforcement agency would have to get involved with the details of business conduct in order to do the job properly would be at a quite unacceptable level and one which would seriously hamper managerial efficiency.

A structural approach would enjoy the advantage of avoiding some of these problems. There would be no need to assess whether high profits were due to monopoly behaviour or to other causes, to assess whether or not research and development was satisfactory, and no need therefore to get heavily involved in the details of business conduct. The acid test would be the industrial structure – if this were judged, on the basis of evidence concerning the number and size distribution of firms, entry conditions to the market, competition from imports and so on, to be satisfactory then that would be the end of the matter. High profits, if they existed, could then be presumed to be the result of efficient management or good luck rather than of monopolistic exploitation.

The argument that competition policy should be structurally based and aimed at preserving effective competition in the economy implies that market structure lies behind market conduct and performance, that a policy which tries to control either of the latter without changing the former will be at best ineffective, and also that a competitive market structure will cause firms to behave in such a way that, in acting in their own interests, a socially desirable allocation of resources is achieved.

One of the major problems with this approach is of course the possibility that as a result of economies of scale and efficient management the workings of the competitive process will lead to market shares inconsistent with effective competition. The UK and EEC have always tried to retain the option on the actual or potential gains from concentration as well as those from competition. The question of what efficiency losses would be imposed by a policy which prevents firms growing beyond a certain size and encourages the preservation of a number of firms in each market allows of no general answer. The desirability of a structural approach clearly depends on the circumstances of each industry, the importance of economies of scale and the size of the market. But it may be argued whether the evidence on economies of increased size supports a neutral case-by-case pros and cons analysis as practised in the UK or whether this should be supplanted by a presumption against concentration with exemption on specific grounds. Those who favour the latter course of action might draw attention to what they regard as a striking result of empirical work – the persistency with which, over a wide range of studies, high market concentration emerges as an important determinant of profitability. Much more important, however, but less amenable to statistical analysis, is the effect which market concentration has on the goods which are available to consumers. Statistical work in this field relates to goods which are actually available. It does not tell us anything about the extent to which this set of products diverges from that which would have been available in more competitively structured markets. Several participants in discussion expressed their anxiety about the effects of growing concentration on the choice of goods available to consumers. More fundamentally, and it is a very simple point, if you want to maintain competition you must maintain competitors. And this brings us right back to the basic problem of the structural approach – that of defining the appropriate market.

The control of mergers

The difficulties faced by the anti-trust authorities in controlling established dominant firms suggests that the best way of dealing with monopoly is by taking measures to prevent the growth of firms to dominant positions. To this end a strong merger policy could make a substantial contribution. However, the history of UK merger policy so far has been totally in keeping with the permissive society. As noted at the beginning of this chapter only a very small proportion of mergers have been referred to the Monopolies Commission. We examine first the basic problems with existing UK policy, secondly we look at the proposed EEC merger policy to see to what extent it may be an improvement on UK practice, and thirdly suggest what needs to be done to make policy in this field more effective.

Problems with UK merger policy

In the UK large mergers have been subject to government control for ten years. How effective has this control been? As with UK monopoly policy, control does not take the form of prohibition, thus its effect depends on the probability of mergers being referred to the Monopolies Commission and of the Commission recommending that the merger should not be allowed. Also, of course, the legislation may prevent some mergers which would otherwise have occurred from even being pro-posed. It may be thought that the Government has at its disposal better information concerning merger activity than concerning monopolistic practices since all sizeable mergers are examined initially by the mergers panel of the Department of Prices and Consumer Protection. However, the effectiveness of the present UK system may be ques-tioned from the fact that of some 800 mergers considered by the merger panel between 1965 and 1974, only about 25 have been referred to the Monopolies Commission. This is a remarkably low referral rate – about three per cent. Moreover, the decision whether to refer a proposed merger rests with the appropriate Minister – at the moment the Secre-tary of State for Prices and Consumer Protection. The Director General of Fair Trading is not able to make merger references. The political element in merger policy is therefore greater than it is in monopoly policy. After a decision on whether to refer a merger proposal is taken the reasons for that decision may be explained to the press. Nevertheless, considerable obscurity surrounds the grounds on which reference decisions are made. And it is to be noted that the political element in competition policy is strongest precisely in the field of policy which potentially could contribute most effectively to the maintenance of competitive market structures. Obviously a greater number of referrals would mean that the Monopolies Commission would have to be enlarged if their reports are to be completed within the statutory time period, but the present probability of referral hardly constitutes much of a deterrent to merger proposals, and there is cause for anxiety about exactly how candidates for referral are chosen.

Of the very small number of mergers which are examined by the Commission, about 75 per cent have not taken place. However, less than half of these were prevented by the Commission recommending against the merger – the others were abandoned either before the report came out or in spite of a 'favourable' finding. In these cases presumably either the Monopolies Commission's investigations uncovered facts which made the firms concerned change their minds, or circumstances changed during the enquiry so that the merger no longer seemed desirable, and these by-products seem to be more effective in stopping mergers than does the Commission itself. Whether mergers which are thus abandoned would have turned out successful in the long run seems at best questionable. It should be reiterated here that a 'favourable' finding by the Monopolies Commission means only that it considers that the merger is not likely to operate against the public interest and this may well mean that a large proportion of mergers 'passed' by the Monopolies Commission could not stand the severer test of having to prove positive benefits to the public interest. In three cases the Commission has been asked to report on mergers that had already taken place and, perhaps not surprisingly in view of the problems of dissolution, has not found that those mergers operated against the public interest. This means that we have yet to see a firm broken up as a result of either a monopoly or a merger investigation by the Monopolies Commission.

Finally, the operation of a merger control system for nearly ten years has produced remarkably little information in the UK on the effects of mergers – there is no provision made for the Monopolies Commission or responsible Department to check that a merger which is allowed to proceed really doesn't operate against the public interest.

The discussion at the Conference was much concerned about the main theme of Dr Utton's chapter – the feasibility of a case-by-case cost–benefit approach to assessing the likely effects of a merger. A limited application of this approach has been applied by the Monopolies

Commission in some of its merger investigations where it has attempted to weigh potential cost savings against the monopoly dangers. The general feeling was that any attempt to refine this approach would be unlikely to pay dividends. The time constraint in merger investigations would not allow for the great increase in the work which would be involved, and even if it did it is doubtful whether the problems inherent in this approach could be satisfactorily solved. One of the major problems is the fact that in merger cases the Commission is having to guess the future, and it is not possible to get enough information on mergers because there is no information on the future. An important distinction, however, has to be made between contested and uncontested bids. With the former the Commission would tend to get more information and at least two views of the future. With the agreed bid, however, there is only one view which tends to be optimistic. On this score it might be argued that those mergers most likely to be in the public interest are those which occur after a tooth and nail contest between opposing interests. On the other hand it might be argued that with agreed mergers the parties have been able to get together so that the acquiring firm should have obtained more information on the internal affairs of the firm to be acquired, whereas with a contested bid the acquiring firm's sources of information are restricted to those which are publicly available.

It seems that in practice quite a lot of emphasis is laid on an assessment of the managerial competence of the people involved. Here again, in a world characterised by change and uncertainty, there are great dangers. There is no guarantee that an efficiently managed firm will remain efficient after a merger. The merger itself may present so many problems that the previously efficient management team is unable to cope. Furthermore, a firm's fortunes in terms of good and bad management are more likely to fluctuate than to remain stable. There is no reason to suppose that the well managed firms of today will always be so favoured.

Another weakness of UK policy which was emphasised by a number of participants was its negative approach. Thus the Monopolies Commission is required to investigate whether a proposed merger is likely to harm the public interest, not with whether it is likely to confer net benefits. Again the Commission is not asked to look at possible alternatives to a take-over bid; it cannot say that 'we are rejecting this bid because we have been convinced that there is a better practical alternative'.

EEC proposals for merger control

The proposed EEC approach to mergers is on the face of it more pro competiton and more hostile to mergers than UK policy and was generally welcomed by Conference participants. The draft proposal gives the grounds on which the 'power to hinder effective competition' is to be assessed as 'the extent to which suppliers and consumers have a possibility of choice, the economic and financial power of the undertakings concerned, the structure of the markets affected and supply and demand trends for the relevant goods or services'. Thus it seems that 'the power to hinder effective competition' is seen as a broadly structural criterion and that structure is viewed dynamically. However, Dr Markert expressed a number of reservations.

First, it may not be possible to prove that a merger will result in such power from structural data alone since the proof that competition is effective requires information on firms' behaviour. This vagueness in interpreting the competition criterion may seriously endanger the effectiveness of the system, and Dr Markert suggests that the present criterion should be supplemented by specific structural criteria prohibiting mergers which increase market share by a specific amount.

A second threat to the effectiveness of the proposed merger control system arises from lack of resources. It seems likely that several hundred mergers a year will be covered by the legislation and each one will have to be examined to see whether it creates the power to hinder effective competition, as well as some being considered for exemption under Article 1(3). Obviously this task would be much easier if there were structural criteria which limited the number of mergers likely to be caught up in the policy to a manageable level.

Third, there is a danger that Article 1(3) which provides for exemptions may be interpreted so widely that the exceptional exemption becomes the rule. This Article exempts 'concentrations which are indispensable to the attainment of an objective which is given priority treatment in the common interest of the Community'.

Finally, a factor which was thought by some to severely limit the effectiveness not only of merger policy but all other areas of competition policy as well is the present organisation of the law enforcement machinery. Dr Markert sees the administrative and procedural problems as the Achilles' heel of the whole system and unless these are dealt with the impact of any extension of competition policy legislation, such as the proposed merger control system, will inevitably be much reduced. In part this is due simply to insufficient resources to deal with even the current workload generated by Articles 85 and 86 and all the other areas such as regulation of state aids to industry, which come within the purview of the Directorate General of Competition. But Dr

Markert's account of the internal workings of the Directorate gives the impression that the resources available are not being used to best advantage. It was felt by several of the EEC participants that the administration of Community competition policy would be made more efficient by setting up a separate independent agency concerned only with enforcing competition policy. Dr Schlieder, the Director General, however, thought that some people had exaggerated the difficulties in reaching decisions within the Commission, pointing to the fact that about 40 decisions a year were now being made in the field of competition policy and another 40 in the field of state aid.

The need for policy changes

The above sketch of weaknesses in current policy towards mergers leads immediately to suggestions for reform.

The majority of those who contributed to this discussion were in favour of introducing guidelines for merger references. US anti-trust policy has a straightforward structural approach to mergers embodied in guidelines which state that horizontal and vertical mergers which increase market concentration by specified percentages (depending on the level of concentration already existing in the market) will be challenged by the Department of Justice and in effect prohibited. A similar system of guidelines based on measures of market concentration and/or size of firm was recommended by a number of participants for the UK and EEC. The opposing point of view was that guidelines would be too inflexible and would create problems for the administrators of merger policy in that they would probably have to explain away a large number of exceptions. The force of this argument clearly depends on the precise way in which the guidelines are drawn and on the number of firms which are caught in the net. Apart from this general point two more specific ones need to be made.

First, the authorities only seem to wake up to the need for a merger policy at all after many dominant firm positions have been established. This means that the introduction of anything like a tough merger policy will discriminate against smaller firms. Once dominant positions have been established, therefore, there may be a case for looking favourably upon mergers involving small and medium-sized firms if there is good reason to believe that this would enable them to compete more effectively with their larger brethren. The alternative is to strengthen the competitive position of smaller firms by taking steps to reduce any disadvantage which they may suffer in the raising of finance and in marketing their products. In addition there are those who argue that there should be provision for unmerging and dismembering large companies in order to restore a more competitive market structure.

Second, a policy directed more strongly towards the prohibition of mergers must consider the viability of the alternative of internal growth or indeed mere survival. There are after all many firms which for personal reasons of the owners, or other causes, want to be taken over. In these cases, where the reasons for merger are found on the side of the acquired firm, merger may be the only alternative to closure and all the consequences of the latter in terms of employment. This still leaves open the question of the identity of the acquiring firm and policy might still serve a useful purpose in loading the dice against the emergence or consolidation of dominant firm positions. This problem also has important international aspects. If all the major countries in the EEC were experiencing roughly the same rate of expansion then the application in all of them of a uniformly severe merger policy would be more feasible in practical terms than in a situation where growth rates showed marked differences. In the latter situation there will be a call for defensive mergers in the slower growing economies. Similarly, the call for a much tougher merger policy in the UK is not likely to receive much sympathy if other countries are not prepared to follow suit. Nor would it be correct to isolate merger policy from other elements of industrial structure such as financial linkages between firms. Thus in Germany, for instance, such financial links operating through the commercial banks may operate to some extent as a substitute for mergers.

A policy change strongly favoured by many participants was that as long as a trade-off approach to merger investigations is used the onus of proof should be placed firmly on the firms to show that a proposed merger would result in net benefits. This would clearly be a far more difficult obstacle to overcome than the present requirement in the UK which is that the Commission should find no detriment to the public interest. It is further suggested in Dr Utton's paper that there should be follow-up investigations of mergers which are completed after a favourable approach by the Monopolies Commission. However, this would lead to additional costs and no benefit unless the authorities were prepared to unmerge companies where growth by merger had 'failed', and it would certainly be difficult to devise workable performance tests on which to base decisions concerning the success or failure of particular mergers.

The more fundamental question of course is whether a cost–benefit or trade-off approach should be used at all. Should not monopoly and merger policy be based entirely on a pro-competitive approach with provision for exemption lying with a separate and higher authority? This is a matter of concern in both EEC and UK policy. In the EEC the Commission is not responsible for competition policy alone but for all areas of policy. The UK includes concerns of other areas of economic policy in competition legislation, so that the Restrictive Practices Court can uphold a restrictive agreement on the basis of its contribution to exports or regional employment and the Monopolies Commission is instructed to take into account 'all matters which appear to them to be relevant'. Under both the UK and the EEC systems, therefore, it can be difficult to tell what are the legitimate concerns of competition policy; whether an agreement or merger has been allowed to continue because it will not appreciably restrict competition, or, in spite of the fact that it will do so, because it has other beneficial effects considered to be more important than the loss of competition. The potential dangers of this situation are noted by Dr Markert with reference to the merger control proposals and by Professor Jacquemin with reference to Article 86.

The draft proposal for the control of mergers poses the potential conflict between the aims of competition policy and other goals in a very clear way: as we have seen, mergers which result in the power to hinder effective competition are prohibited unless the concentration is indispensable to the attainment of an objective which is given priority treatment in the common interests of the Community. Dr Markert suggests that a separate competition law enforcement agency should be set up to examine, among other things, the competitive effects of mergers and decide whether they should be prohibited. The Commission would retain the right to grant exemptions by overriding the competition agency's decision for reasons of public policy. This is a similar separation of functions to that practised in West Germany where the Federal Cartel Office decides whether to prohibit mergers for competitive reasons and the Economics Minister can reverse decisions in the 'overriding interests of the public'. This has the advantage that the public can see clearly on what grounds the merger is or is not allowed.

In the application of Article 86 problems may arise in determining what types of conduct constitute an 'abuse' of a dominant position and are prohibited. The practices specifically mentioned by this Article are only examples and it has been argued that abusiveness should be judged in the light of the general goals of the Community. Article 86 has no exemption provisions and so the whole weight of determining the legality of monopolistic practices rests on the interpretation of abuse. Is behaviour which could not have occurred in a competitive market necessarily abusive or can it be justified by reference to beneficial effects? Professor Jacquemin considers that the amount of discretion allowed in the interpretation of this Article could become 'the source of a dangerous discretionary and discriminating power'. In trying to judge cases on the basis of their contribution to macro- or micro-performance the Commission will often in fact have to make a political choice between conflicting goals. For clarification of the issues behind such a decision the Community needs a clearer delineation of functions. Again, the argument follows that instead of the Commission having sole responsibility for all the potentially conflicting goals of economic policy a separate independent agency should be established for the enforcement of competition law. This agency would decide whether the conduct of a dominant firm constituted an abuse against competition and if so would suggest remedies, and the Commission could say whether this was justified in the light of other goals of the Community.

A strong argument can therefore be made out for the need of an independent agency concerned with competition policy. This would have the distinct advantage of focusing the attention of competition policy on those goals to which it is most applicable, leaving such goals as the balance of payments and regional policy to other more suitable policy weapons.

The problem of harmonisation

It was mentioned in chapter 1 (p. 17) that at the time of the formation of the EEC its constituent countries held varying attitudes towards the regulation of competition and had correspondingly different apparatus to enforce the law in this area, so that until the EEC developed its own mechanisms the enforcement of Articles 85 and 86 varied from country to country. How has seventeen years of the EEC succeeded in eliminating this problem and harmonising the competition laws of the nine member states? Membership of the EEC has not yet brought all these countries round to a common view of what constitutes a threat to competition and how to deal with the problem. Reference was made at the Conference both to the small number of cases considered by the Commission involving French and Italian firms (see de Jong, p. 59) and to the possible non-coincidental lack of French or Italian participants (Sutherland, p. 127). Such facts are evidence of a continuing divergence of opinion among the member states of the EEC about the importance which should be attached to the preservation of competition.

Of the six original EEC members only West Germany has a national system for the control of mergers, although merger legislation is currently under consideration by some other member countries as well as by the EEC itself. In 1957 only West Germany, France and the Netherlands had cartel laws but the formation of the EEC and pressure from these countries induced the others to introduce such legislation. In 1957 the Netherlands and West Germany had laws to control the activities of dominant firms, France passed such a law in 1963 and Italy and Belgium introduced legislation to cover both cartels and abuses of dominant position in 1964 and 1960 respectively (although the Italian law had not actually been passed by March 1972).

Thus as far as the original members of the EEC are concerned, harmonisation of competition laws meant that in some cases laws controlling restrictive practices and dominant firms had to be started from scratch and in other cases the concepts contained in national legislation were changed so as to be more in line with EEC policy. With the exception of mergers, these countries now have laws that are broadly comparable in terms of coverage and attitude, although this doesn't mean that the implementation of these laws is pursued with equal enthusiasm in all cases.

The enlargement of the EEC in 1973 introduced a new problem for harmonisation in the shape of UK competition policy which in fact predated any legislation in continental Europe and had developed along quite separate lines from EEC policy (see chapter 1). Of the other new recruits to the EEC, Denmark had a long-established law to control both monopolies and restrictive practices, passed in 1955, and Ireland had just passed a new law consolidating and extending previous legislation on restrictive practices and was proposing to introduce further measures of control over monopolies, oligopolies and mergers. At the time of the UK's accession to the EEC, legislation was being planned which altered substantially the administration, if not the basic policy attitude, of UK competition policy. However, it is not possible to discern in the Fair Trading Act 1973 any marked impact of Community membership – in fact the definition of a 'monopoly' share of the market was reduced from a third to a quarter in spite of the vastly enlarged market in which UK firms were now able to compete on equal terms. The Fair Trading Act did extend the scope of policy to cover restrictive export agreements and the products of the nationalised industries, both of which would certainly come under EEC legislation, and also made more explicit mention of the desirability of competition than previous legislation in the UK, but all of these changes may be attributable to internal developments rather than to the influence of the EEC.

Dr Howe mentions the effect which EEC competition policy has so far had on that in the UK – this seems to boil down to consultation between the Office of Fair Trading and the Directorate General for Competition of the EEC on possible future developments. Thus as the EEC proceeds towards integration more consideration will have to be given to whether the whole EEC rather than the national market should be used in assessing market shares, dominance, etc. It seems unlikely that there are many restrictive agreements which remain outside the scope of UK law yet would be prohibited by the EEC, and unlikely also that the UK's large firms will be much troubled by investigation under the little used Article 86 unless the pace of the EEC's monopoly policy is hotted up. However, the prospective enactment of merger control laws is likely to affect UK firms since mergers of a certain size will have to be notified to the EEC Commission as well as scrutinised by the UK Government's merger panel. Merger proposals involving British steel firms are already subject to EEC control through the rules of the European Coal and Steel Community. Indeed as things stand a trans-national merger involving a steel company may be subject to four separate laws – EEC, ECSC and possibly two national laws.

But even if a much greater degree of uniformity could be achieved in monopoly legislation there would still be the problem of enforcing it uniformly and in ensuring that it did not pinch some economies much more severely than others. A major problem here is the differences which exist between countries in the relationship between industry and the state, and also between industry and financial institutions. Thus, for instance, where government and industry are closely involved in indicative planning it will be more difficult to enforce effective restrictive practices policy than where such arrangements do not feature prominently in economic policy. To give one example, if firms are encouraged to exchange information on investment plans as part of an indicative plan this may have the advantage of enabling capacity to be adjusted more accurately in relation to changes in demand, but it could also form the basis for market-sharing agreements. Again, where financial links between companies differ between countries, a uniform application of merger policy may have a stronger pro-competitive effect in one country than another.

There is also the question of what progress has been made towards harmonisation of those aspects of competition policy which involve state aid to enterprises. Professor Mathijsen tells us that most state monopolies by which certain firms were granted exclusive rights to buy or sell have been adjusted so as not to prevent the free movement of goods between member countries. Public enterprises are covered by Articles 85 and 86 in just the same way as private firms unless they provide services of general economic interest. However, it can be no less difficult to ensure the absence of abuse in the case of public enterprise than in the case of large firms in the private sector. The whole field of state aid to industry, including regional policy and selective assistance to firms in difficulty, has been, and indeed still is, one of the most controversial areas of EEC policy. The amount and types of such aid which can be granted are subject to EEC control but this has not been accepted lightly by all the countries concerned.

Future developments

Finally, we must consider what are the likely future developments in competition policy, for we cannot suppose that policy in either the UK or the EEC has evolved to a point which makes future change unnecessary. The concerns of competition policy must change to take account of the evolution of the competitive process. Thus the latest development in EEC policy is the proposal for a system of merger control, provoked by the rapid increase in concentration in many industries in Europe and by the part played by mergers in that process. The 'market structure–market conduct–market performance' chain is above all a dynamic system which is affected by policy moves: thus the prohibition of many forms of restrictive agreement may cause firms to find other ways to keep the intensity of competition down to what is considered a tolerable level. If firms react by making less formal 'information' agreements or by joining together in mergers the intention of the legislation to promote competition will be frustrated and the need for further policy initiatives becomes clear. They are certainly needed. A merger wave has led to increased concentration, dominant firms continue to grow and to increase their dominance, and the growth of the multi-national, multi-product firm has given the authorities still more to think about. Will an effective competition policy eventually emerge or will the ingenuity of firms continue to outpace the development of policy?

Another point which needs repeating is that the post-war progress in fostering competition has owed much to the high levels and growth rates of demand in the Western world. This has provided an important element of safety to firms, and in general has contributed much towards that favourable balance between safety and competition which is so difficult to define and yet in practice so important. Any hope of further strengthening competition policy depends heavily on a continuation of these demand conditions.

The suggestions made at the Conference pointed on the whole to the desirability of using competition policy above all else to maintain or restore competitive market structures, and such an approach would probably offer a better chance of a comprehensive solution to the problems of competition policy than our present piecemeal policies which involve separate legislation procedure and criteria for different aspects of the problem. As part of this pro-competition approach special attention would have to be paid to concentrations of economic power which are not adequately characterised by conventional structural measures such as concentration ratios – e.g. multi-product firms and conglomerate mergers. There would also have to be a far tougher line taken towards mergers. Since there is such an obvious asymmetry between the costs of preventing concentration and of enforced deconcentration, the policy conclusion to be drawn for Europe appears to be the urgency of passing and rigorously enforcing laws to control industrial structure before the benevolent deconcentrating effect of economic integration is totally eroded.

INDEX

Index